A GESTALT COACHING PRIMER

THE PATH TOWARD AWARENESS IQ

DOROTHY E. SIMINOVITCH, PH.D., MCC

Copyrighted Material

A Gestalt Coaching Primer: The Path Toward Awareness IQ

Copyright © 2017 by Dorothy E. Siminovitch. All Rights Reserved.

No part of this publication may be reproduced, stored in a retrieval system, or transmitted, in any form or by any means—electronic, mechanical, photocopying, recording or otherwise—without prior written permission from the author, except for the inclusion of brief quotations embodied in critical reviews and certain other noncommercial uses permitted by copyright law.

Many of the names, locations, and actual events have been changed to protect the privacy of those involved.

Every attempt has been made to source properly all quotes.

Neither the author nor the publisher shall be liable or responsible for any loss, injury, or damage resulting from the reader's use, application, implementation, or imitation of any information or suggestion in this book.

Address all inquiries to the author:
Dorothy E. Siminovitch, PhD, MCC
dorothy@gestaltcoachingworks.com
www.gestaltcoachingworks.com

Library of Congress Control Number: 2017930705

Published by:
Gestalt Coaching Works, LLC
www.gestaltcoachingworks.com

ISBN: 978-0-9973781-7-7
E-book ISBN: 978-0-9973781-2-2

Printed in the United States of America

Cover and Interior Design: 1106 Design

Back Cover Photo: Yanka Van Der Kolk Imaging and Photography

Praise for *A Gestalt Coaching Primer*

In this book Dr. Dorothy Siminovitch lays out a useful structure for understanding and applying Gestalt Coaching. Her approach to presence, for example, provides a road map for developing this essential yet elusive competency for coaches. She combines simple anecdotes with deeper theory to unlock the layers of ambiguity and skill required for master coaches. This is no small feat, and Dr. Siminovitch accomplishes the task while keeping the writing highly readable and engaging. This book is recommended for coaches with all levels of experience. The writing evokes reflection and provokes action.
 —C. Ross van Horn, CEO, Van Horn Consulting, Nairobi, Kenya

Anyone reading *A Gestalt Coaching Primer* will come to know the process and practices of both universal coaching and specifically, the transformational aspects of Gestalt Coaching. As a result, the coach will go beyond steps and tools to hear what is needed to evolve the client's awareness, leading to a personal discovery of possible actions. I applaud Dorothy for putting Gestalt coaching into print so it is accessible for coaches worldwide.
 —Marcia Reynolds, PsyD, MCC, author of *The Discomfort Zone: How Leaders Turn Difficult Conversations into Breakthroughs*, past President of the International Coach Federation

For all of us in leadership development who need to hone our craft, Dorothy Siminovitch gives us important and fresh angles on how to help leaders grow. She makes an elegant case that leadership performance and presence meet in the world of Gestalt coaching. Her contributions are practical and profound, meaningful and replicable.
 —John P. Schuster, PCC, Executive Coach, faculty at the Hudson Institute and Columbia University Coach Certification Programs, author of *Answering Your Call: A Guide for Living Your Deepest Purpose* and *The Power of Your Past: The Art of Recalling, Recasting, and Reclaiming*

In this seminal book on Gestalt Coaching, Dr. Dorothy Siminovitch is generously sharing her extensive experience, expertise, and wisdom on supporting others through transformational growth. Written words have rarely done justice to the Gestalt approach: The work is highly experiential, and the transformation is not in the words but in the existential moment and sensory experience. Yet Dorothy has masterfully tackled that challenge and captured the magic of the moment in a Gestalt coaching session on paper. A must-read for any coach, leader, or Gestalt practitioner who wants to explore their untapped potential to become better interveners.

—Dost Can Deniz, MCC, Executive Coach, author of *Cesur Sorular*, founder of MareFidelis Coaching and Consulting

This powerful book on Gestalt Coaching is an exceptional gift to the coaching world, as well as for practitioners and coaches from multiple disciplines. It is greatly experiential and existential in its magical language, simple to read and understand. In this book, the multidimensionality and complexity of Gestalt theory has been masterfully woven to its simplest form, and integrated by multiple real life examples to increase the reader's curiosity and create inspiration, and it will serve well for applying the approach. Dr. Dorothy Siminovitch, a pioneer in the coaching world—and my partner, teacher, and mentor—has created a phenomenal piece of "art" through her wisdom and savvy, which is a legacy to the whole coaching world. This is a must-read handbook for every Gestalt coach and practitioner, and for practitioners of any approach who would like to expand and explore their personal range and potential to create greater impact.

—Gila Ancel Şeritçioğlu, MCC, Executive Coach, founder of Increa Coaching & Consulting

Praise for *A Gestalt Coaching Primer*

There is an absolute need for *A Gestalt Coaching Primer* by Dorothy Siminovitch. While other schools of psychological and philosophical thought have their well-articulated writings about professional coaching, the most comprehensive—and some would say important—school, Gestalt, needs its foundational work, and Dr. Siminovitch provides it. She not only articulates the spirit of Gestalt coaching, but also offers specific tools and processes, illustrated by engaging case examples. Dorothy Siminovitch's work is truly "Gestalt"—engaging all aspects of human experience, from the biological to the epistemological. As Dorothy intended, she offers a lovely "dance of horizontal and vertical development."

—WILLIAM H. BERGQUIST, PHD, AUTHOR OF *THE POSTMODERN ORGANIZATION*, PRESIDENT OF THE PROFESSIONAL SCHOOL OF PSYCHOLOGY

Gestalt psychology and coaching is the foundation for many somatic approaches that are so relevant today. Dorothy Siminovitch beautifully shares the essence of Gestalt coaching with the focus on awareness, experiments, and learning. The ability to be aware without judgment and with compassion is the key to growth, aliveness, and new possibilities. Not only does Dorothy share and masterfully embody herself the magic of Gestalt coaching, she marries it with the practical skills and competencies required of a coach. All coaches and leaders will greatly benefit from this book.

—ANN VAN ERON, PHD, EXECUTIVE COACH, AUTHOR OF *OASIS CONVERSATIONS: LEADING WITH AN OPEN MINDSET TO MAXIMIZE POTENTIAL*

Dorothy's work on the "presence concept," which is often so elusive, is now, finally, made clear with a model that gives guidance for how to recognize presence and articulate its active dimension. This is presented with depth and experienced practice. Thanks for this lifelong treasure.

—DIDEM TEKAY, MANAGING PARTNER, MANAGEMENT CENTRE TÜRKIYE

We shall not cease from exploration
And the end of all our exploring
Will be to arrive where we started
And know the place for the first time.
—T. S. Eliot

For my husband Jeffrey, my eternal optimist
For my mother Raja, my ever-amazing inspiration and paradox

Table of Contents

INTRODUCTION		1
CHAPTER 1	Why Gestalt Coaching?	11
CHAPTER 2	Awareness and Change	39
CHAPTER 3	The Cycle of Experience	55
CHAPTER 4	Resistance and the Challenge of Development and Change	81
CHAPTER 5	Presence and Use of Self	105
CHAPTER 6	The Power of Experiment(s) in Unit of Work	143
CHAPTER 7	Group and Team Coaching	167
CHAPTER 8	Universal Coaching Competencies—International Coach Federation and Gestalt Coaching	205
CHAPTER 9	The Relevance of Gestalt Coaching Today by Barbara Singer	241
APPENDIX A	The ICF Certification Process	263
APPENDIX B	Sample Coaching Agreement	265
APPENDIX C	Coaching Supervision	269
BIBLIOGRAPHY		297
ENDNOTES		307
INDEX		331

Introduction

Awareness without action leads to regret.
—Gestalt working wisdom

This book, and the journey it represents, feels like a quest for new possibilities in supporting growth and development. In 1995, in a moment of professional and entrepreneurial insight, I linked Gestalt theory and practice with professional coaching and began building the conceptual and training basis for what became known as Gestalt Coaching.[1] I could not fully know that what then seemed like a moderate shift in Gestalt thinking and application would become a vibrant force in the world of professional coaching. What captures that memory now is the Turkish phrase, *küçük ama büyük*—"small but big," which suggests that even little steps can have enormous outcomes.

Gestalt coaching was an adaptive innovation which recognized that psychotherapy was not serving the needs of those challenged by increasing complexities of modern work and life, and that Gestalt organizational consulting could not adequately address the sensitive issues of emotional and social intelligence involved in complex systems. In observing these gaps, a new vision and field for Gestalt practice emerged. Although Gestalt coaching was almost indifferently received at first, in the past decades I have witnessed its conceptual breakthroughs reverberating around the world. The growing number of organizational and life coaches who encompass a Gestalt approach speaks to the relevance and transformative power of Gestalt-based coaching.

The aim of this book is to make accessible and available what is often obscured by academic language. Gestalt coaching offers practical, workable support for those seeking new prospects and different choices, but this process-based approach often seems mysterious to the uninitiated. What is missing from the literature is a trusted guide, a primer that demystifies the Gestalt principles, concepts, and applications that provide meaningful and compelling resources for coaching practice. Because of the power of the Gestalt approach, it often gets labeled as magical to those new to working with a process approach. After years of teaching the practical ways of being able to recognize process, my aim in this book is to be revealing about theory, cases, coaching credentialization, and illustrations. I often use the pronoun "we," even when it seems most intuitively natural to use the singular pronoun "I." I do this in part to signify that I am attending to all the influential voices who have guided me and who still walk with me, and in part to signify that no Gestalt coach is without communal resources of fellow practitioners and a written body of work. On the other hand, I use the pronoun "she" to describe the Gestalt coach's action, as this relates directly to me, as author and as a Gestalt coach. I also tend to avoid the use of "he/she" or "he or she" as compound pronouns when addressing the hypothetical circumstances of coaches and clients, preferring to either use the appropriate plural form or to alternate between the use of the "he" and "she" pronouns. These gendered pronoun choices are random, but are used to signify an acknowledgment of gender in the learning and skills involved in Gestalt coaching. So I intend this primer to be valuable to you, regardless of gender, and regardless of whether you are new to coaching or a seasoned practitioner looking to add the robust power of a Gestalt approach to your practice. This book comes after many years of practice and reflection, but it responds to a growing need to articulate and describe this twenty-year-old phenomenon that is now recognized as Gestalt coaching. It is also important to articulate what Gestalt coaching is and is not in comparison to Gestalt therapy and Gestalt consultation—and, critical to the voice of Gestalt coaching, to identify it as the collaborative yet innovative stance that fully embraces the Gestalt process approach.

Years ago, Rainette Fantz—a founder of the Gestalt Institute of Cleveland (GIC) and a renowned lecturer on dreamwork—regularly earned student and client adulation as a "magical" practitioner. In the past several years, it has become clear to me that all master Gestalt practitioners receive similar adulation when their work with ordinary phenomena yields unexpected outcomes. What is immensely gratifying is that people can, in fact, be taught how to skillfully apply the theory and practice of Gestalt process. And when Gestalt principles, theory, concepts, and methodology are embodied and masterfully delivered, the outcomes do feel like magic. Because we can teach people this approach and successfully transmit its key learnings and wisdom, I have come to describe Gestalt as "the pragmatics of magic."[2] This magical feeling has a great deal to do with the sense of energy, renewal, and self-liberation released by acting with informed awareness in the moment that holds the greatest possibility for choice and change.

In coaching encounters, clients typically come to us as well-functioning individuals who are seeking new possibilities or are stymied by challenges that may have answers just outside their comfort zone. The process approach of Gestalt coaching is delivered in an "experiential, experimental, and existential" manner, which values experiencing and engaging in the present over reviewing historical narratives.[3] The Gestalt approach makes the common organic processes of human relations and interactions, which are usually out of awareness, "visible"—a phenomenon that makes Gestalt coaching so surprising, yet also so immediately compelling, for our clients and students. Bringing what has been invisible into the visible realm allows the Gestalt coach to fulfill her mandate: to assist her clients to become aware of what they are missing or ignoring in relation to their needs, wants, or goals. Becoming aware of what one has been unaware of is the catalyst that unleashes the energy to conceive, explore, and embrace alternative perceptions or behaviors. For the client, accessing such new awareness, in all of its manifestations, becomes an integrative, holistic potential for change. I name this integrative awareness competency Awareness IQ, and thank Barbara Singer, CEO of Executive Core and coach extraordinaire, for collaborating with me to create the Leadership Awareness Index, a 360-degree assessment of awareness that is truly needed in our volatile and almost frenzied life. This development, too, was unexpected: if writing this book was an achievement, that work is what has led to this next ambitious assessment initiative, which would have thrilled the founders of the Gestalt approach.

The post-World War II history of the Gestalt approach is most intimately connected with the founders of the Gestalt Institute of Cleveland, who were considered by many to be intellectual revolutionaries. In the WWII aftermath, they argued against Freudian-based psychoanalysis, the dominant dogma of the day, and took a divergent approach to the practice of making people "whole" and "functional." First articulated as a theoretical and methodological psychotherapy in the 1940s, the

Gestalt approach eventually gained prominence and found its way into mainstream psychology and social psychology, and has subsequently been adopted and adapted by many professionals. Numerous well-trained practitioners within the Gestalt community have richly re-thought and found different applications of the original conceptual models to meet shifting 21st-century paradigms and demands.[4] A Gestalt approach has also recently been re-conceived and integrated by other coaching methods, though oftentimes without official acknowledgment. And in this age, when "disruptive" theory espouses the power of novel possibilities, it is valuable to see how these divergent ideas come together to enrich the evolution of Gestalt theory and practice.

Today, we are witnessing serious contention among various Gestalt-based training centers, many suggesting their approach is either unique or most satisfactory. Not all of this dissension is unexpected. The late Richard Kitzler, a pioneer of Gestalt therapy, wrote that "[e]very organization ultimately dulls the charismatic call that quickened it. Integral to this process is bureaucracy as the organization wraps itself in the corruption of respectability."[5] A later Gestalt writer has pointed out that "[i]n keeping with their anarchistic roots, Gestalt institutions invariably self-destruct and reconstitute. Training institutes differentiate into new organizations as a result of theoretical differences, practical considerations, or personality conflicts."[6] This lively struggle is possibly more pronounced in the comparatively fresh field of Gestalt coaching, where increased market competition guarantees that new organizations will proliferate—often with a sense of disconnection from the espoused Gestalt values of community and colleagueship. The fact that the power of relationship and the call for community are embedded across all Gestalt centers yet are often lacking does not diminish the value of either. An appreciation of paradox is also embedded in Gestalt theory, because paradox is such a natural part of the human experience and awareness of it is linked to change. We even have a concept called the paradoxical theory of change, which is discussed in Chapter 2.

Some Gestalt colleagues have not been satisfied with re-conceptualizing the models for the purposes of evolving their applications. Rather, they have occasionally waged public campaigns to claim proprietary control over the originating ideas—ideas that remain fertile and resonant for others precisely because they continually escape such control. The shadow side of all revolutionary movements is that those who are most visible or most established mistake themselves to be the personal owners of every nuance of the movement. The concepts we teach and practice in Gestalt coaching, first introduced by thinkers who are now long gone, have circulated in the Gestalt community, as well as in the public mainstream, for decades without copyright.[7] Oral history and directly reported published practices have been as (or more) potent forces in the continued vibrancy of a Gestalt approach in the professional fields as any copyrighted publications.

All Gestalt teaching centers have certain family resemblances, and Gestalt coaching may in fact come to serve as a unifying practice within the global community of Gestalt theorists and practitioners. Each Gestalt training center, and their practitioners, has played a role in arriving at this moment when the Gestalt approach is reaching worldwide recognition and appreciation for its significance and resonance in contemporary life. Recent writing has proven valuable in bringing different approaches together for attention.[8] My decision to integrate Gestalt theory and methodology into professional coaching was a gift—a moment of insight that was shared by my colleagues in an inaugural training program called the International Gestalt Coaching Program, the first formal Gestalt coaching program and the first to achieve

International Coach Federation accreditation. The Gestalt Center for Coaching (GCC), started in Istanbul in 2009, is the "alma mater" claimed by a vibrant alumni community whose accomplishments range from ensuring more effective organizational leadership in international corporations to equipping individual HR directors, executive coaches, external coaches, and life coaches with the awareness and sustained-learning tools that enable them to realize their goals. This Center and its Gestalt coach training workshops and programs are the natural evolution of the work that began at the Gestalt Institute of Cleveland over 20 years ago.

Our work in Istanbul is testament to the power of being disrupted from one's original home base, but then, through the power of relationship and valued partnership, being able to re-ground and to re-organize into a dynamic new program and training center. The productive fertility of the GCC may have as much to do with its quality of social richness that has worked to strengthen the fullest expressions of Gestalt practice across mental, emotional, physical, cultural, and spiritual levels. Working in Istanbul has brought a deep psycho-spiritual richness to our work where the strength of community is visible in the accomplishments of the individual. Gestalt coaching has been embraced by the business community, coach practitioners, and others who stand to benefit.

Though begun under my leadership, "Gestalt coaching" is not owned by anyone. What we all share as Gestalt coaches is the knowledge and skills we can model to our clients, who are facing complex challenges, some never seen before, that call for creative intervention and experimentation to spark innovative thinking and adaptive behavior. A marvelous vitality and sense of purpose accompanies the creation of new workshops, programs, and schools for Gestalt coach training. Partnering and collaborating with so many talented and dedicated Gestalt practitioners around the world, and witnessing the difference that a Gestalt approach makes in people's lives—these experiences are testaments for me to the continuing value of Gestalt in the 21st century.

I have had the honor of co-founding our international Gestalt Center for Coaching along with my dear colleagues and excellent teaching partners Dost Can Deniz and Gila Ancel Şeritçioğlu, as well as the great pleasure of working with an outstanding faculty in our coach training programs—Belkıs Kazmirci, Elif Biçer Suner, Yeşim Özlale Önen, and Zeynep Evgin Eryılmaz. I express deep gratitude to Martha Lannoch for her painstaking attention to this work and for her partnership in all my projects. My additional thanks go to Eti Ben Ziv and Avi Hadari for partnering with me in the early days of bringing this work to Israel and then to Istanbul. Thanks as well to Joan Kofodimos for stepping into the work with me to provide her perspective, to Deb Halinski for her contributions to my presentations, and to John Schuster, Alper Utku, and Ann Van Eron for their ongoing collaboration(s). I am grateful to Leslie Virag and Esra Sertoglu for their generous reviews of book chapters, and to Meyzi Elhadef, Ahmet Akın, and Ann Hawkins for their ongoing encouragement. Dear friends Belleruth Naparstek, Pamela McBride Land, and Bonnie Fowke are always with me. The tenacious resilience of my mother has always acted as a reminder to press on, and the achievements of my brother, Paul Enker, MD, are a source of inspiration. The memory of my father reminds me of the strength and grace that are needed to rebuild after all is lost. But the most important pillar of support has come from my husband, the remarkable Jeffrey Siminovitch, MD, who always delivers on all the promises of excellence and the quality of his character, and who never failed to remind me that I could write this book. He is an ongoing inspiration, and the blessing in my universe.

Groups of people who have influenced my journey have been: Adler International, Association of Coach Training Organizations

(ACTO), Case Western Reserve University Department of Organizational Behavior, Coaching Beyond Borders, Executive Core, faculty of the International Gestalt Coaching Program, Gestalt Institute of Cleveland (GIC), Gestalt International Study Center (GISC), Hudson Institute of Coaching, International Coach Federation Global, International Coach Federation Toronto Chapter, International Consortium for Coaching in Organizations (ICCO), ISRAGIC training program, Jonno Hanafin & Associates, Lake Health Systems (Cleveland, OH), Management Centre Türkiye, MKB Leadership Coaching, New Management Network, Newfield Network, Search Inside Yourself Leadership Institute (SIYLI), Strozzi Institute, Team Coaching Zone, and World Business Executive Coach Summit (WBECS). I extend my deep gratitude to my dear students and clients who have endorsed and honored my work with their presence. Each student and each client renews my commitment to this field of practice and my gratitude for your trust.

Whatever your current coaching approach or career path, learning and practicing Gestalt coaching can be an insightful and exhilarating vehicle that supports you to become more self-aware and personally fulfilled, but most importantly, more aware of the needs, wants, or goals of your clients and how they can effectively realize these. My aim here is to provide you with enough theoretical knowledge to support your understanding of what a Gestalt approach entails while also giving you practical aspects of this approach. I invite you—whether you are new to coaching or a seasoned professional who has used a different approach in the past—to learn a powerful, experiential coaching-process paradigm that inspires both coaches and clients.

As I have traveled the world teaching this approach, I realize that beyond typical sightseeing, Gestalt-based coaching has enabled me to experience moments of soul-seeing, as the power of this approach is revealed in the invitation to greater awareness that has far-reaching depth. Gestalt work evokes a sense of awakening, or as we say in Turkish, *uyanis*. When individuals, teams, or groups can awaken from their unaware habits in favor of choosing what offers new possibilities, there is the sense of arriving to what is familiar but with a sense of more resources and imaginative possibilities. We welcome you to the Gestalt path, which will always feel new even as it also feels intuitively familiar.

CHAPTER I
Why Gestalt Coaching?

The illiterate of the 21st century will not be those who cannot read and write, but those who cannot learn, unlearn, and relearn.
—ALVIN TOFFLER

To capture the robust richness involved in Gestalt coaching, we offer the Integrated Gestalt Coaching graphic to illustrate relationships between Gestalt theory and concepts, on the one hand, and the premises of Gestalt coaching on the other (Figure 1.1).

As the graphic shows, the elements of theory, concept, and method are "all of a piece": together, they form an interactive whole. Mastery of Gestalt coaching practice is founded on having all of these elements accessible for whatever necessary coaching work emerges "in the moment"—when it's most serviceable and impactful for the client. This commonly used phrase in Gestalt work—in the moment—is the living embodiment of years of thought, practice, and wisdom. Gestalt coaching has a robust lineage that gives proven depth to its principles and theory.

12 | A Gestalt Coaching Primer

Figure 1.1 Integrated Gestalt Coaching

An Overview

In 1970, Alvin Toffler's *Future Shock* was a wake-up call for the world. It drew attention to the radical changes taking place in all spheres of life and made clear that learning strategies were key to avoiding "obsolescence," whether personally or professionally. In 1980, Peter Vaill introduced the metaphor of "permanent white water" rafting to describe the context of the rapid, turbulent changes that organizational environments were experiencing as the new normal. Then, in the early 1990s, the US Army War College coined the acronym VUCA—Volatility, Uncertainty, Complexity, and Ambiguity—to sensitize their leadership to the trials of change, and to better prepare their personnel for unexpected challenges: the discomfort of volatility, the confusion of uncertainty, the chaos of complexity, and the disorientation of ambiguity. The pace of change and the rush of information have only increased as globalization creates more disruptions and a sense of fragmentation.[1]

Today, the central need for those in leadership positions is the capacity to respond adaptively and effectively in order to manage the volatility, uncertainty, complexity, and ambiguity in their own environments. The adaptive responses to confront VUCA are the power of vision, understanding, clarity, and agility. We offer Gestalt coaching as the most dynamic and most productive approach to assist us in meeting these contemporary VUCA challenges. Gestalt coaching, first offered in 1996, differentiated itself from therapy, consulting, mentoring, and teaching (see Chapter 8 for further clarification). What Gestalt coaching provides is a safe environment for clients to reflectively and experimentally explore their learning and performance demands. Gestalt is an integral approach that allows clients to access and make meaning of their inner experiences of change as well as attending to contextual challenges. After 60 years of evolving Gestalt theory, Gestalt coaching can be used to aid clients in recognizing VUCA issues while also assisting them in the innovative actions that could move them forward.[2]

A common start in describing Gestalt coaching is the obvious question: What is Gestalt? The first clarifying answer is to address the German origin of the word. Even in German, the word *gestalt* has multiple definitions. Though these definitions are related, maintaining "gestalt" as the descriptor of the approach evocatively calls attention to the need for meaning-making. One of the primary definitions of *gestalt* is the capacity to see in wholes, what is referred to as the "big picture." For example, the word *gestalt* derives from the German for "organized whole," which came from the Gestalt psychology of the early 20th century that defined perception as a matter of seeing wholes rather than just parts. Our natural tendency is to create wholes (the big picture), even from fragments, and to give meaning to that big picture. So if we are shown two parallel dots and an upward-curved line below them, we connect the contours and see a graphic "face" we've all become familiar with: ☺. The capacity to perceive coherent wholes—the big picture—when rapid change and fragmentation are occurring is the strength and value of the Gestalt approach. This book outlines the primary principles, conceptual models, and strategies of using these strengths and values.

When introduced in the 1940s, Gestalt practice was offered as a non-adjustment, individualized need-fulfillment psychotherapy. The psychotherapy model that dominated most of the first half of the 20th century was the Freudian approach: basically, the therapist cognitively determined ("analyzed") what was "wrong" with the client according to ideal, normative social mores and behaviors, and then helped the client to better conform to those normative expectations. In contrast, Gestalt focused on holistic perceptions, organic processes, and the individual's unique sense of integrity in the present. The Freudian approach is foremost an historical assessment, with interpretations of memory serving as data. But "in its theory, its methodology, its practice, and its application, Gestalt . . . is a present-centered approach."[3] Recognizing the important role that *awareness* plays, the Gestalt approach focuses on the process of paying attention to something, which is what shapes awareness. Gestalt theory articulates that what a person needs (or wants) will influence how she perceives her environment and the meaning she will make from her interactions with it. When a person has awareness of a need, she will look to her environment for the available resources to meet it. At a rudimentary need-fulfillment level, for example, if she's thirsty, she'll look in her surroundings for something to drink. This is a Gestalt maxim: that once one becomes aware of a need, this awareness creates motivation and action for its fulfillment.

Of course, complex psychological needs or desires are rarely, if ever, so readily identified or so easily met. These are simplistic depictions of Freudian psychoanalysis and Gestalt psychotherapy. The crucial difference between the two approaches lies in the practitioner's relationship with the client: in the Freudian model, the practitioner is the expert who knows what the client really needs or desires; in the Gestalt model, the practitioner is the agent who supports the client to become aware of what she herself really needs or desires. The aim of Gestalt coaching is to assist clients to become aware of what they need or want. The power of awareness acts to catalyze their responses to fulfill that need or want. Gestalt coaching is the process of enabling clients to become aware of what they need or want, the means toward fulfilling those desired goals, and the learning strategies that engender new possibilities. In supporting clients to become aware of what they need or want, an accompanying collaboration occurs where the client joins the coach to design the work that then needs to occur.

Need-fulfillment can be thwarted by a skewed awareness. As Aldous Huxley said, "Experience isn't what happens to you—it's how you interpret what happens to you." If a person is lonely, for example, he may perceive others in his environment to be equally lonely, and he may presume that his loneliness is also the reality of others. Or he may believe that he is lonely because others are uninterested in him or coldly aloof, which only reinforces his sense of isolation. These responses are influenced by his own subjective "reality." The psychological phenomenon of making meaning from what we see, relative to our subjectivity, is central to how we respond to the world and the opportunities it presents. The Talmud teaches, "You do not see the world the way it is, you see the world the way you are." This ancient wisdom captures the process of perceptions being shaped by unaware, habitual responses to needs and desires. The process of perception is filtered by one's own subjectivity, which blocks capacities to see differently and respond adaptively. Awareness is central to Gestalt theory and practice, and is applied and prompted by Gestalt practitioners in multiple ways. To better understand awareness, we first start with how it is captured in the concept of figure/ground, which influences perception.

Figure/Ground: Perception and Change

The Gestalt concept of figure/ground is the core element of awareness work. The figure/ground perceptual process is a natural human activity, and refers to what we pay attention to and how we respond to what we see. While figure/ground is basically understood as a visual phenomenon, it is also a psychological phenomenon in Gestalt. What we pay attention to—the "figure of interest"—among all other available things in the environment—what is referred to as "ground"—will focus our awareness and will influence the meaning we make of that figure and the actions we take in response to it.

For example: I'm presenting a major project proposal in a meeting. As I'm about to speak, my cellphone hums with a text message from my home security company about a possible security breach—I have to respond to that call quickly. Within the span of a few minutes, I need to let the meeting facilitator know that I have to step out, I have to call the security company and report in, and I then need to return to the meeting and give the presentation. My presentation is a very important figure of interest to me—it has dominated my time and energy for months. At the same time, this security breach at home has suddenly and unexpectedly become a new figure of interest that I can't ignore. My psychological work, then, is to shift between my long-term figure of interest (the presentation) and my in-the-moment figure

Why Gestalt Coaching? | 17

of interest (the security breach). I need to effectively manage both figures. The best outcome? I call the security company and resolve the issue quickly and satisfactorily, and I return and deliver my presentation, fully focused and present. In that ideal scenario, I feel a sense of relief and completion.

In Gestalt practice, whether as coach or as client, managing multiple figures of interest is an important skill to master. Our continually shifting local and global environments create a kind of figure frenzy, making it difficult to know what to pay attention to and challenging to be grounded and focused. In its emphasis on managing awareness, Gestalt practice is thoroughly aligned with the growing interest in mindfulness, best defined as "paying attention . . . on purpose, in the present moment, and nonjudgmentally."[4]

To be aware of and to navigate between competing figures of interest is known as figure/ground reversal, and that capacity demonstrates that we *can* choose how we will respond to multiple figures. The ability to manage multiple or competing figures requires a form of "bracketing," which takes discipline and personal mastery.[5] The genius of Fritz Perls, originator of Gestalt psychotherapy in the mid-20th century, was to identify the link between perception and motivation: our needs and desires not only motivate us, but also ultimately determine what we are able to see in our world and how we then respond to what we are able to see. So in Gestalt practice, the first substantive question for our clients (and ourselves as coaches) is: "What are you aware of that holds your attention?" The second substantive question of Gestalt practice is: "Are you ever aware of what you are *not* aware of?" The idea of becoming aware of what one is not aware of may sound paradoxical, but this may be the crucial awareness that could change both your perceptions of the world and your responses to the world. We tend to be quite good at "keep[ing] out of our own awareness what we do not want to know. By doing so we deceive ourselves and protect ourselves at the same time."[6] In Chapter 2, we will expand on how habitual, unaware patterns result in reduced awareness and therefore reduced choices.

The role of awareness in our physical or psychological environments is usually not obvious to us. Instead, we function economically through habitual, virtually invisible processes, which usually are functional and serve personal efficiency. Certain activities and behaviors become routine and no longer require our attention or energy (personal habits like putting your car keys in a designated spot, for example, or customary habits like shaking hands with people you're just meeting). Sometimes, though, we're unable to see that a change has occurred in our environment that requires a different response from us; or we sense that there's been a change, but we can't articulate just what it is or what response it calls for. Sometimes, what has become our habitual process also limits our ability to function effectively or to respond well to new situations. For example: The organizational leader who keeps doing "business as usual," despite environmental demands for technological changes, is probably headed for obsolescence. Obsolescence has to do with the inability to see and adapt to unexpected possibilities emerging in our field of activity. The person who has prepared extensively for an important presentation but can't convincingly answer an unanticipated yet relevant question "in the moment" will inevitably feel diminished and regretful. So another core question of Gestalt practice is: "Are you aware of the figures that need your attention?" Recent work by Otto Scharmer speaks to the relevance of being able to respond to emerging new figures in the moment that test our capacity to be adaptive.[7] This capacity to pay attention to what is emerging requires combining a nonjudgmental attitude with a curiosity to open oneself to what is new or different, which holds an element of wonder. "Without the capacity for wonder, we will most likely remain stuck in the prison of our mental constructs."⁸ The capacity to pay attention is critical to learning, as it is linked to the critical strength embedded in resilience, which is adaptability. An emerging understanding of adaptability is being able to recognize and discern figures as they emerge from the ground of our experience. This idea of ground in relation to figure is also what gives meaning to the concept of awareness.

Gestalt's figure/ground concept is often explained through optical illusions, presented in introductory psychology classes and entertainment venues as perceptual games. Let's look at one example, the "Columns or People" illusion (Figure 1.2).

Figure 1.2 Columns or People⁹

Which do you see first and most easily? It may take a while to see that both images are there because you can't see both images at the same time, only one image at a time. When you see the columns, the people are the shadowy background out of which the columns emerge. When you see the people, the columns are the shadowy background out of which the people emerge. To recognize that both images exist simultaneously in the field, you need to consciously and willfully shift your visual attention.

What is important in terms of Gestalt practice is that once you are aware that two images are available to you, then you have the capacity to choose where to focus your attention. The premise of all such illusions is deceptively simple but serves an important teaching point: What we're not aware of—whether objects or people, viewpoints or perspectives—may be the very figures that we need to be aware of, as they give us lively new perceptual possibilities, new cognitive interpretations, and new behavioral responses. The mindfulness of Gestalt practice is learning to be aware of one's awareness, which involves internal states of thoughts and feelings as well as the external states of one's environment.

The power of awareness was captured by the concept of the paradoxical theory of change, developed by Arnold Beisser in 1970 in a now classic essay (the theory is discussed more fully in Chapter 2).[10] Beisser wrote the paper intending to clarify Fritz Perls's somewhat indistinct ideas about how Gestalt theory and practice understands change for patients/clients. Beisser summarizes the paradox of change this way: "Change occurs when one becomes what he is, not when he tries to become what he is not." Like all paradoxes, the statement seems contradictory at first, but it reveals an essential truth from a Gestalt perspective, and captures what many experience as a surprising mystery that is only revealed when "seen" with awareness. When people shun aspects of their self-definition (their identity), whether purposefully or without awareness, they experience "inner conflict" and are unable to engage with the motivating energy and emotional openness that are necessary for change to occur. For example, surveys and inquiries reveal that many people, after years of hard work, are dissatisfied—they were never optimally aligned with their career choice. But when people are able to embrace who they are "right now," with acceptance and self-awareness, no matter their status, they experience a sense of psychological integrity and renewed energy. They are able to embrace emerging opportunities for growth and change.[11] Awareness is a present-state phenomenon that differs from the recollection of the past or the anticipation of the future. Awareness enables the power of choice, in the moment, which is what makes the present-centered power of the Gestalt approach so compelling.

Mel Zuckerman, the visionary behind Canyon Ranch Spas, is famous for creating a groundbreaking approach to health and well-being, which ignited a revolutionary approach to the health spa industry.[12] As the story goes: Though he had initially gone to a weight loss camp for his health, at the end of two weeks he called his wife to tell her, "Come to Tucson—I've found out what to do with the rest of our lives." At the age of 50, Zuckerman had the awareness and capacity to see a new possibility for his own well-being, which he had always disowned in early life, yet at midlife his disowned concern about his well-being became the catalyst for his entrepreneurial success. He incorporated the work and business skills learned earlier into new dreams built on reclaiming his capacity to live in a healthy manner, gaining renewed energy and purpose. The issue for Zuckerman—really for all who seek growth—is how to awaken from unaware habits or habituation to an awareness of new possibilities and change: how to move from what was to what can be.

The Gestalt approach places awareness in the central role for self-regulation and self-development, and integrates multiple forms of intelligence.[13] We propose that personal and practitioner mastery is advanced through intelligently and strategically using one's awareness. We identify this evolutionary Gestalt process as Awareness IQ, which involves awareness across all senses (vision, hearing, touch, taste, smell) and all modalities (head, heart, gut), as well as the ability to intelligently use that awareness information to strategically provoke a needed action.[14] The concept of Awareness IQ arose primarily through my own recognition (in myself and in my clients) that failure to use one's awareness fully and astutely leads to the regret of lost opportunities. These contrast with experiences of mastery, where successful use of awareness leads to positive and, at times, magical outcomes. The story of Mel Zuckerman and Canyon Ranch is exemplary because he was willing, at the age of 50, to become fully aware of his needs and to act on that awareness to enable and realize new possibilities. When such initial awareness is compelling yet disowned or avoided, Gestalt coaches can creatively inquire of the client whether that disowning or avoidance was or will be a cause for regret.

Process: Gaining Awareness through the Cycle of Experience and Unit of Work

As awareness is the key phenomenon that drives Gestalt work, the Cycle of Experience (Cycle or COE) is the central theoretical model of a Gestalt approach (discussed fully in Chapter 3). It is a powerful conceptual tool to determine correspondence among awareness, resistance, choice, and responsibility for taking action. One of the early influences on Gestalt psychology and theory, Kurt Lewin, once remarked that there is nothing so practical as a good theory, and the COE is an illustration of that maxim. The COE serves foremost as an organic process model of what one is aware of about oneself and one's environment, and how one acts on that awareness in relation to satisfying needs and wants. The COE also serves as an assessment of how need and want processes are being engaged or avoided through patterns of resistance. The optimal process of the COE starts with sensation, which gets recognized as a figure of awareness, which causes emotion that generates action, which is satisfied by contact and assimilated through closure. This seemingly simple sequence has profound diversity and depth. The

Gestalt practitioner works with the COE to facilitate clients' self-identification of their response patterns. Gestalt clients often experience an energetic sense of "liberation" when they discern patterns that they have not been aware of and, through that understanding, are then able to make more satisfying choices (Figure 1.3).

Figure 1.3 Cycle of Experience

The conceptual partner of the Cycle is the Unit of Work (UOW), a four-step model for designing and implementing deliberate—that is, "intentional"—interventions which will serve the client's agenda of learning and development (Figure 1.4).

Figure 1.4 Unit(ing) of Work

THE DRIVER OF CHANGE is The Paradoxical Theory of Change

When we say "work," we are referring to the processes of change and development clients need to address, whether naturally arrived at through awareness or deliberately orchestrated through an intentional process called the UOW. The guiding questions for the UOW are:

In Step 1: "What issues is the client dealing with?"

In Step 2: "What will the client choose to explore?"

In Step 3: "What new experiments can be co-created with the client?"

In Step 4: "What has the client learned in this UOW that offers new possibilities?"

Where the Cycle is used to support awareness, the UOW is employed to strategically support a learning experience. The COE can assist recognition of the awareness process in the moment while the UOW applies the awareness data of the COE in a designed learning process. The UOW also incorporates the awareness power of the COE, but invites the client to focus on an issue that has been avoided, alienated, or never considered. The UOW is a purposeful guide for coaching interventions, which we further review in

Why Gestalt Coaching? | 25

Chapter 6. The COE and the UOW together assist both coach and client in moving forward with agreed-upon work, allowing them to assess articulated goals and to identify whatever forces serve or hinder those goals.

We introduce these two concepts here with some concern, as they deserve the in-depth attention given to them in later chapters. A short overview, especially to those who have never heard these concepts, is not enough. As our approach is experiential, it is against our strengths to ask you, the reader, to first be introduced to these powerful concepts only in written form. As author, I am uncomfortable even trying to introduce COE and UOW in this manner, and I am aware of my sensations of discomfort. My figure of awareness is that I already feel this introduction will not serve you, and my emotional energy is anxiety. Feeling this, my action is to take this energy and describe this to you, and I now feel moderately satisfied that I presented you with the dilemma of presenting COE and UOW in written form. And the power of this approach is so compelling that I invite you to go to Chapter 3 for COE and Chapter 6 for UOW, if you immediately wish further clarification.

The Gestalt coach uses the Cycle and UOW as central awareness-work process tools, the primary objective being to mobilize clients' attention and energy toward a targeted outcome in service of their goals and sustained learning. The COE and UOW enable clients to discern their needs and wants and then to manage their self-development through a learning process directed to moving forward on their goals.

The COE reflects a natural process that is always occurring, since we are all always engaged in some action to satisfy a want or a need. Even reading this book is part of the reader's Cycle. The UOW, however, is a coaching tool that requires a conscious commitment to a chosen aim or intervention in order to assist clients with specific work that could further serve their goals. The effectiveness of Gestalt-based coaching comes from working with awareness and choice for which the COE and UOW are core to coaching mastery. Recognizing how to work with the COE comes first through the self-work of understanding one's own COE as well as learning how to use oneself effectively to manage the subtle steps of the UOW. We further review this in Chapter 6.

Contexts: Systems and Field Thinking

Even when dealing with individuals, Gestalt coaches are mindful that clients are involved in multiple environmental fields, so the coach needs to have an understanding of both the obviously visible as well as the not-so-visible forces affecting them in relation to these linkages. Two significant conceptual influences play a role in how the Gestalt coach works with clients: system and field theories. System and field are often used interchangeably in Gestalt approaches, which results in some confusion. They are, in fact, "two different ways of understanding and describing how discrete things are put together," and these differences in meaning-making assumptions are equally useful for purposeful coaching.[15]

Systems theory and thinking can be thought of as a kind of "mechanistic" approach that emphasizes system integrity related to identifiable boundaries and levels. Systems thinking expects cause-and-effect phenomena: i.e., if something happens at a certain level of the system, then *that* phenomenon will inevitably occur at another level of the system. So, in group or team coaching (further reviewed in Chapter 7), if one person voices a concern in relation to a group task, chances are great that this individual-level concern will also manifest at the subgroup or even group level. Since Gestalt theory posits that change occurs at the boundary affected by the work, a Gestalt coaching competency is to determine the level of system which "holds the work," i.e., the motivation and energy for change. Executive and organizational group coaching, where any individual issue will involve other levels of the related system, particularly benefits from this kind of strategic systems understanding.

For this reason, we spend time teaching our students how to recognize these boundary choices at individual, interpersonal, group, and organizational levels of system because clients so often get stuck when they cannot identify which level holds the issue. In determining the environmental interconnections that affect clients, Gestalt coaches look to discern whether the presenting issue is primarily at the individual, interpersonal, group/team, or organizational level (or even socio-cultural system level). Each system level is connected to, but different from, all other levels, but change at any one level of the system will to some degree impact all the other levels. For example: If something changes for the client individually, people at other levels of the system that this client deals with will also experience a difference in their interactions with the client. So the Gestalt coach asks: "At what level of system is it most productive to intervene for the greatest learning and development?"

As an example: A client has difficulty offering direct feedback to subordinates. The client considers this "my problem." Nevertheless, while she feels she "owns" the issue, the coach requires an understanding of the various levels of organizational system at which the client may want or need to give feedback. The coach is therefore interested in who else would be involved if the client were to actively experiment with improving her feedback skills. Being adept at identifying and managing system-level boundaries is critical for effective coaching—particularly for executive or organizational group coaching, where the clients are always interactive with and responsible for multiple levels of system. In addition, recognizing which boundaries hold the work makes the coaching effort more effective in reaching desired goals.

Making an intervention which is a system boundary error can damage the coaching effort. Working what is an individual-level issue at the group level, for instance, risks a significant boundary error, even if that person's issue may affect the group as a whole. Working one person's issue at the group level could be effective, but doing so neglects the important confidentiality if that person is not ready to work her issue at the group level or if she would prefer to work her issue at the individual level. Conversely, working a group boundary issue at the individual level can limit the full understanding of what work is really needed. When a person speaks for a group without involving the group, the group level is misrepresented by that person speaking "for" the group.

Field theory (or field dynamics) involves both social and personality dynamics in interaction with each other in a given environment—in other words, an engagement simultaneously encompassing both the individual's unique psychological pathways, made up of past experiences and future expectations, as well the unique environmental circumstances in which the individual is currently present.[16] It is a more complex conceptual model that invites intuitive options for sensing the invisible, intensely interconnected ways of perceiving and interacting with systems and their participants. Field theory thinking invites the Gestalt practitioner into a nonlinear thinking which can appreciate phenomena beyond simple cause and effect. It honors the unique nature of situations and people, as no individual's experiential field is the same as another's. It is relativistic and non-dichotomous where fields interconnect, overlap, and co-influence one another. Field theory thinking is a process approach that is present-centered and that acknowledges a world in flux. Above all, the field itself becomes a kind of living gestalt of all the energies, vectors, or influences existing in the psycho-social fields that one is part of. So, for example, if we enter a different country, we might be sensitive to differences in culture and ways of engaging which are connected to that field, but which we also influence by the field we bring.

Otto Scharmer, along with Peter Senge and others, has envisioned a new leadership model informed by states of "deep attention and awareness" termed "Theory U." In this re-conception of a "unified field," the Gestalt precept of being and staying in-the-moment is described by Scharmer as a call for empathic, generative listening; inquiry-based dialogue; "presencing" (a portmanteau word merging *presence* and *sensing*); and a fluid adaptability of the self to the "flow" of the current situation, allowing one to see "the future possibility that is wanting to emerge." Transformative action is realized through "intentionally reintegrating the intelligence of the head, the heart, and the hand in the context of practical applications."[17] This work suggests that we have an interior field that connects to the exterior field we are part of.

Nick Petrie's recent work on horizontal and vertical development derives similar axes of capabilities, where leadership development can be seen as progressing along a horizontal knowledge axis and a vertical developmental axis (Figure 1.5).[18] On the knowledge axis, the focus is on learning and attaining new skills and competencies. The vertical development axis is a measure of leaders' ability to interpret their experiences and transform their learning into environmental change. Horizontal leadership development focuses on enlarging leaders' knowledge content: learning additional information, skills, and competencies. This long-established and favored approach in virtually every teaching and training program may well account for the ongoing obsession with accumulating official certifications as testaments to one's presumed "development." Vertical development, which Petrie calls the neglected but more relevant model for today's leaders, refers to furthering leaders' ability to think in more complex, systemic, strategic, and

Figure 1.5 Horizontal and Vertical Axes of Development

Adapted from Nick Petrie

interdependent ways. To succeed in the VUCA-propelled world and its 21st-century organizations, leaders must meet these conditions from a stage of vertical self-development "equal to or superior to the complexity of the environment."[19]

The dynamic power of awareness and the relationship of perception to new learning possibilities is in the realm of vertical development. For Gestalt practitioners, whose practice is rooted in comprehensive awareness that can be described by Awareness IQ, the work of being aware of the complexities of our inner and outer fields reinforces the need for continual self-development beyond common, institutionally derived tools and techniques to provide master coaching. Petrie's work has strengthened the understanding of how the soft skills of awareness can empower delivery skills of knowledge acquisition.

Whereas systems thinking provides a strong strategic intervention framework, field thinking provides a more fluid, dynamic intervention framework that allows us to consider broader contexts, including emergent and uncertain boundaries, conditions, and influences. To work with sensitivity to the field is to employ "a set of principles, an outlook, and [a] way of thinking that relates to intimate interconnections between events and the settings or situations in which these events take place."[20] Defining the field is a matter of first defining the coaching purpose and then further defining that field "in relation to its parts and to the larger field of which it is a part."[21] There are highly subjective elements to such definitions, and the coach values these as part of the client's reality. Field thinking is perhaps more adaptive to new research and discussion related to social contagion, emotional intelligence, mirror neurons, positive psychology, and the elements of the vertical (developmental) axis.

Being and Learning: The Gifts of Presence

I have been defining presence as one's embodiment of identity which evokes an impact on others. Presence is an interpersonal and relational construct, as we can only find out about our presence in the company of others. This allows us to consider the powerful instrument that the Gestalt coach brings to the coaching encounter, which has an immediate influence on the client: the coach's *presence*. Clients often respond immediately—positively or negatively—to what gets evoked in them when in the coach's presence. Masterful Gestalt coaches have typically followed an ongoing path of personal and professional self-development, and are attuned to how they "show up" to the client. They are often aware of qualities they convey and have worked to understand, e.g., whether their physical stance is aggressive or inviting; whether their facial expression is harsh or soft; or if the timbre of voice is unfriendly or welcoming. A key question is whether the coach is able to "be with" the client in a manner that allows clients to find their own space of possibility.

Gestalt theory has been influenced by Eastern philosophy, particularly the notions of receiving energy and active energy, which are popularly known as yin and yang. How we show up to others sends an identity message of congruence or incongruence with self, a statement of who we are. Biologically, we are neurologically wired to attune to the presence of others—their stance, their expressions, their behaviors—through mirror neurons, which allow us to sense others' feelings and intentions.[22] Coaching presence in itself, then, can be considered a "being" intervention. When we resonate with someone's presence, we are drawn positively to that person. When we feel a sense of unease or dissonance in someone's presence, we react negatively to that person. Accordingly, one measure of self-work that Gestalt coaches actively invite is to become aware of what they evoke in others. It takes commitment and a form of courageous inquiry to explore what gets evoked. This often is the self-work that is enhanced by taking specific presence-focused workshops or training programs where the design will support participants in accessing this sensitive material from others willing to share what is evoked in them. Often, people only share what gets evoked when it is a positive experience, such as the warmth of friendship or pleasant memories. But there is great value in learning about the negative aspects of what our presence evokes in others, as this provides important information for potential self-development, acceptance, and understanding.

Many years ago, I worked with a senior male colleague who presented me with many work challenges. As he was senior, and seemingly more skilled, I truly thought that I was responsible for our work difficulties. Only with a great deal of self-work and inquiry did I come to understand that some of the issue concerned what I evoked in this partner and what I could do to manage our challenges. The learning about what I evoked in this colleague became the catalyst influencing the work I began on my leadership presence for myself and others.

The intentional or *provocative* aspect of the coach's presence is revealed through her intentional interventions, which is called "use of self as instrument" in the coaching encounter. Which facets of our presence we act from in service of the client are limited only by the range and depth of our presence across physical, emotional, cognitive, and spiritual dimensions. Where presence is the domain of self-development, use of self is the way we strategically access our resources, which determine how effective we are in provoking an outcome that serves the client. The difference between presence and use of self is important since we can get feedback about our effectiveness in how we use ourselves. When we hear what we evoke in others, what we are hearing is their response to our being. It is relevant to know what we evoke, as it guides our understanding about ourselves and what to be aware of as we engage with others. When people give us feedback on what we did to provoke something, that feedback is about our behavior in using ourselves.

This distinction between evoking and provoking is critical to appreciate and requires further elaboration, offered in Chapter 5. Presence and use of self are the integrative elements of Gestalt-based coaching. As the concept of social intelligence suggests, when we are present and then act authentically from our intentions, we create resonance with others, who then engage more openly and vibrantly with us. Cultivating presence and leveraging presence through use of self is a Gestalt coach's primary responsibility. Chapter 5 presents additional dimensions of presence and the skills of use of self. Chapter 7 on group and team coaching offers considerations of how to be aware of one's presence and use of self across the different levels of the social system, from the level of ourselves to the level of group and organization. As leaders, coaches, or consultants, if we wish to influence others, we first have to be aware of ourselves: our strengths, limitations, and areas for development.

Why Gestalt Coaching?

Gestalt coaching unites principles, concepts, and methodologies taken from Gestalt psychotherapy and from Gestalt organizational consulting, both of which have long histories and are effective for their targeted purposes. The central principles and concepts for trust development, intimacy, dialogue, and inquiry-based learning come from Gestalt psychotherapy; the integration of systems theory and level of system intervention cues comes from Gestalt organizational consulting. But Gestalt coaching isn't distinctly identified with either of these.[23]

The primary definition of coaching, worldwide and irrespective of methodological differences, holds that coaching is a collaborative relationship between coach and client which is designed to support the client's acting upon goals or new possibilities. The coach-client collaboration is one key differentiation from therapy and consulting.[24] An egalitarian relationship with the client creates a quality of transparency and energetic possibility, which in part explains why coaching as a profession has so quickly become a global phenomenon. It is also why Gestalt-based coaching in particular, with some 60 years of thoughtful theory development, is positioned so powerfully within the field of professional coaching. The distinctive strengths of Gestalt coaching are based on its core values, chief among which is seeing the client as a collaborator in the learning and change process. Gestalt practice has always had this collaborative orientation embedded in how to work with the client, and this orientation is the distinct example of the alignment of Gestalt-based coaching with the practice of contemporary coaching.

Clients present themselves to coaches asking for support and deeper meaning, or to find renewed energy in moving toward new possibilities. By applying Gestalt theory and practice, Gestalt coaches support their clients' ability to act in the moment—with experiential, experimental, and existential responsiveness—as an instrumental skill. And of course, the more proficiently coaches embody this skill in themselves, the greater their mastery in coaching others.

Mastering the ability to spot opportunities and to act assertively on them comes through a developed and disciplined practice. To meet client needs, Gestalt coaches must become competent in staying fully aware in the existential moment as well as in staying experientially engaged and experimentally curious. In partnership with an experienced Gestalt coach, clients' situational awareness and intervention skills are strengthened, their vision of opportunity and possibility is sharpened, and they are empowered by processes of ongoing self-support and sustained learning.

Early on, Gestalt coaching students recognize the malleable creativity of the Gestalt approach, which is in part a result of its focus on the organic processes and multiple awarenesses that undergird human experience. Gestalt coaching provides an integrative paradigm that is:

- Both intuitive *and* pragmatic
- Both holistic *and* capable of individualized specification
- Both focused on the present moment *and* appreciative of past influences

- Both change-oriented *and* identity-preserving

Gestalt coaching has the conceptual and practical range to be immediately effective across cultural boundaries, which is particularly significant in this era of globalization. The power of being a practiced observer allows the Gestalt coach to notice what is universal while being curious about cultural differences. Gestalt models of organic processes for understanding perception and meaning-making are pan-cultural. This accumulated cognitive and experiential knowledge can be artfully applied in culturally unfamiliar circumstances because the inquiry with others is always honored with permission for exploration and exchange.

The principles that inform, guide, and support Gestalt coaching are rooted in values that are deeply integral to these human processes:

- **The Gestalt coach facilitates a co-created environment of trust** wherein clients are able to explore alternative ways of behaving with no risk to their professional well-being (the "safe emergency" of Gestalt practice).[25]
- **Clients are believed to be innately capable and competent.** The Gestalt coach's primary responsibility is to assist clients to identify (and to own) their available resources.
- **Gestalt thinking holds that learning and change occur through experience and experimentation,** both of which are often contingent on emotion and "failure" to ignite new insights and new perspectives.
- **The Gestalt coach helps clients understand and appreciate their resistance to change.** Resistance is honored for its service to clients, and through coaching clients determine whether identified resistances still serve or instead obstruct their needs.

Why Gestalt Coaching? | 37

- **The Gestalt coach works appreciatively and co-creatively** with clients to assist their self-identification of needs, wants, and resistances, and to then shift their focus to opportunities and possibilities.

When Gestalt coaches engage with clients, whether executive leaders or task teams or others, they are calling upon an inner "toolkit" of competencies, and the selection of any particular tool depends on the orientation questions that are foremost in the moment. Such orientation questions about the client will include:

- What is the client aware of? What is the client unaware of?
- Is the client aware of needs or wants and able to satisfy them, or is the client blocked at some point in the recognition and/or experience of satisfaction?
- What field is the client part of? What level of system holds the work that would best serve the client?
- How aware is the client of his identity in relation to the wider field? Is the client aware of how he impacts others?
- If the client is in a leadership position, how aware of others does she appear to be? To what degree does the client demonstrate awareness intelligence? What is she missing?

The Cycle of Experience and the Unit of Work are central to Gestalt practice, but they are not easy concepts to fully master. Beginning coaches may learn the models quite well, but applying them in the moment will at first be awkward and challenging. With dedicated practice, though, Gestalt coaches will witness the magic of seeing clients move forward with greater energy, agility, and confidence as they begin to learn how to track their own Cycle for sustained self-development and self-support.

Incorporating an awareness of both system and field thinking is also a skill that can be taught to Gestalt coaching clients. The Gestalt coach supports clients' experiential and experimental practice in recognizing and working across multiple levels of system. The perceptual concept of figure/ground is enhanced by an understanding both of levels of system and the field, making more salient the existence of multiple realities and multiple contexts, and therefore of more choices. This awareness heightens clients' emotional and social intelligence, and tutors them in the art of identifying what "holds" the energy for any given change effort. When the coach skillfully uses core Gestalt principles and methodologies to teach clients the means to achieve on their own what they have been imagining, hoping for, dreaming about—that is, indeed, a powerful and intensely pragmatic kind of magic.

Gestalt theory and methodology have depth, breadth, and power for both individuals and larger human systems. Central Gestalt principles—e.g., collaboration, co-creation, awareness intelligence, experimentation, deep listening—are in perfect accord with the core competencies that the International Coach Federation (ICF), the leading professional coach accreditation organization, has made the established universal standards for coaching (we will expand on the ICF and core competencies in Chapter 8).[26] Moreover, key Gestalt theoretic, conceptual, and methodological principles are repeatedly affirmed in a number of different fields: by recent research in neuroscience, quantum physics, and systems theory; by greater and more nuanced understanding of the significant impact of emotional and social intelligence for successful leadership in any number of professional arenas; and by compelling new developments in learning theory.[27] The more I explore the explosion of professional coaching programs and their philosophies, the more assured I am that this particular constellation of Gestalt concepts, as applied and practiced by masterful coaches, uniquely serves our clients in meeting the VUCA demands of our modern world.

CHAPTER 2
Awareness and Change

From a Gestalt perspective, the three most important elements in the work are awareness, awareness, and awareness.
—Jonno Hanafin

Change the way you look at things, and the things you look at will change.
—Wayne Dyer

Clients seek coaching in order to achieve change, whether externally demanded or self-motivated or both. Their reasons and sense of urgency vary, but the fundamental aim is to better themselves, professionally or personally. Despite talent and focused ambition, these clients are unable to clearly understand or evaluate what frustrates their ability to realize their change goals since habitual processes operate to reduce their awareness. Habitual processes, those habits we constantly do, work to maintain the status quo as well as personal efficiency, but over time, when habitual process becomes fully unaware, blind spots are created in our awareness. Change, even desired change, then becomes difficult to *intentionally* affect or effect, and clients sometimes experience strong resistance or what has been called "a kind of personal immunity to change."[1]

In mobilizing the needed energy to make big or even small changes in the world—to right a wrong, to alter social priorities, to reallocate available resources—one has to catch others' attention by offering new data or by bringing ignored conditions into view. In the 1960s, these tactics were called "raising consciousness"; today, the preferred phrase is "raising awareness." This shift to *awareness* is the first step in learning and change. Our awareness is the essential material for choice and responsibility. Whether we're talking about changing the world, changing our organization, or changing ourselves, the objective of raising awareness is to make what was background and unaware, or even invisible, now visible and figural, and to therefore make it available for choice and action. This seems obvious, but the impact that awareness generates ranges from heightened interest to radical surprise. This impact is the essential message of the mantra *küçük ama büyük*—"small but big"—that I so love to use. A small piece of revealed awareness at the right moment is what ignites the most energy for new possibilities.

Gestalt coaching is differentiated from other coaching approaches by a perspective that emphasizes awareness as both the path and the method. Where Organizational Development practices made "change agent" the stance for OD practitioners, Gestalt coaches take their stance as *awareness agents,* a role that calls upon them to catalyze clients' self-awareness as the key asset for current and future goal attainment. Most clients want to know "what to do" about some situation they may define as dysfunctional or threatening. But for the Gestalt coach, the first questions are: "What are you aware of in your world? What are you seeing or maybe not seeing? What is getting your attention as you answer this?" The intent of working to encourage clients' awareness is for them to become aware of their aware and unaware processes.

The role of habits is to provide efficiency, and, by practice, those habits support one's identity. The issue of unaware process is that, often, not paying attention to certain things serves our habits and can be understood as an evolutionary skill. Self-deception can be understood to serve an evolutionary function as it helps hide the truth from ourselves, though it also makes it easier to lie to others: "Self-deception is any mental process or behaviour the function of which is to conceal information from one's conscious mind."[2] So pervasive is the need to maintain one's identity that people perceive their world through the filters of previous experience rather than present-moment awareness. This filtering acts as a "premature cognitive commitment," where commitment embeds beliefs that can block the unfolding of an awareness process.[3]

Gestalt coaches do not position themselves as experts whose job is to diagnose or to fix client problems. Rather, they believe that the ability to heighten clients' self-awareness is what gives the client more choices—it is then up to the client to act on what is brought into awareness. The coach supports clients' awareness processes with a stance of compassionate curiosity and dialogical inquiry, offering select invitations to clients about processes that may not be in their field of awareness. This prompts clients to be intimately engaged in "learning from within," which grounds and nurtures authentic change.[4]

All Gestalt approaches are distinctive in requiring a collaborative relationship with the client. But Gestalt coaching heightens that collaboration into a pivotal creative partnership as the foundational condition of successful coaching work. Gestalt coaches are interested, in collaboration, in supporting the client in appreciatively discovering how he may be obstructing his goals. The consequential work is to identify perceptual and behavioral patterns that may no longer serve the client but which continue to have influence without his full awareness and to effectively bring these patterns into his awareness. Looking *intentionally* at something, including one's patterns of functional self-deception, pushes us beyond habitual ways of seeing, and often beyond our comfort zones. In unearthing these unaware patterns, coach and client together explore the cost of such patterns and what other choices exist to attain the client's designated goals. This is why a stance of compassionate inquiry on the part of the coach is so critical. Encouraging clients to become aware of what they have been unaware of can be liberating, but can also evoke a sense of shame about outdated beliefs or values or allegiance to knowledge that has been disproved. There have been times I have shared this memorable quote: "The truth will set you free, but first it will make you miserable."

The power of clients experiencing new possibilities is what happens when new perspectives are perceived.[5] But for that to occur, the process of reflective awareness needs to occur, and that has surprising challenges. As Schopenhauer said, "Every man takes the limits of his own field of vision for the limits of the world." That statement could be a pithy definition of the concept of the *umwelt* (literally, our "surrounding world," the milieus we live and work in). Umwelt is a term coined by the early 20th-century biologist Jakob von Uexküll to describe the "micro-realities" that organisms of any given ecosystem inhabit. In Uexküll's conception, multiple organisms may live in the very same environmental conditions, but each will perceive and experience the physical reality of that environment differently based on what it is capable of detecting, and each will respond and act accordingly.[6] As the Zen enlightenment tale says, the fish cannot tell you about "the water": the fish isn't aware that it's in water or that the water is what holds its being. Our *inward* umwelt, where our emotional and psychological processing happens, encompasses a great deal of undetected phenomena. To appreciate the concept of umwelt is to "appreciate the amount that goes undetected in our lives" and to be reminded that our awareness is limited by our umwelt.[7]

We usually remain unaware of our umwelt until we encounter someone else's contradictory or surprising perspective. For example, when I am facilitating group meetings, it is always illuminating to ask people to name what others have noticed that surprised them. Their revelations always reveal a range of small to significant surprises when participants become aware of the perspectives of others. The power of Gestalt coaching lies in noting and offering such unexpected perspectives that help clients see the limits imposed by their umwelt, as well as finding ways to guide clients toward greater awareness in relation to their unaware, habituated ways of looking at their world and processing their experiences. The Gestalt coach does this knowing that heightened awareness is the catalyst for change. Bringing unaware perceptual or behavioral patterns into the orbit of the client's awareness commonly shifts the client's horizon of opportunity: it's what releases *new* awareness and *new* choices.

Maybe we have never been exposed to alternative methods of recognizing certain data, or maybe we are unwilling to acknowledge certain cues that seem obvious to others. But the range of what people might miss is only relevant if what they miss is important in relation to their needs, wants, and goals. Clients who feel professionally passed over and alienated, for example, may be unaware of the negative impact of their behavior on others, whether it's bad manners, inappropriate remarks, or questionable ethics; that impact can impede their career advancement. So the Gestalt coach works to discern what the client doesn't, can't, or won't see. This is where the coach's curiosity, intuition, and boldness develop into artful practice. The Gestalt coach invites clients to work with unaware elements and to raise such awareness intentionally and collaboratively in order to support the clients' own needs, wants, and goals. Again, we cannot stress how critical it is for the coach to maintain a compassionate stance in the awareness heightening process.

Gestalt coaches repeatedly note how surprised clients are when they are made aware of perception and response patterns so deeply ingrained as to be "invisible" to them. This surprise indicates that awareness work is not only difficult, but also somewhat risky. Gestalt coaches train and practice to "develop exceptionally acute powers of observation and articulation" but must also accept responsibility and accountability for their part of the coaching work.[8] Gestalt coaches are tasked with sharing their observations selectively and non-judgmentally (separating "data from interpretation") because new awareness can sometimes be unsettling, even threatening, to clients' self-perception. Awareness *in itself* has power, and the profound ethical commitment of the Gestalt coach is to maintain an inquiring stance toward awareness, and to use awareness in ways that best serve the client. There is both a skill and an art in sharing one's observations, as it demonstrates intentional use of one's presence (further explained in Chapter 5).

When I was a young practitioner, I worked with an executive client in a professional development workshop. Though he presented as amiable and self-confident, he had gotten feedback about being aloof and hard to approach. He was annoyed and confused by this feedback but interested in learning how other people saw him. His interest invited me to observe him attentively—his vocal qualities, speech patterns, physical posture and gestures, and so on. Each time I shared my observations, he would respond with what appeared to be a slight shock of dismayed recognition and say, "You saw that?" With each such confirmation, I felt the value of what was being uncovered for him. In my effort to serve him, I offered him more feedback. While my observations were given with good intent, I didn't then, almost thirty years ago, understand the impact they were having on him. And because I didn't yet fully appreciate the power of my observations, I could not then "own" their power.

Looking back, we had no agreed-upon coaching contract regarding "safe emergencies," which would have assisted us to work directly with unsettling observations in more supportive ways. The safe emergency concept of Gestalt practice works to give more collaborative accountability to the client-coach dyad by inviting the client to say when the interventions offered feel too risky.[9] The coach can then scale down the intervention to something more digestible for the client. The idea of safe emergency is to keep the work risky enough to be interesting but not so threatening or anxiety-provoking that the client finds himself tipping into his perceived states of emergency. Again, this reflects the value that there is no learning without emotion. But it is the responsibility of the coach to be vigilant in her awareness in collaboratively managing this useful tension with the client.

After that workshop, I never heard from the client again. Today, I speculate—from a place of compassion for both of us—that my well-intentioned observations provoked in my client what in the neuroscience fields is known as an "amygdala hijack": With each observation, my client felt increasingly exposed in ways neither he nor I could anticipate.[10] I realize now I was seeing things he was not consciously aware of but that rang true for him. Every startle-response was an opportunity to explore that further; his emotion was a valuable entry point for deepening the work. But we hadn't established an up-front coaching contract around this kind of discomfort. Since he probably experienced the feedback as threatening, in hindsight, I could have scaled down the interventions to assist him in becoming aware of what was so surprising. In the years since, particularly when giving supervision to other coaches, I have learned to offer this wisdom: Those moments that take the client by surprise are the moments to slow down and create more safety for doing the deep work that's needed but may feel uncomfortable to the client.

My example is the kind of learning failure that can serve to teach Gestalt coaches how to be more aware, responsible, and accountable about how to deliver observations to clients. With the guidance of today's Gestalt coaching process tools and coaching agreement concept, this executive client would have been invited to receive an observation, share how this observation affected him, and if the observation was too surprising, client and coach would collaboratively negotiate how to proceed further. With today's clearer understanding of how deeply embedded habitual processes are, the corresponding skill when offering observations as learning feedback is to invite and support clients' interest and willingness to explore new possibilities. In keeping with the Gestalt belief that clients are innately capable, the Gestalt coach can trust that clients are just as smart as or smarter than their coaches, and will not allow themselves to be in a vulnerable space if they see that the coach is too ambitious or moving faster than they can tolerate. The failure in this instance is a strong reminder that Gestalt coaching is challenging and calls for skill and art in delivering perspectives and awarenesses that clients may wish to know but need the container of the safe emergency to manage the discomfort that most probably will be triggered.

Gestalt's Distinctive Theory of Change: From Change Agent to Awareness Agent

Arnold Beisser articulated what was only suggested in Fritz Perls's work (Perls is considered the founder of Gestalt psychotherapy), and thereby gifted Gestalt practitioners with an innovative and seminal change theory, which Beisser called the paradoxical theory of change (PTC):

> [C]hange occurs when one becomes what he is, not when he tries to become what he is not. Change does not take place through a coercive attempt by the individual or by

another person to change him, but it does take place if one takes the time and effort to be what he is—to be fully invested in his current positions. By rejecting the role of change agent, [Gestalt practitioners] make meaningful and orderly change possible.[11]

In determining how change occurs, Beisser described the process of becoming aware of and consciously acknowledging parts of ourselves that have been disowned or alienated. This is a transformative awareness process and a profound act of self-acceptance, which paradoxically ignites change. Demanding or coercing change will not result in sustainable change and will most likely lead to superficial change or a quick relapse. Client complaints about their good intentions are familiar: "I *tell* myself not to be or act this way, but I keep doing it anyway." Leadership coach Kevin Cashman popularized a truth embedded in the PTC: Authentic change is *ignited from within*—it emerges as an integrative function of our character, and cannot be forced or legislated externally, either by oneself or by another.[12]

The PTC reorients the "expertise-driven" change agent approach to an awareness agent approach. The change agent model sets up the practitioner as a proactive expert who has all the necessary knowledge, tools, and techniques to determine the right answers to solve any personal or professional issue. Thus the change agent's role is to tell the client what's "wrong" and what she needs to do to fix the problem. Recent developments in neuroscience and collaborative learning research are demonstrating that this paradigm negates clients' full engagement and self-awareness, which genuine and sustainable change requires. The PTC compels us to appreciate that instead of being change agents, Gestalt coaches are awareness agents.

A common coaching issue that illustrates how alienated parts become the client's umwelt is when his perceptions or behavior, which are disowned, negatively influence others. For example, a client comes seeking better work relations with staff but has received feedback from them that he is combative, controlling, and authoritarian. The client is upset by this feedback and denies its veracity. Yet the consistency of the feedback indicates this client is unaware of, ignoring, or rejecting habitual behavioral patterns that affect and are obvious to others. This alienation of some integral part of his behavioral identity may be the obstruction of his ability to achieve his desired goal of being a better leader. These behavioral patterns need to be brought into his awareness, and their role in his leadership persona needs to be explored. As these behaviors are brought into awareness, the questions for this client become: "Do I still want or need to choose this response? What are my other options?"

Awareness is at the heart of Gestalt theory, concepts, and methodology. "Awareness is like the sun," Thich Nhat Hanh tells us. "When it shines on things, they are transformed." As an awareness agent, the Gestalt coach works from these grounded principles of the PTC:

- People naturally strive to be whole and integrated, and have the innate capacity to be so.
- Change cannot be manufactured through predetermined or cognitively plotted behavioral modifications, and therefore the Gestalt practitioner rejects the role of being a "change agent."
- The Gestalt practitioner is herself an active and mutual participant in the work.
- The work is here-and-now, process-oriented, experiential, and experimental. The data of emotions, perceptions, and responses are more vivid in the moment, which is where the power to choose a new way of responding resides.

- An adaptive capability to adjust to changing environments is the goal of the work.
- The Gestalt change theory is applicable to larger social systems and promises "orderly change . . . in the direction of integration and holism." This is why working at the individual level with leaders can have such an important impact at the larger macro system.

Paying Attention to the What-Is, Right Now

"Know thyself," an insight from ancient Greece, is a piece of perennial wisdom that promotes self-inquiry. This adage implies more than self-absorption, as it has become a core focus in the field of emotional intelligence and, in the 21st-century, approaches to leadership development. Contemporary leadership "demands . . . self-awareness, awareness of others and organizational awareness . . . . Furthermore, [effective leaders] are able to identify [and correct for] unhelpful defenses or reactions in themselves—perhaps a fear of failure, perhaps a fear of conflict and a desire to appease."[13] In knowing oneself, an important self-inquiry question is "who am I?" The answer reveals a person's operating narrative and personal values. When people can answer that question in such a way that the cognitive, emotional, and behavioral dimensions of self are aligned, trust for oneself and trust from others increases.[14]

However, Beisser observes that clients are often immobilized by a perceptual distortion: they get stuck between who they think they *should be* and who they think they *are* without fully understanding or accepting either one. These conflicting concepts of self block clients from inhabiting either conception with any sense of security or integrity. There has to be a "home base of self" from which to step out with confidence and optimism into a new self-conception, but confidence and optimism have to be experienced as emerging organically, from within, which the client recognizes and experiences as real phenomena.

The PTC reminds us that what was initially ignored or blocked from our awareness for good reasons can, over time, become habituated and limits how we pay attention to and what we can see in our changing environments. These self-limits are what sabotage intentional change until the client becomes aware of, and thus choiceful about, who she *is* and who she *could be*. The skill and art of Gestalt coaching lies in the coach's ability to identify and heighten the client's awareness about what she is unable to detect for herself. This is the core intervention that yields extraordinary outcomes. The PTC reveals the power of awareness to ignite change.

Experiential Learning: The Importance of Process

The VUCA world has changed the learning landscape, and now "experiential learning is the pedagogy of choice" because current, never-before-seen situations require applying awareness into action. Experiential learning involves "a whole contextual set of lessons that you have to learn almost at the muscle memory level to make them real."[15] The Gestalt coach keeps clients focused on whatever emerges in the moment, because however hidden or obscured, these are the experiential data that connect to both short- and long-term challenges. The Gestalt coach recognizes that using what occurs in the moment, experientially and existentially, allows coach and client to explore and experiment with new possibilities.

Working with the PTC is a "radical challenge" that requires discipline on the coach's part, and courage and commitment from both coach and client, because "[a]wareness and contact with self is anxiety-provoking, for each time people allow themselves to know themselves and grow through awareness and contact, they destroy part of their old habits, identity or self-image . . . ."[16] Bluntly put: To enable a new possibility requires the death of an old way of being. Even if that new identity or self-image is desired, stepping out from the known and predictable into the unknown and uncertain can be daunting. Nevertheless, this is the essential work of self-awareness, which is never without risk of discomfort. Genuine, sustainable learning forces us to embrace the possibility of failure. But failure in itself is a profound learning experience: if embraced with awareness, we can learn something that had been previously alienated but, with awareness, will allow for new learning.

What Matters: The Energetic Heart of Gestalt Coaching

In our data-overloaded world, we have trouble identifying and paying attention to what really matters. This challenge is a big invitation to the global hunger for mindful practices linked to well-being, improvements in decision-making and productivity, teamwork, and even peace-making initiatives.[17] Rapid technological, social, economic, and political challenges are all demanding attention and understanding, and there is a growing trend of inability to pay attention or even attention fatigue. In a 2012 *Wall Street Journal* article, Holly Finn remarked on today's pervasive cultural phenomenon of inattention:

> Today's signature move is the head swivel. It is the age of look-then-look-away. Our average attention span halved in a decade, from twelve to five minutes, according to a study commissioned by Lloyds TSB Insurance. (And that was in 2008.) We miss almost everything.... What makes a person stand out now is the ability to look and keep looking.[18]

In response to a VUCA-driven world, programs devoted to the education and development of leaders now have a diminished focus on functional competencies, instead demanding an increased focus on "learning agility, self-awareness, comfort with ambiguity" and on "more complex thinking abilities and mindsets."[19]

Incorporating Nick Petrie's dichotomy between the horizontal knowledge axis and the vertical axis of transformation, the realm of awareness as vertical development increases what we are aware of, or what we can pay attention to, and therefore what we can influence and integrate and transform.[20] The importance of the vertical axis to leader development is that it clearly identifies awareness as the distinguishing variable that supports the application of knowledge to produce change. Otto Scharmer and Katrin Kaufer make a connecting link when they suggest that to meet the complex challenges of our times, we need a shift in consciousness from an ego-system to an eco-system awareness.[21] Where today's economy is a set of globally interlinked eco-systems, where elements interact in the social, intellectual, spiritual, and ecological spheres, they lament that the consciousness of the players within is fragmented into a set of ego-systems. Instead of having macro-system awareness, the "gap between eco-system reality and ego-system consciousness may be the most important leadership challenge in business, in government and in civil society."[22] Despite the importance of consciousness and awareness for development, it is only in the last 20 years that awareness has become a mainstream variable in the learning agenda toward emotional and social intelligence. Awareness is now being recognized as critical to breaking through the blind spot of staying with the patterns of the past and instead connecting to the emerging future. Scharmer and Kaufer are inviting a global discourse by breaking the habituations of past patterns through learning to pay attention to emerging future opportunities that only in the moment of awareness can be discerned. We see Gestalt practice as having the awareness-related training tools to support and guide this activity, especially in executive coaching, which focuses on supporting the awareness competencies leaders need in these tumultuous times of rapid change.

More than 20 years ago, I had the privilege of interviewing Ron Barbaro, President and CEO of the Prudential Insurance Company of America, Canadian Operations (1985–1990), then President of Prudential's Worldwide Operations (1990–1993). He came to my attention as an example of generative leadership for his ground-breaking work in altering the insurance benefits for those patients who were dying of AIDS. The idea for offering some value to these patients came after he was approached by AIDS patients while he was volunteering at Casey House, a Toronto specialty HIV/AIDS hospital with community programs. An industry shifted when he engineered an experimental policy to have Prudential of Canada offer a "living benefits" plan, then a radical innovation.

In his words, Barbaro reported his feelings of discomfort when he was approached by people he could see were dying and who he wished he could help. If these afflicted people held a policy with Prudential, his response was "why not?" And he could point to many more examples of innovations that he championed because of his capacity to be aware of ideas and possibilities that others could not see. While he would downplay his role in stimulating the innovation, the story behind each started with his awareness. When he was interviewed, he displayed an eco-systems awareness, where "doing good" in the world could be equated with the "rent one has to pay while one is on earth." The living benefits policy innovation that he spearheaded while at Prudential later brought him many awards, but at the time his awareness of the gross neglect that AIDS patients suffered sparked his ascension on the vertical development scale.

Barbaro took a courageous, committed chance in a stable and fixed insurance industry where few leaders dared to make radical changes. Barbaro listened to his deep interior, his inner awareness, that something needed to be done to serve those completely ignored at the time, and so established a new industry norm. Conforming to social or organizational expectations (habituating oneself to one's environment) is usually positive and productive. But the VUCA world has essentially gutted the inherent value of such expectations and replaced them with new and even more demanding expectations. We now require and endorse flexibility and adaptability as characteristics central to success, and these in turn entail greater personal risks—all tied to the ability to learn from unexpected and unlikely sources, to being open to alternative ways of thinking or acting or being, and to embracing a "world awareness" behavioral paradigm. Too many leaders miss the opportunity to capitalize on this internal guidance system. The best leadership today keys in on "inspiring people and tap[ping] into what they truly desire to achieve in terms of growth and contribution."[23]

This is a huge shift. And many of us are experiencing the difficulties and anxieties of adjusting to it. Yet the Gestalt approach has always had these goals, skills, and capabilities of flexibility, adaptability, and personal risk embedded in its concepts. So now that we are in the throes of this VUCA shift, we can more fully recognize Gestalt's relevance and power.

Awareness intelligence, which involves sensations, emotions, intuitions, and scanning of the environment, is at the heart of Gestalt practice. Using skilled observations of clients' experiential processes and interactions with the environment, the Gestalt coach can ignite clients' available energy toward new perceptions and behaviors. The core Gestalt principles of a collaborative stance and of co-created experiential/experimental work between coach and client is what engenders the client's trust in the work and in their ability to choose for themselves with full awareness. When the Gestalt coach skillfully and artfully uses herself to support the client's awareness of and experimentation with new possibilities and choices, she has facilitated making visible to the client what had been invisible (and unaware) and supported the client to see and to experience the liberating power of self-determined change—we see this as a contemporary version of genuine magic.

CHAPTER 3
The Cycle of Experience

The Cycle of Experience (COE, or simply the Cycle) is the conceptual tool that describes the alignment between awareness, choice, and responsibility for responding to wants, needs, and goals.[1] The COE serves as the foundational model of human processes in Gestalt theory and is a kind of tracking map of the processes of recognition and satisfaction. The COE illustrates, as process, how needs and wants are sensed, articulated, engaged with, acted upon, satisfied, and assimilated through meaning-making processes (Figure 3.1). For all Gestalt practitioners, the COE is the profound concept to master. Students are continually amazed that such a "simple" model holds such complexity that can allow us to observe the need-satisfaction process as influenced by one's habit pattern.

There are almost as many graphic representations and interpretative applications of the COE as there are Gestalt practitioners, but the principal elements of the model and their significance for understanding human systems, from self to organizations, captures organic human functioning in relation to perceiving and acting on needs and wants. The COE is a model taught differently by different Gestaltists, and over the years has been called different names,

Figure 3.1 Cycle of Experience (COE)

reflecting different emphases and orienting points of interest.[2] To explain the COE in writing, we are forced to describe a nonlinear, interactive, multi-layered process in linear terms that "arrest" and identify particular moments, which does not adequately address the fullness of the COE. Any graphic modeling therefore belies its deep power and complexity. Yet the fact that people name, represent, and teach the COE differently, while still adhering to its central tenets and structure, reflects the model's intrinsic power—its ability to capture the organic core movement through human experience in relation to need fulfillment.

The concept of figure/ground, this core construct of perceptual psychology, is central to the awareness process of the COE. Something going on inside or outside of us attracts and focuses our attention—that's the figure, or "figure of interest." The same context may evoke different figures for different people, because what drives a particular figure of interest for an individual is influenced by motivational triggers embedded in one's identity, life story, and meaning-making processes. A figure of interest is something that captures our attention and generates energy; it's what that "something" evokes or means to us that makes a figure *figural*, that is, of immediate notice and relevance (e.g., comfort/discomfort, pleasure/uneasiness, attraction/revulsion). And when we are no longer interested in that figure of interest (we've "figured it out" or are "done" with it), the figure is no longer figural, and therefore it recedes and again becomes an undifferentiated part of the ground. This process, so easily described, is far more complex because of how motivation affects perception—and when perceptions become habitual process, awareness becomes narrowed.

We are always being stimulated, internally or externally, in our awareness process, and it is our understanding of our awareness pattern that determines the responses we make and the options we have yet to explore. Viktor Frankl said that "between stimulus and response there is a space," and that space is the place for awareness, which influences choice.³ All too often, people are not aware of their awareness patterns, or that there is a jump from perceiving a figure into action rather than choice. Think of the executive who gets a call that there is conflict between an important stakeholder and a top sales manager. If the executive tries to solve the problem before he understands the issue, he is moving from figure to imagined solution. It's a common pattern. What is often needed is to slow down, gather data, and then decide what the real figure is or what plan of action is needed. In this case, there are multiple cycles: the stakeholder's, the sales manager's, and the executive's. Slowing down to gather data by moving through the COE process is an act of discipline that yields important information.

The Discipline of Moving through the Cycle: Six Points

The COE lays out a process-pattern that is organized around need fulfillment. Ideally, each point has to be adequately completed in order to move forward toward cycle completion. Learning and growth are the outcomes of satisfying our needs and wants in relation to challenges confronted.

To understand the basic process, we start by exploring the ideal situation. The COE identifies organic need-fulfillment processes across six differentiated points: sensation, awareness, excitement/anxiety, action, contact, and withdrawal/closure. The phenomenon of hunger, because it's a basic human need that must be satisfied, is a classic way to describe and explain the ideal process of the COE.

Sensation: I notice a sensation in my stomach. The sensation may be triggered by something external, such as the aroma of bread baking, or internally through a feeling in the stomach. I begin to pay attention to this sensation, and I feel a desire to eat.

Awareness: Once the sensation and desire enter my consciousness, I shift to thinking, "I haven't eaten in four hours. I must be hungry." The cognitive act of "framing" the sensation as a verbal statement marks the beginning of figure formation. Here, the figure that's formed is the awareness of wanting food. Framing the figure as "hunger" makes hunger *figural* and the priority over other sensations and needs. I may still have other figures in progress (maybe I'm on the way to a particular destination, or maybe there's an important meeting I'm anticipating). But the clear figure of hunger becomes my uppermost figure, the one that has my awareness and focus.

Excitement/Anxiety: If the figure of wanting to eat is compelling enough to take priority over other figures, I'll feel a sense of excitement that impels me to do something about it. Alternately, I may feel the other kind of energy—anxiety—if I don't have time or resources to satisfy my hunger. The subtle distinctions between excitement and anxiety are important for how we move toward or hold back from action.

Action: The energy of either excitement or anxiety can mobilize me to take action to find the food that will satisfy my hunger. Maybe that action will be to find a small snack from the kitchen cupboard, or maybe I'm looking for a more elaborate and hot meal. Whichever I choose, I'll need to keep myself moving forward and taking the actions necessary to satisfy my hunger. Action steps are dynamic and defined strategically to satisfy the uppermost figure, which in this cycle is hunger.

Contact: The action steps of satisfying hunger are what move me to make contact, the point where my need meets and merges with conditions of satisfaction. A palpable shift in energy occurs in the experiential difference between the driving energy of the hunger and the settling energy of hunger being satisfied: contact happens when the figure of hunger is satisfied by the food being eaten, and a change is then experienced. Contact is the experience of meeting the conditions of satisfying the figure so that the boundary of the figure is changed. In our example, making contact describes an energetic shift and a figural boundary change from "I am hungry" to "I am satisfied." A change in boundaries signifies a shift in energy and is central to figure satisfaction. If no sense of shift occurs, no change occurs. No satisfaction has taken place. Noticing the shift in energy and the boundary change allows for understanding when contact has happened.

Withdrawal/Closure: Having eaten, the figure of hunger is satisfied and can recede into my background, emerging only when it again becomes figural. In satisfying and letting go of the original figure of hunger, the energy I experience is that of withdrawing from and closing out the activity of eating, driven by both physical and cognitive acknowledgment that my hunger has been satisfied. Figure satisfaction can be sensed as an inner pleasure or spoken of with appreciation. Withdrawal and closure are often used interchangeably as ways of signifying figure satisfaction, but there is an important distinction. Withdrawal indicates being able to step back from a figure of interest "for now," even with incomplete satisfaction. Closure, on the other hand, indicates an existential completeness, a sense of being satisfactorily finished with a figure, either permanently or until it reemerges. Satisfactory functioning permits figures of interest to continually emerge and recede in relation to needs or wants. Challenges and problems may arise when clients do not complete their Cycle because of habitual perceptual and behavioral patterns that interrupt or block its completion. This is the issue of resistance, which we will attend to in Chapter 4.

The example of the phenomenon of hunger seems straightforward, but in fact it can be used to demonstrate the complexity of figure satisfaction in our modern world, where some people eat when they're not hungry and some people are hungry but cannot satisfy themselves. For many of us, the physiological cues that would naturally bring the figure of hunger to our attention have been confused with sociological cues that become the habitual "shoulds" and "oughts" around food and eating. Satisfying one's hunger literally changes the biology of hunger but may also be a metaphor for satisfying other needs.

Optimizing Movement through the Cycle: Assessment Questions

Clients often think they know what they need or want, but they may be unaware that their language or behavior suggests otherwise, what we may describe in phenomenological or existential terms as an alternate "what is." The Gestalt coach recognizes the significance of clients' frustrations around figure satisfaction, whether these are needs, wants, or goals, and can use the COE to help clients become aware of their own process. Let's return to the hunger example as the figure of interest and use pertinent assessment questions raised by the COE's figure-satisfaction process across the six points.

1. Does the client pay attention to his sensations? Does he scan his feelings and sensations to determine what he is experiencing? In scanning his internal landscape, is he unduly influenced by external cues? Focusing attention on what we are thinking, feeling, and sensing is an important first step in data gathering in order to accurately identify what we're experiencing. People often mistake thirst for hunger, for example; a glass of water may satisfy them as well as a meal. Preset meal times (e.g., lunch is always at noon) or the sight of other people eating can also trigger a false identification of hunger when what is actually desired may simply be the social connection linked with eating meals together.

2. Does the client use context to determine what she needs? Or is she simply accepting whatever her surroundings offer? The move from sensation to awareness involves scanning both internal and external cues. If the cues are "in sync," she will accurately identify the experiential need and strategize her behavior successfully to meet that need. If the cues are muddled, the need can be misidentified and the associated behavior will fail to satisfy. Mistaking "I am thirsty" for "I am hungry" may not, in the short run, matter much.

Repeatedly mistaking "I am bored" for "I am hungry," however, can lead to chronic inappropriate eating habits. Misreading sensory and environmental cues can seriously affect clients' ability to identify their needs and reach personal or professional satisfaction. As we become less and less connected to agriculture-based work rhythms, health problems become more closely related to poor eating habits. We're also continually confronted with marketing reminders for food and drink we have no immediate urge for. Without a great deal of self-awareness and discipline, people easily succumb to damaging eating habits that have little or nothing to do with biological hunger.

3. Does the client have the capacity to hold the energy aroused by his awareness? Is he physically, emotionally, or cognitively able to stay with the energy caused by the awareness? Does energy of either excitement or anxiety trigger a reactive response? If the client knows that food he likes is available and close at hand, he may experience a surge of pleasant excitement as he mobilizes his energy to access that food resource. However, if there are shoulds about satisfying his hunger (when he should eat, the kind of food he should eat, how much he should spend on food, how he should look while eating the food), he may instead experience a surge of anxiety; in turn, the experience of being anxious may generate even greater anxiety, and he might become immobilized—unable to move to action. Excitement around food has promoted a glut of cooking shows, and we delight in them. But that same excitement and pleasurable interest around food has also resulted in heightened awareness around the act of eating—diets, body-image, and eating disorders are now understandable causes for anxiety.

4. How does the client move to action? Once the client is aware of and energized by a need, is she open to the energy of action, which is the natural next step? Does the client move quickly or slowly?

Does she move promptly with the clarity of a plan, or slowly with excessive complexity? Does the client move with easily available energy, or does she hold back the needed personal energy? Energy is what mobilizes us for action. If the client moves too quickly to action, she may be skipping essential mobilization processes involved in figure formation and the heightening of energy. If she prioritizes convenience and speed in her action plan to satisfy her hunger, for example, she may continually choose a fast-food meal, which may be detrimental to her long-term health. Is the action she thinks she wants really necessary? Could she have a better plan to make more satisfying choices?

On the other hand, if the client noticeably holds back from taking action, she may have some action-related anxieties. Perhaps she has an experiential history of spontaneous decisions she later regretted (letting friends decide where to eat), or perhaps she is frequently tangled up in shoulds that frustrate her personal choices (eating undesired foods at business meetings to be polite). Being overly concerned about her actions impacts her ability to take any satisfying action, and to observers, she therefore may appear indecisive or confused.

5. Does the client experience contact? Is he able to effectively engage in activities that lead to satisfaction? Does he feel and is he aware of a shift in energy as he meets his need? In Gestalt terms, contact occurs when the boundaries that define the need change. A bounded, clear figure of interest points us to something that requires attention, a need that is pressing enough, or figural, to stand out from other possible needs. Contact is the point at which the conditions for satisfying that need (biological, psychological, cognitive, spiritual) are met. Satisfaction is experienced as a shift in energy, which is also the experience of change. This shift, or change experience, identifies that the need has been successfully satisfied. When contact is made and the energy alters, we can observe that the client's affect may appear different, or he may verbally express a felt difference.

6. How does the client withdraw from or "close out" the experience? Does she feel a satisfying sense of completion? Can she observe her experience and learn from it? Is she able to reflect on her experience with appreciation of satisfaction? Is her completion of the Cycle "good enough" to allow her to move to other figures of interest? At times, people complete their COE without closure, that is, without the sense of being finished with that experience. Their experience might be constrained by time limits, or there may not be sufficient resources or support in the environment to reach closure. The client's *withdrawal* in this moment is a stepping-back that helps bring the experience to a satisfactory end for now. She can adaptively "bracket" what is unfinished with the understanding that she can return to the need later with greater energy and intention.

Closure, though, requires time spent savoring, reflecting on, and assimilating the experience. In that regard, the experience of closure is subjective. Some people may take years, even a lifetime, to reach closure around pivotal experiences while others require far less time. People often don't give even a few minutes to ending their experiences. Yet the end of experiences is where the learning occurs around figure satisfaction: Did we do, and learn about, what is needed? Closure is vital to the assimilation and learning process. Our culture now perceives time to be in short supply, and we live and work under pressure to keep moving on to the "next thing." Even five minutes devoted to reflection can sometimes feel excessive. Closure is thus becoming neglected or marginalized. Withdrawal without closure is increasingly the "new normal" for leadership. The Gestalt coach learns, however, that clients' inability to reach satisfactory closure ensures that they will have the same experiences, with the same unsatisfactory results, in other situations. This stuckness around closure becomes the experience of "unfinished business."[4]

People may then inappropriately respond to new figures according to submerged tensions generated by unfinished old business and be continually unable to reach satisfaction.

At stake is a conscious, integrated sense of well-being, whether we're speaking about physical or metaphysical "nourishment." The satisfaction, reflection, and appreciation that ideally close out the Cycle are key elements not only for self-management but for ongoing evolution and learning. Closure is vital for successfully ending and savoring an experience as well as for learning and growing from that experience. Daniel Kahneman tells us that "what defines a story [of an experience] are changes, significant moments, and endings."[5] Kahneman explains that "endings are very, very important" in that they determine how the given experience will be remembered and incorporated into our life story (and into our perceptual and behavioral responses). If you have a positive experience that ends badly, that experience may become "a disaster"; if you have a horrible experience that ends well, that experience may become "a blessing." In terms of closure and unfinished business, if you have an experience that doesn't really end one way or the other, you will find ways to close that experience in your meaning-making process (e.g., "that's the best that could happen") or you will actively experiment with ways to close. Or, it can remain as unfinished business, which always carries an ongoing energetic charge. Closure is vital to learning and therefore a process that needs attention in all aspects of coaching, particularly executive coaching where learning from experience is the key element in goal attainment.

Experiential, Data-Based Feedback: Teaching Sustainable Learning

The COE is integral to what allows the Gestalt coach to pay attention to what is visible about the client while also raising questions as to what may be invisible to the client. What the client is unaware of is, in fact, invisible to him. The COE prompts the coach to use phenomenological data (those movements involving what we see, hear, feel, and do) in the moment of actual physical experience. This integration is what holds central importance and value for the Gestalt practitioner. The Cycle model is our vehicle for engaging in the existential moment, and being able to see and use the data of that moment. Sonia Nevis, a renowned Gestalt practitioner, engages clients' interest in their own process with an invitation: "Can I offer you something that I notice?" or "Are you interested in something that I notice?"[6] Offering this kind of experientially-based data is a basic tenet of most contemporary coaching schools, but using the lens of the COE enables the Gestalt coach to begin teaching clients how to track their own process, which empowers clients with greater awareness and choice.

The "data of the moment," observed through the COE lens, gives experienced Gestalt coaches the opportunity to skillfully heighten client awareness in the coaching encounter by observing, tracking, and assessing what is occurring at the sensory (physical), affective (emotional), and cognitive (thoughts and ideas) levels. As a meaning-making lens, it is especially adept at bringing into focus unaware perceptual or behavioral patterns that disrupt movement toward achieving and/or satisfying what is needed or wanted. Gestalt coaches use the COE to help clients become aware of what they have been ignoring (not "seeing") or avoiding (resisting). Through an interactive inquiry process, the Gestalt coach teaches these Cycle points and observational skills to clients and supports their self-empowerment through awareness work. Where there are chronic patterns that interrupt satisfaction of needs, wants, and/or goals, there are opportunities for the coach to offer clients a learning experiment toward new possibility. The structure and creative power of Gestalt experiment is reviewed in Chapter 6.

Leadership clients understand the increased empowerment that comes with identifying new possibilities and the capacity to choose how to see and respond to future threats and challenges—and they are best positioned to pass that learning and energy on to others in the organization. A female executive client who came to coaching because of a concern that she was failing in her leadership mandate became fascinated with the awareness that in talking about how she tried harder than others realized, she had a way to avoid paying attention to what she was feeling. What emerged from working with her COE was how little support she gave herself in her leadership challenges. The observations that were offered to her seemed to both surprise her and then invite further exploration. She had no idea how stern her face was as she relayed her frustrations, and she became more interested in the non-verbal messages she was sending that unintentionally communicated coldness, arrogance, and disinterest. The coaching exploration of her somatic portrayal (those non-verbal messages) illuminated other possibilities that energized her and proved successful to her leadership agenda.

Countless figures compete for our attention every day and, in our everyday lives, we easily attend to some and ignore others. For leaders and executives living in a VUCA world of relentless change and ambiguous events, however, it's easy to be overwhelmed by the sheer number and complexity of competing figures. When a figure that had been prioritized can so easily and quickly be displaced by another figure, we experience loss of focus. Within what could be understood as a kind of "frenzy of figures," many experience disorientation—a kind of organizational attentional deficit disorder that throws content and process out of sync. The inability to gain closure or completion around specific figures of interest often creates dissonance, dis-ease, and distress. Those who habitually withdraw from figures of interest without reaching closure well enough to feel content run the risk of feeling chronically unfinished and unsatisfied—the experience of being stuck. The impact of this stuckness is that clients may be unwilling or unable to mobilize the necessary energy to successfully engage with new and potentially more relevant figures of interest that could move them forward.

Similarly, when one figure of interest dominates and suppresses other valid figures of interest and begins to shape habitual response patterns, that figure can prove harmful to clients' personal and professional lives by constricting the emergence of alternative possibilities. Perceiving the same figure across different contexts could be understood as having a "frozen gestalt." Common coaching challenges in organizational contexts offer many examples of people laboring under the burden of conceptual and behavioral patterns that have outworn their usefulness yet live on in the workplace culture. Where such "frozen" mindsets hold sway, new possibilities and different choices are very hard to come by. Many business leaders still stubbornly prioritize function-specific expertise as the desired quality in management hires. But new evidence-based surveys and analyses suggest that employees more deeply value leaders who display emotional intelligence, who ask provocative and relevant questions in relation to industry challenges, and who express authentic interest in employees' professional lives. The permission for many to be more emotionally sensitive is withheld if people hold emotional sensitivity as an alienated part.

Until recently, for example, Google's core practices included valuing deep technical expertise and encouraging hands-off management of employees, only engaging them when specific technical guidance was required. When best-practices studies showed that social intelligence skills were instead the strongest indicators of high performance and professional satisfaction, Google began selecting, training, and coaching for those skills, while also ensuring that this new orientation was rolled out to employees company-wide.[7] The

Google project attracted a lot of internal and external notice, but from a Gestalt standpoint, the "buzz" confirms that stepped-up energy, creativity, and satisfaction inherently emerge from bringing in the alienated figures that hold value and energy.

Beyond the cognitive content of feedback, the process and quality of the feedback are equally critical to successful change efforts. Although offering experiential, data-based feedback is highly touted in the professional literature, in practice, giving feedback carries many challenges. Edie Seashore, an authority on the art of giving feedback, suggested it takes a great deal of personal courage to speak directly to the client about performance issues, especially those issues whose impact the client has brushed aside or denied—that is, what the client cannot or will not see on her own.[8] The challenge of giving feedback to clients is to work with them to increase their awareness about what has been disregarded or often, without that awareness, alienated by them.

In leadership training and organizational development fields, practitioners have made a business of implementing the 360-degree feedback method to assess personal strengths and weaknesses for employee performance appraisals. In this method, data used in feedback to employees is usually collected anonymously through questionnaires from those who work with them (e.g., manager, peers, and direct reports). The organization is actually advised to hire "professional and neutral consultants" or a "professional coach" to deliver the feedback because giving feedback—especially negative feedback—can be "demoralizing" and/or hard to hear.[9] What can we deduce from that advice?

What is significantly missing in most feedback scenarios is an in-the-moment, process-oriented inquiry into how the employee is receiving and taking in the feedback, which could better facilitate assimilation and integration of any recommended changes. More than simple agreement is necessary to assure the employee's assimilation and implementation of the feedback. Supporting the employee's awareness of her responses in the moment of the feedback (which the coach sees by tracking her Cycle) can uncover subtle but significant distinctions between perceived agreement and the unaware resistances that continue to serve the employee's unspoken sense of identity and integrity. Bringing these distinctions into the employee's awareness better serves the client by using the Cycle to see how she is scanning the data, checking to see what she is aware of, what emotions get stimulated, what she is actively looking to make contact with, and what she has learned that is different or new. The Cycle is used to support clients' ongoing evolution and to help them question whether their COE pattern continues to serve them.

Change Stakes: Re-Assessing Threats through Awareness

Coaches often see clients who are fixated on a verbalized agenda. This agenda becomes their content, and their interpretation of what they need or want adheres to this narrative agenda that holds their conscious energy. To the skilled Gestalt coach using the Cycle as guide, however, it may become clear that clients aren't recognizing their own energetic patterns or in-the-moment shifts in their sensory, affective, or cognitive responses. Examples of clients' unawareness may include: the client who wants to work on a specific business goal but keeps talking about family issues; the client who tells a sad story but who affects a frozen smile and is oblivious to his discordant somatic messages; the client who talks endlessly about preparing for a project that she assiduously avoids or delays doing; or the client who has had the same frustrating experience repeatedly but who hasn't yet made the link with his role in those experiences. Such patterns are disruptive to both personal and professional goals but are oftentimes not

The Cycle of Experience | 71

obvious to clients. Therefore, they are not able to consider other options with awareness and choice.

Habituation is a process of continued behavior, as habit, that has served one effectively. Habits that become unaware can threaten personal development and new opportunities when not responsive to changing circumstances. By evolutionary design, we are programmed to ward off perceived threats (whether physical, emotional, or cognitive) while seeking to enhance personal well-being—that is, normative health seeks to minimize threat and maximize reward. There is a neurological basis and value for habitualized social behavior: The brain uses the same neural networks to identify and respond to social threats as it does to identify and respond to physical threats. In our civilized era, social threats have become more prevalent than physical but are just as serious.

David Rock's five-domain SCARF model clarifies the threat/reward matrix that drives social behavior: **S**tatus (relative importance to others); **C**ertainty (ability to predict the future); **A**utonomy (a sense of control over events); **R**elatedness (a sense of safety with others); and **F**airness (a perception of what constitutes fair exchanges between people).[10] What the SCARF model makes evident is how easily physiological dimensions of social threats can be provoked and how easily resistance is triggered in order to maintain perceived status, how anxious we become over uncertainty and issues of autonomy, and how emotionally invested we are in our relationships and in our perceptions of fair treatment.

Using the Cycle as a guide, Gestalt coaches learn to measure the accuracy of what they're noticing about the client by dialoguing with the client about perceived figures. Cognitive theorists have described positive habituated patterns of perception and behavior as those that support successful navigation through routine, everyday obligations. It's a welcoming habit to smile when introduced to a stranger, for example, and it's strategically useful to always put one's car keys in the same place. Habits that successfully support efficiencies are credited as good discipline. But chronic habituated processes inevitably result in some degree of diminished awareness, which can be costly when important decisions must be made but *aware* choices are limited or unavailable. Diminished awareness results in limited perceptions, and therefore a diminished capacity to choose something different. The extent to which people are able to scan their interior and external landscapes promotes their awareness, which is what empowers them to manage their choiceful responses to the environment. This is key to mastery of self and leadership of others.

The range of behavioral cues that are outside clients' awareness is always fascinating and usually enlightening to them. For example, if an executive client is talking about his intense work schedule, we may notice he appears to be speaking quickly and with shallow breath. When we point out this observation, all too often we get a familiar response that speaks of a habituated response of not breathing deeply, as if he had no time. These simple phenomenological observations ("I notice you breathe faster when you talk about that") tend to surprise clients because behavior seems obvious once it's verbalized, but when habituated, clients no longer notice that behavior. We often aren't aware of personal traits that others easily see and quickly respond to: how we're standing, the affect our face shows, what our hands or feet are "saying." When awareness is heightened around these observable cues, clients can begin to see new behavioral possibilities and choices emerging. They begin to reclaim and redefine perceptions or behaviors that had been lost through habituation (what has become the unaware, alienated part). Clients experience a renewed energy as well as a regenerated sense of integrity when able to be in conscious choice-making. Imagine someone trying to reverse parallel park without a rear view mirror, continually bumping up against obstacles she can't see and getting too far away from or over-running the curb. Giving clients feedback on what they're "not seeing" is like giving them that missing rear view mirror. So the COE is used to help clients become aware of themselves and of habituated patterns that no longer serve their stated goals or even their well-being. With this new and newly available awareness, clients can see the obstacles for themselves and gain better control over choices that could satisfy their goals and needs.

Inquiring into the clients' experiential data makes Gestalt coaching work dialogical, process-focused, relational—and risky. This speaks to the important role the coach has in offering a safe place to give observations and feedback about the client's cycle. Phenomenological inquiries ("What did that gesture mean for you?" or "Are you aware you closed your eyes just then?") are in-the-moment interventions that heighten client awareness but may also heighten client anxiety. These observations can be provocative for the client, and so the Gestalt coach is encouraged to ask the client's permission to speak about such observations or to follow up with equally provocative questions. "May I offer you an observation?" is a necessary invitation, but it is also wise to remember that focused awareness is potentially unsettling, so the coaching encounter has to occur in a co-created, confidential, trusting space that honors the sensitivity inherent in unmasking old patterns while also inviting new patterns.

Even positive or desired change invites some degree of disorientation, uncertainty, and loss. Coaching for high performance typically must help people adapt to the disorientation and anxiety involved in moving toward even a desired new position and new possibilities. Any coaching approach benefits from understanding the innate need to minimize threats and maximize rewards. Coaches need to consider what the client perceives to be a threat to personal, professional, or social well-being because identifying a threat arises from individual perceptual patterns (what is a threat to one person may not be to another). What and how people perceive is in part driven by the figures that populate their inner landscape, even if these do not accord with the figures of others. The phrase "a figment of the imagination" refers to a figure that may realistically be an illusion but is nevertheless strongly relevant to the person who holds that figure. The concept of the umwelt reminds us of how much we are unaware of, but the paradoxical theory of change reminds us of the power of calling into awareness what we have been unaware of, especially those parts of ourselves which have been alienated through denial, fear, or lack of use.

The coaching encounter needs to establish a place for "safe emergency," where deep learning takes place. The context for learning must be safe enough that clients feel empowered to push the boundaries of what they consider acceptable. Yet the invitation for work must be at the edge of their discomfort, which breaks up habituated processes and feels risky but interesting. In beginning any coaching work, the Gestalt coach establishes a context and relationship of trust with the client. Essentially, Gestalt coaches must "invite" themselves to engage with clients in what matters most to the clients and receive their "permission" to pursue serious work. The Gestalt coach makes clear that she is interested in offering her observations of what is happening "in the moment" for the client, and that her work is to share observations she trusts will most benefit the client. The coach negotiates with the client that when observations or invitations feel too risky, more support will be offered to maintain the experience of safety. Conversely, if there is too much safety and not enough risk, the experience of emotional flatness will weaken learning possibilities. The safe emergency tension as the created learning environment for the client requires that the coach track the COE for herself, her client, and for the encounter they are managing. Managing the safe emergency tension with the client is what also supports the client's trust.

Gestalt coaches work from an appreciative stance through observational curiosity and awareness inquiries—they share their own awareness of how they experience the client and inquire into the client's process. When the coach asks, "What are you aware of right now?" the coach then pays particular attention to hesitations, incongruences, or resistances that may reveal what the client isn't aware of. These are the process figures that the coach can offer back to the client and, from the client's response, offer further observations that are connected to the data from the client's COE. The coaching work is done in an aware, co-created environment of trust, where clients can safely explore alternative ways of behaving. As the work proceeds, coaches teach clients how to use the Cycle to further their own learning and development. Gestalt coaches teach clients how to be agile, adaptive, and resilient in their personal and professional lives "on their own," in self-generated and self-supported ways.

Practicing the Cycle: Awareness Is a Two-Way Street

Working productively with the COE requires an unwavering stance of attentive curiosity regarding behavioral phenomena, a nonjudgmental consideration of process, and a commitment to report on observations of sensation, awareness, excitement, action, contact, and closure as essential process data. These can be considered as embedded mindful practices—being curious and appreciative about clients' every movement through their COE and paying attention to those movements in an alert, tolerant manner. Such a stance is integral to the Gestalt coach's work, but must become integral to the client's self-work as well.

For while the coach is attending to the client's COE, she is also using her own COE to help her accurately bring into awareness her own hesitations and resistances. She shares observations from her own COE as an invitation for the client to similarly engage in the awareness work from his COE, which is so critical for the client's growth and learning. The skilled Gestalt coach uses her observations and tracking of her own COE in service of the client's learning, using immediate phenomenological examples from her own COE to identify and articulate potential figures of interest for the client. The coach's ability to report her self-aware, experiential data as she observes the client almost always proves interesting and potentially motivating for the client. We further review the coach's use of self in Chapter 5, but reference here the skill required to selectively share one's self-observations as a way of supporting the client.

For example: A corporate client talks about her most pressing work issues in a very calm voice with little affect. But as I listen to her, I am aware that my heartbeat has quickened as she tells me about having to fire four long-term employees. I share my physiological responses with her. I ask her to tell me again that she had to let those four employees go. She does. "What do you notice this time?" I ask. This second time around, the client acknowledges an uncomfortable feeling in her stomach. I invite her to say again that she had to fire four long-term employees, this time more slowly. After she does so, I ask: "What do you notice now?" Repetition and slowing the pace of the words is an awareness experiment (detailed in Chapter 6) that allows the client to pay more attention to her sensations and to cognitively acknowledge that she was deeply sad and even angry about this situation. She's able to reconnect with her emotional need to grieve over this action, even though the decision was out of her hands and organizationally justified. Doing this allows her to realize the personal sacrifices she is making for this organization and opens up alternative possibilities and choices about her response to the situation.

For the Gestalt coach, tracking a client's Cycle of Experience occurs in tandem with tracking her own. That is, the Gestalt coach must have adequate self-knowledge of her own Cycle before she can effectively use her self-observation skills in service of others. This dual awareness takes extensive training and practice until it becomes a process assimilated and embodied into the coach's being and use of self. Self-mastery of one's own COE is an identifying marker of the masterful Gestalt coach. When a Gestalt coach has not attained competency using the COE, we observe some of the following:

- If the coach has difficulty scanning her own interior landscape in the moment, she will be less skilled in "seeing" if clients are similarly skipping over scanning their interior landscape.
- If the coach struggles for a clear figure of interest or moves too quickly to action before determining a clear figure, she will be less able to direct clients' awareness to this tendency in themselves.
- If the coach misses her own "aha" moments (when contact is made, a shift of energy occurs, and change happens), she will more likely miss these pivotal instances when this happens for clients.
- If the coach moves on from contact to new experiences without first reaching satisfying withdrawal or closure, she will have trouble discriminating when this happens in clients' COE process.
- If the coach fails to attend to, track, and address her own awareness processes, she will diminish her capacity to help clients learn how to slow down, pay attention to emerging figures, express their own awarenesses, and integrate and assimilate the experience of satisfying an important need or want.

Hidden Dimensions: The Pragmatism and Complexity of the Cycle

The Cycle of Experience isn't meant to anticipate or define all possible variants of complex human behavior. It's an ideal representation of need fulfillment and, of course, life isn't ideal. When we see clients who miss certain parts of their Cycle—e.g., when they move immediately to action—we can offer that observation to the client and inquire if that feels familiar. In our achievement-oriented world, the pace of work has become so fast that often people develop a characteristic style of moving straight to action or of bypassing closure. There is even a style that we call "ready, fire, aim." As coaches, we offer this as an observation, and when the client looks interested, we can follow up with the pertinent question: "So how is that pattern working for you?" Again, we see this style as a reflection of the larger worldwide work environment, which encourages swift responses yet recognizes that the consequences of haste in work are considerable. When scanning and awareness are consistently missed in the pattern of self-management, the outcome is that people may feel they are working hard but not necessarily achieving success. Scanning means getting data in the moment, and the awareness process means deciphering which figure to attend to. Moving to action without accurate scanning and awareness-framing may mean that the course of action is impoverished and will result in a poor outcome. The COE offers a mindful manner to give clients data about their process so that alternative choices and new possibilities can be brought to bear on patterns of which the clients, without that data, had been unaware.

The representational simplicity of the model is at odds with the complexity of its application. For one thing, multiple cycles are often occurring simultaneously. And meeting our needs, even one as presumably straightforward as hunger, can become surprisingly intricate. As mentioned before, the satisfaction of hunger has become a favorite example of contemporary Gestalt trainers not because it's so simple, but because it's so nuanced and layered—it can be metaphorically extrapolated to help consider how clients approach other needs or "appetites" and how they satisfy or "nourish" themselves. Even while we may be attending to our most urgent figure, inner biological or external work figures can also be vying for our attention. An important skill is being able to pay attention to the most relevant figure that needs attention and completion. Additionally, it is a skill to be able to bracket an unfinished Cycle with awareness and return to it for completion and satisfaction.

And while presented graphically as a compact "step by step" conceptual model, the COE becomes notably multifaceted when we need to look at different levels of human systems. The COE is a valuable tool that can be used at all levels of system: individual, dyad, group, and organization. While many coaching models are based on coaching just the individual, the Gestalt approach embraces the relevance of seeing individual issues in relation to dyadic, group, or organizational realities. The COE is one of Gestalt's great gifts to the field of coaching, enabling us to track the influences affecting a client's issue across system levels. It allows us to see different data across these levels, and we can therefore assist clients to have greater self-awareness, to be cognizant of multiple contexts, and to envision more and different choices and possibilities. For example, the executive client who comes to strengthen his articulation of his organizational vision, which may look like an individual level issue, will benefit from getting coaching assistance as to how this vision is delivered across the different levels of system.

Understanding, assimilating, and applying the COE is obviously challenging, but the Cycle is the essential model and instrument of awareness, which can be used toward learning and growth. It is a critical vehicle for coaches and clients to strengthen their awareness, which is the dimension of vertical development necessary in this VUCA era. It can be applied to any aspect of our lives in relation to biological, intellectual, emotional, social, or spiritual needs, or to any projects or figures of interest that attract our attention and energize us. When used with competence and agility, the Cycle opens up alternative viewpoints and strategic choice points for both coach and client. The pragmatic power of the COE is that it helps to discriminate between multiple figures and to heighten awareness around those figures most relevant for the client. The late Ed Nevis, who pioneered the application of Gestalt to organizational consulting, described the skilled Gestalt practitioner as one

> who has internalized the Cycle of Experience as an orienting principle through experiencing it as both a client and a consultant. One must not only believe intellectually that this theory of awareness is a powerful perspective, one must have assimilated the value of the awareness process into his or her *visceral* and *skeletal* being as a fundamental biological orientation.[11]

The Gestalt coach learns to use the COE as a way to observe and track clients' interactions with the environment, looking for those habitual patterns that may interfere with clients' ability to satisfy their stated needs or goals, then facilitate the clients' responses to this new knowledge. Gestalt clients commonly experience an energetic sense of "liberation" when they become aware of those patterns and get interested in other possible choices. This is what ignites the sense of liberation—the experience of being able to make new choices and the possibility of becoming more whole.

CHAPTER 4
Resistance and the Challenge of Development and Change

Most of us build our identity around our knowledge and competence in employing certain known techniques or abilities. Making a deep change involves abandoning both and "walking naked into the land of uncertainty."
—ROBERT QUINN

The psychological concept of resistance originated with Freudian psychoanalysis as a negative construct, as the repression of uncomfortable or traumatic memories or thoughts. Such repression was seen to cause dysfunctional behavior that interfered with clients' self-integrity and the ability to act in a socially successful manner. This dysfunctional behavior, according to psychoanalytic approaches, could only be ameliorated by articulating these memories through in-depth and sustained analysis.

The Gestalt approach, a post-psychoanalytic paradigm, articulated a different stance toward resistance. While Gestalt thinking accepts that most resistance lies outside the awareness of the conscious mind, resistance is not considered purely dysfunctional. Instead, resistance is seen as an adaptive behavioral phenomenon that serves to preserve self-integrity in certain circumstances. Resistance is connected to the need for stability and safety, which can protect our well-being. As an example, when a person who has a food allergy makes sure that she does not get exposed to the aggravating allergen, she is functioning in a protective and potentially life-saving manner. Similarly, the doctor who needs to administer life-saving surgeries adaptively de-sensitizes to sights and experiences that cause negative reactions, such as fear or even revulsion, in others.

One of the productive aspects of human development is the capacity to make particular responses an automatic part of our lives, "buried so deeply in the inner workings of our subconscious that they no longer require conscious thought."[1] While we've looked at the role of habituation in relation to awareness, we now look at how we deepen our understanding about how habits affect the function of "learning and unlearning." Researchers at MIT have been able to map what may be the habit genome. It seems that the nucleus of a habit has a three-part neurological loop: It begins with a cue that sends a message to the brain to switch to automatic mode. Next comes the routine, which we think of as the habit itself and which can be psychological, emotional, or physical. And last is the reward, the cue that tells the brain to reinforce this process. This is the "habit loop," and it is easy to see why as time goes on it becomes more and more automatic, more and more difficult to break.[2]

As we know, positive habits that serve us are supported by habituation and increased efficiency because habits bypass the time requirement of the meaning-making process. But habits that have outworn their usefulness may be hard to become aware of and become a non-productive and non-adaptive resistance. Resistance can become a force that interferes with and sabotages new possibilities. The paradox of resistance is that while a resisting behavior may once have served one's integrity, over time, the usefulness of that behavior can become outdated. In the Freudian model, resistance—and the dysfunctional thinking or behavior it engenders—emerges from repressed trauma or deep psychic discomfort. Gestalt thinking rejected those interpretations. The Gestalt approach is process driven, and rather than offering prescriptive suggestions, Gestalt practitioners offer an awareness process for clients to consider how their resistances have served them and whether those resistances continue to be adaptive and responsive to their needs.

Habitual patterns of thinking and behavior serve to define and support character and consistency as well as to strengthen one's self- and public identity and so to inspire trust. However, these needs for stability and consistency are often battling the urge to innovate and to change. Gestaltists have described habituation as a force for stability that slows down or minimizes change. Gestalt practitioners become interested in a client's resistances when it appears that the client is unaware that his resistance no longer serves to fulfill his needs and wants. For example, if a client receives repeated feedback that he is interpersonally aloof, yet he himself believes he frequently extends himself to others, a Gestalt coach would immediately be interested in exploring the dynamic behavioral pattern this person exhibits when interacting with others. In offering the observation to the client, the coach uses the Cycle of Experience to make figural the interpersonal behavior that the client may be blind to, and thereby raise his awareness. The Gestalt coach as an active witness and participant supports the client to become aware of how he creates closeness or distance in his interpersonal interactions. The client would be supported to both experience what is familiar and, using the coach's feedback, to experience and become aware of unfamiliar (unaware) patterns and the alienated or suppressed parts of himself that contribute to the gap between others' perceptions and his self-perception.

In early life, the child needs the guidance of clear sanctions regarding what she should or shouldn't do to stay physically safe in the world. Over time, and with the best intentions, other authority figures will transmit different should/shouldn't rules to ensure the child's social success. Our mentors and teachers will tell us directly what we should learn and how we should behave to be granted acceptance, inclusion, and reward. We identify "shoulds" as the primary way that values get transmitted across all levels—in families, schools, and social institutions. To accommodate shoulds, the individual has to say "no" to other opportunities and construct further invisible structures to assist the process of being in the world relationally and strategically.

Adolescents, on the other hand, endure a period of especially strong social forces determining acceptance and inclusion, particularly where inclusion demands accommodation and assimilation. Similarly, institutional work life carries with it expectations about "success" in terms of which values should be honored to gain advancement or reward. The shoulds of powerful figures in our lives, both intrinsic (respected role models, family authority figures) and extrinsic (superiors at work, institutions, corporations), carry vital information that helps us navigate our way through youthful development to adult identity. Yet the shoulds of these same powerful figures can become outdated or irrelevant in relation to what we need or want, and to how we might grow and change. The world of parents, teachers, mentors, and role models cannot speak fully for the world and the choices we are required to respond to and, even where their wisdom was once useful, it is a measure of personal mastery to be able to discern what best serves our personal and professional lives.

Resistance and the Challenge of Development and Change

To move forward requires change. Habitual perceptual and behavioral patterns happen out of conscious choice or control—*without awareness*. The relevant question is: Are these patterns serving the individual's needs and wants? When clients narrate incidents of frustration, blind to a self-defeating behavioral pattern that is discernible to the coach, the challenge is to bring that pattern into awareness. The coach must determine where best to offer an observation about a pattern the client may be unaware of, because doing so invites the disorientation of moving from a familiar and stable zone into an unfamiliar zone of discomfort.

The incentive to step out of one's comfort zone is supported by the belief in the potential of better choices to yield better outcomes. There has to be a sense of recognition that things are not working out in intended ways, and that maybe there are factors outside one's awareness. The self-awareness process undertaken to examine habitual behaviors is best served by articulating one's patterns, by exploring and experimenting with them, and by accurately assessing their observable impact on personal and professional life. A coach works to assist this process, and to help the client access and manage the deep emotional residue the process stirs up. When a trusted coach poses "the powerful question that breaks through our protective trance of habitual process, the brain is required to restructure long-term memory information." And for any shift in thinking or behavior to occur, that moment of recognition inevitably evokes an unnerving but essential visceral response—"there must be an emotional stake in the game for restructuring to occur."[3] A core belief of Gestalt coaching is that when there is no emotion, there is no learning. Clients are naturally prone to resist moving into discomforting and uncertain territory, and therefore the coach's invitation to enter that territory must carry a compelling acknowledgment that it is part of the learning process.

Individuals need to explore their resistances to see which are valuable and which are hindering. Hank Karp's work on personal power allows us to see the value of resistance used intentionally and with awareness as well as the burden of unaware resistances (Figure 4.1).

Figure 4.1 Karp's Power-Resistance Model[4]

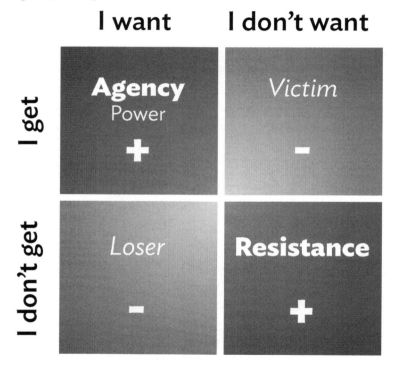

Positive use of resistance helps maintain the personal power of self-integrity and identity, but unaware resistance leaves us vulnerable to "loser" or "victim" status that seems to be beyond our control. In habitual processes, awareness has become constricted, and we do not see the choices that would give us a sense of control.

Positive resistance is the capacity to functionally set a boundary to not receive what one does not want. But without awareness it may become habitual to not get what one *does* want and feel like a loser, or to get what one does *not* want and feel like a victim.

For example, a hard-working professional learned early in her career that desensitization to the soft signs of fatigue enabled her to get an impressive amount of work done outside of working hours, and this had always helped her productivity and overall career success. In ignoring her fatigue, she was recognized as a high leadership talent. While the price of this desensitization to the fatigue of overwork could be afforded when she was in her early 20s, in her 40s, she complains that she is feeling less effective (loser) and that she is getting angry at what she is experiencing (victim). Until she entered the coaching encounter, she ignored feedback that there may be other options for her to explore.

Karp's model allows us to understand that dysfunctional uses of resistance invite us to fall into patterned roles that are self-defeating and distressing. When the issue of career derailment is reviewed, one clear reason why high-talented professionals fail to make the most of the opportunities offered them can be traced back to unaware patterns that work to restrict choice. Alex, a talented surgeon, appeared as an ambivalent coaching client who shared how angry he was about how others treated him and how he saw his colleagues as always undermining him. Alex was more interested in being energized by how unfair his world was rather than look at other choices he could make to change his status of victimhood. His distress was a chronic pattern that he continued to present rather than establishing positive resistance by setting better boundaries that could protect him from being taken advantage of. As his coach, I had to remember that habituations can become comfortable as a role pattern that does not serve one's goals. There is a pattern that identifies being invested in resignation or resentment rather than in ambition.[5] An important part of coaching is being able to differentiate those clients who are interested in the uncomfortable work required to alter old patterns of being that can, without awareness, become the experience of resignation or resentment. Alex's pattern, while so distressing to him, persisted because he remained more invested in the familiar discomfort of being in the loser/victim role than in engaging in the vulnerable work of moving to a more choiceful, adaptive, and powerful way of being in his work life.

The role pattern that people can fall into can be understood by studying the Karpman Drama Triangle (Figure 4.2).

Figure 4.2 Karpman Drama Triangle[6]

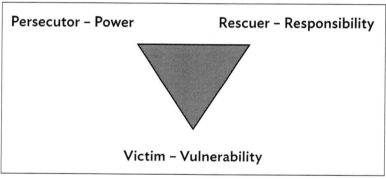

Steven Karpman's Drama Triangle is an inter-relational paradigm of "the interplay and behavioral moves between two or more people," specifically gauging "the connection between responsibility and power, and their relationship to boundaries."[7] The Drama Triangle schematically represents how cycles of aggressive domination, vulnerable martyrdom, and aggrieved responsibility become a dramatic and obstructive relational enactment of habitual perceptual and behavioral patterns. Each role is adopted without overt intention or purpose—each, in fact, plays out without self-awareness of the price being paid for living in that role.

As an example, Katherine, a hard-working executive coaching client, has been involved in a project that needs greater sponsorship from key company stakeholders. The scheduled company retreat is an ideal opportunity for her to present her project and gather sponsorship and support. Though she is prepared to offer her ideas, she nevertheless keeps deferring presentation time to others until, finally, there is no time for her project to be reviewed. Critical project time is lost—or worse, the very possibility of moving the project forward is lost. When asked why she had not been more forceful in asking for the needed presentation time, Katherine remarks that she was "waiting for the right time." In closing reflections, she shares how she does this often to herself, but she appears to have no insight into her role in co-creating this lost opportunity. This high-potential young leader needs to become aware of how her unaware resistance patterns are sabotaging her success. This is the invitation that Gestalt-trained coaches can offer their clients—this small but incredibly powerful invitation: "Are you interested in understanding the habitual patterns that may be blocking your success?" The need to overcome failure and arrive at success is what motivates clients to follow the coach into the discomfort zone, where exploring unaware habitual patterns leads to new possibilities, conscious choices, and new learning.

Gestalt coaching works carefully to distinguish between supportive habits that strengthen the individual's self-identity and obstructive habits that no longer serve the individual's needs or wants. The primary intent of Gestalt coaching is to assist clients to see for themselves what they truly need or want and to support them in satisfying that need or want. Marcia Reynolds observes: "For the same reason you can't tickle yourself, you can't fully explore your own thoughts. Your brain will block and desensitize you to self-imposed exploration."[8] Working with clients to support them to uncover and understand their habitual patterns demands a relationship of trust, as this exploration evokes vulnerability in clients. It is important to recognize that when a client shows reluctance or refusal to change his habitual processes, whether unconsciously or choicefully, this means that his resistance has a value that has to be further appreciated. Change is ignited from within, and the client who is resistant to changing a habitual behavior needs greater support and understanding for this sensitive exploration.

Gestalt theory reminds us that any change will be greeted with ambivalence, even if that change is desired. Deep-seated fears can be aroused and stable beliefs shaken when change is intentionally pursued. In such instances, despite a voiced commitment to change, the client may unintentionally disrupt the change effort in an attempt to preserve the status quo and to maintain his accustomed sense of self and perceptions of how the world works. Resistance of this sort, as Robert Kegan and Lisa Lahey describe, "does not reflect opposition, nor is it merely a result of inertia." Instead, it usually arises from "applying productive energy toward a hidden *competing commitment*," resulting in a psychological stalemate that "looks like resistance but is in fact a kind of personal immunity to change." Kegan and Lahey give the example of an African-American manager whose hidden, competing commitment kept him from engaging in an exciting new business venture. He feared that close and successful collaboration with his mostly white colleagues would "estrange him from his ethnic group" and thus "compromise his personal identity." For this manager, safety was preserved by *not* engaging in a new business opportunity, even though that opportunity appeared at the same time exciting and desirable.[9] As Kegan and Lahey observe, resistance to acknowledging the competing, unconscious commitment may not be obvious, since resistance of this type is an adaptive function that bolsters some self-preserving purpose. But the resistance can become a habitual process, which then limits awareness. For learning and enhanced choice, the critical strategy is to bring the competing commitment into awareness, and with this awareness, this manager could then determine for himself how to reconcile the internal and external commitments.

Kegan and Lahey's discussion of "immunity to change" aligns well with the Gestalt conception of resistance and Gestalt methods of working with resistance. Gestalt coaches recognize the reluctance and ambivalence clients feel around change as a normal human response. Gestalt thinking encourages appreciating resistance for its "protective, curative, [and] creative aspects," and explores it respectfully in ways that offer clients new perspectives and an awareness of self-determined choices.[10]

A key competence for the coach is to recognize resistance when it either serves or undermines the client. One measure of self-awareness is to know what one wants and to know what one doesn't want. Gestalt theory maintains that clients are innately capable of appreciating their habitual processes as serving some need. This perspective permits Gestalt coaches to assist their clients to identify new possibilities that will serve them to successfully adapt to the relentless pace of modern change.

Poet David Whyte poignantly described the visible and invisible force of resistance when he wrote: "We shape our self to fit this world, and by the world are shaped again." Sometimes, the shaping we submitted to earlier in our lives no longer meets the realities of a world that demands adaptive new possibilities and confident action.

Assessing Resistance Patterns

We view our clients' awareness and their ability to satisfy their needs and wants through the lens of the Cycle of Experience. When clients move fluidly through their Cycle, we can assume their needs and wants are being met with sufficient awareness and that they make choices to engender a sense of well-being. By moving smoothly through the Cycle and being in touch with their figural awareness, they may then notice some emotional energy that activates them toward getting satisfaction and then, once satisfied, closing that figure and allowing another figure to emerge from the ground of their needs and wants. When clients' movement through their COE is hesitant, interrupted, or blocked, the Gestalt coach looks to make meaning of these particular patterns.

In Chapter 3 we introduced the Cycle of Experience, which we now revisit by acknowledging that resistance is actually embedded within everyone's COE, and reminding ourselves that resistance is a normative part of being functional. One definition of resistance Ed Nevis made famous was that when a client says "no" to a new behavior, she is also saying "yes" to another behavior. We therefore look at the patterns of where the COE is interrupted or blocked to get interested in the particular meaning of the client's resistance.

Interruptions to the COE present opportunities for interesting questions through which to explore identifiable resistance patterns. Some sample COE questions and attendant skills are:

In the Sensation stage: Is the person desensitizing in order to manage overwhelming physical and emotional challenges?

> *COE skill: To recognize the sensation-numbing qualities of desensitization*

In the Awareness stage: Is the person aware of what she notices yet, because of old sanctions that dictate what she should or shouldn't pay attention to, she interrupts or negates what she notices?

> *COE skill: To recognize the shoulds of introjections*

In the Excitement/Anxiety stage: Can the person hold the power of his energy, or does he feel he needs to manage his excitement or anxiety by projecting this onto others?

COE skill: To recognize when the intensity of excitement, anxiety, or disowned feelings are managed by projections onto others

In the Action stage: Can the person take action on a figure of need or want, or does she feel the need to restrain action in an unaware gesture of retroflection?

COE skill: To recognize the somatic way of holding back, through retroflection, of movement to action

In the Contact stage: Does the habitual pattern of interrupting contact serve to protect the person from the threat of change? Does the person notice his need or want to maintain what is familiar by being confluent with others rather than risk the threat embedded in change, which is the experience of contact?

COE skill: To recognize how merging one's needs and wants with the wants of others promotes confluence rather than the differentiation that supports choice

In the Closure/Withdrawal stage: Can the person reflect on and articulate her experience of what did or did not occur, or does she stay unaware and unfinished?

COE skill: To recognize when the importance of endings is avoided through the distraction of deflection or the numbness of desensitization

The Gestalt stance allows us to see that there are common resistance patterns which have both positive and negative values and consequences. There are infinite ways that one can interrupt awareness, action, and change, but we focus on six classic resistances that Gestalt theory describes as appearing at the individual, dyadic, group, and organizational levels of system.[11] Recognizing patterns of resistance is a required skill competency for using the COE. These six classic resistance patterns are: Desensitization, Introjection, Projection, Retroflection, Deflection, and Confluence. These patterns can occur at any point of the COE, but for teaching purposes, we offer them at the COE's six energy points (Figure 4.3).

Figure 4.3 Cycle of Experience and Resistances

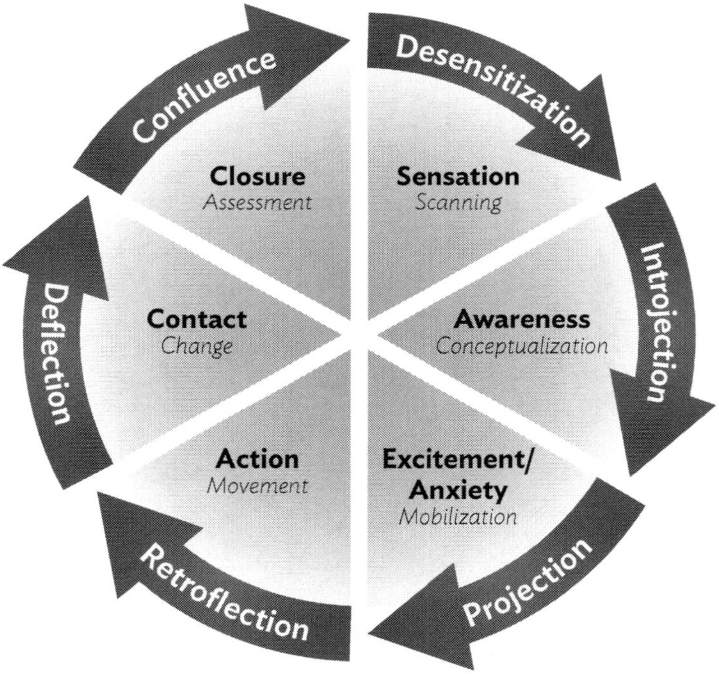

(Diagram: a circular cycle with six inner segments labeled — Closure/Assessment, Sensation/Scanning, Awareness/Conceptualization, Excitement/Anxiety/Mobilization, Action/Movement, Contact/Change — surrounded by six outer arrows labeled Confluence, Desensitization, Introjection, Projection, Retroflection, Deflection.)

DESENSITIZATION occurs when there is *a numbing of any aware sensation, whether of pleasure or of pain, whether physical, psychological, or emotional.* Desensitization as an adaptive strategy allows one to perform effectively and safely under highly stressful circumstances, anything from engaging in combat to working through the night to meet a deadline. As mentioned, to be effective, physicians must sometimes desensitize to acutely distressing smells, images, and emotions in service of delivering life-saving interventions. There are many examples of the value of disregarding sensations in order to accomplish an urgent or necessary matter.

If desensitization becomes chronic and habitual, it can block relevant sensory or psychological signals that alert us to significant personal or environmental danger. Desensitization has a way of exacting a higher cost in the long run than we are willing to recognize, especially when the cues we choose to ignore end up being cues that were literally trying to save our lives. In one case, a very busy executive had to suddenly relinquish an important project when his gallbladder ruptured. Asked if he had experienced stomach pains in advance, he acknowledged that he had experienced abdominal "discomfort" but had decided it was trivial and continued working on his project. Desensitization can also pair with other resistance patterns: e.g., where there is a should that one work hard, desensitization assists the hard work by blocking out awareness of fatigue. A desensitization pattern can be undone with an intervention that encourages clients to breathe more, as breath is the key intervention to bringing more life to the senses, re-sensitizing what has been desensitized.

INTROJECTION occurs when *one uncritically accepts, as if "swallowing whole," the ideas, behaviors, or values of an authority figure (e.g., a mentor or a corporate entity) without regard for personal meaning or resonance.* Introjected ideas, behaviors, or values are taken in but not assimilated; they become an undigested but active should. So while they remain, in a sense, foreign to the individual's persona, they are habitually enacted. Positive introjections could include the parent's injunction to not touch a candle flame or a hot stove top (ensuring physical safety), or the cultural injunction "do not steal" (which functions as a measure of personal integrity). Negative introjections could include the parental injunction to "eat everything on your plate" whether you're hungry or not (which can lead to dysfunctional eating habits), or the organizational injunction to "work hard," where we are finding that there may be better introjects, like "work smart," which could serve the professional even better.

Because it is hard to disregard or flout what those in a position of authority or power tell us we should believe or do, the shoulds of public behavior and values often trump the inner shoulds of personal beliefs and principles. Over time, we discover cognitive or psychological dissonances between what we've learned from others and what we've learned for ourselves. Sometimes we choose simply not to acknowledge the contradiction.

These introjects hold sway over our beliefs and behaviors and become habitual patterns that help keep us safe, stable, and predictable to ourselves and to others. Such unexamined introjects are widespread and difficult resistances to uncover and dislodge. Because these introjects have been imparted to us by authoritative figures, we tend to dismiss evidence that what our parents, mentors, or trusted colleagues may have told us is no longer effective or valuable for us. When thought or behavioral patterns become habitual and fall out of awareness, we lose the visceral or deep emotional engagement necessary to assess the relevance of the introject. The difficulty of becoming aware of an introject that is unconsciously embedded is often likened to the parable of the fish in water: Who can tell the fish about the water they live and move in? Certainly not another fish. Recognizing and letting go of an outdated introject can be experienced as immensely liberating and energizing, allowing new possibilities to emerge.

PROJECTION occurs when ***one attributes one's own feelings, thoughts, or actions to other people in the environment rather than experiencing them as part of oneself.*** The positive use of projection is linked to what we now understand as emotional intelligence. Projecting our internal experiences onto another person can be received by that person as understanding, empathy, and connection. Used with awareness, projection supports the capacity to build possibilities with others as well as the capacity to include people in what is important for us. But when one's own feelings, thoughts, or actions are disowned because of perceived taboos or should-nots, the emotional or psychological discomfort impels unexamined and unaware projections.[12] When our personal introjects of how people should or shouldn't behave are activated and make us uncomfortable, to reduce discomfort, we can assign blame to someone else. A projection is often recognized by use of the pronoun "you" instead of "I," the personal reference. Shifting responsibility for one's own feelings or thoughts (whether anger or aggression, reassurance or praise) to another is a way of managing what feels like difficult-to-accept or hard-to-practice introjects. Projection can reinforce self-alienated parts by attributing to others what we find hard to manage in ourselves.

For example: Emma has internalized the introject that one should never be loud or demanding in public. When she sees Jacob in a business meeting being "loud" and "demanding," she immediately forms a negative impression and tunes him out, as she projects that he cannot be of value to the meeting. Jacob may have been contributing positively to the meeting, but Emma is unable to accurately assess what he has to say because of her habitual introject, which influences her projection. On the other hand, in that same meeting, Michael, another member, proposes a different approach that emphasizes empathy and shared values. Michael may not have added anything relevant to the meeting's agenda, but Emma isn't able to evaluate Michael's contribution because of her unaware introject that advises her that empathy is usually a ruse to lure in the unwary. Emma's projection is that Michael is trying to manipulate the group. She cannot differentiate between the speakers—her unaware introjects, which confirm her projections, paralyze her ability to attend to what is said with awareness and therefore to assess others clearly.

Uncovering unaware projections is powerful work. It is one example of the deep self-work required to be able to recognize and own the feelings and thoughts that belong to us and to see what belongs to others. When we are able to be clear about our use of projections, we engender greater self-trust as well as trust from others.

RETROFLECTION occurs when there is ***an experience of holding back from requesting something from others and the environment, and doing to oneself what one wishes to receive from others.*** Positive retroflection can be seen when someone holds back intense emotions but then channels those feelings into creative work (e.g., poetry, painting, design innovations) or when a person withholds thoughts during vocal exchanges with others but later publishes an article using the ideas he withheld.

Retroflection becomes dysfunctional when it results in "a chronic standoff . . . between mutually opposing forces/energies within the individual," often leading to physical illness manifested in forms such as migraines, ulcers, or muscular aches.[13] Witness the person who cannot voice a disagreement but develops a headache as a somatic manifestation of retroflection. Retroflection is often linked to other resistances. For example, introjections ("don't do this") can also influence what people hold back from doing or saying. "Never ask others for help" is an introjection that may prompt a retroflection, "Thanks, I'll handle it myself." The retroflection then becomes a behavioral pattern that causes the individual to feel isolated and unsupported without perceiving how he contributes to his own condition of being isolated and unsupported. Some somatic cues that retroflection is occurring are visible when people hold a finger to their lips, rub their necks, play with or twirl their hair, bounce their legs while sitting or speaking, or rocking back in their shoes. An unchanging smile on a person's face could signal retroflection—as he holds back other expressions, the smile can appear inauthentic, as it is no longer connected to the vibrancy of positive feelings but rather to a hidden should that triggers holding back rather than expressing more. Retroflection can be undone by asking the client to breathe at the same time that we invite the client to release what he has been holding back.

DEFLECTION occurs when there is ***an avoidance of contact with others by diverting awareness or attention away from an issue.*** The power of deflection involves strategic choice to avoid direct engagement with a person or situation that induces tension. One could consider diplomacy as an artful function of deflection, serving to interrupt heated, complex debates to allow tempers to cool. Humor can also serve as an enjoyable and effective deflection, permitting people in a difficult setting to relax and to regain their sense of goodwill.

Deflection becomes unproductive and dysfunctional when, in an unaware manner, a person repeatedly or irrelevantly interrupts or disrupts others or activity as a way of managing personal anxiety. Consider the person who must give difficult job performance feedback to another but, because it makes her uncomfortable, continually reschedules the meeting or cuts the feedback exchange short, complaining there simply isn't enough time. Consider, too, how often people will check their smartphones when they are in conversation with others, unaware that they have diverted (deflected) their attention. Deflection can interrupt any point of the COE, and a simple but powerful question the coach can use to undo deflection is: "So where did you just go?"

CONFLUENCE occurs when there is ***agreement for the sake of gaining acceptance from or identification with others, particularly those admired or feared, in order to minimize or eliminate tension or conflict.*** Being intentionally confluent often serves to build trust and psychological support in relationships of all sorts—in work groups, in project partnerships, in marriages. Confluence creates an experience of bonding and togetherness that can strengthen collaboration and develop the energy needed for successful endeavors.

On the other hand, often a person will make a choice to maintain some degree of safety, stability, and predictability to manage being in a relationship with a controlling and demanding person. This is considered a confluent choice for sustaining the relationship. When confluence dominates in relationships or groups, innovation and differentiation are weakened.

Practiced without awareness, the personal costs of confluence can be high. Unaware confluence is a frequently encountered resistance that denies self-differentiation. The corporate "yes man" is an illustration of a more common behavior for making peace with others at the expense of our own needs or wants. When people fear losing love or respect, either in private life or at work, and choose confluence, they may stop listening to their own needs and wants. The member of a partnership or marriage who develops a pattern of always deferring to the other eventually will stop trying to influence the other in relation to his needs and wants. The way to work with a client who is exhibiting confluence is to invite somatic exercises and activities with cognitive inquiry for client self-exploration with one core question: "What is it that you are aware of wanting?" By supporting the client's self-ownership, we counter the self-diminishment of unaware confluence.

Working with Resistance

Coaching clients toward new possibilities necessitates a willingness to explore habitual processes that may surprise or dismay them. Gestalt coaches are interested in what a client works to keep hidden that may be obvious to others and in what is self-alienated that may be obvious to others but not to the client. In working with resistance, the Gestalt coach is using herself as an instrument, paying attention to the phenomenological data embedded in her COE while tracking the client's COE. We are looking for what is obvious to the client and for what is out of his awareness.

The Johari Window represents obvious and hidden information within or about a person—feelings, experience, views, attitudes, skills, intentions, motivation, etc.—in relation to others from four perspectives.[14] This model makes it clear that we are always keeping some aspect of ourselves hidden from others, but we are also unaware of something obvious to others that is hidden even from ourselves (Figure 4.4).

Figure 4.4 Johari Window

	Known to Self	**Not Known to Self**
Known To Others	**OPEN** *Presentation of Self*	**BLIND** *Unaware/alienated*
Not Known To Others	**HIDDEN** *The private self*	**UNKNOWN** *Umwelt*

Working to help clients become aware of their unaware resistance patterns is akin to managing one's "swamp work," a term that may have influenced Ron Heifetz's formulation of adaptive leadership development and learning skills.[15] The work of confronting unaware resistance patterns can be discomfiting.

When we enter into this swamp work of undoing unaware resistances, the Gestalt coach becomes the trusted guide who assists clients in identifying and exploring past and current realities. Through the awareness work involved in designed experiments, clients are encouraged to try on new behaviors and embrace new opportunities. We will be looking at how to create and work with Gestalt experiments in Chapter 6.

The coach is required to be impeccably trustworthy, both in presence and methodology, so that clients are both challenged and supported to enter a zone of safe emergency, where they are prompted to take risks in perception and in behaviors in order to achieve their goals. If the risk is too large, clients will be reluctant to commit to the work. If safety is the predominant structure, the work will feel boring and lack emotional energy. In supporting clients to confront unaware resistances that may be blocking new possibilities, we are inviting them into vertical development work, identifying the unaware "protective frames" of resistance that seem to keep them safe and comfortable. It is challenging to dismantle those frames by engaging in alternative and potentially risky paradigms of perception and behavior.

Unaware resistances are an integral part of our umwelt—the parts of ourselves that we are *not* aware of. We all possess blind spots and alienated parts of ourselves with which we resist making contact, even though that alienated part might give us permission to be more verbally or physically expressive, to be more socially bold, or to embark on an innovative new business venture. In the environment of safe emergency, with a trusted coach, clients can self-determine whether their related resistances are of continued value, and experiment with alternative perceptual and behavioral options. They can confront their self in service of reclaiming more of their own resources which have been ignored, alienated, and discarded.

Mahatma Gandhi expressed: "I have only three enemies. My favorite enemy, the most easily influenced for the better, is the British Empire. My second enemy, the Indian people, is far more difficult. But my most formidable opponent is a man named Mohandas K. Gandhi. With him I seem to have very little influence."[16] It is always surprising how the greatest challenges involve one's very self. When we support clients to undo or retire outdated resistances, we are inviting them to redefine themselves. If a client has a pattern of desensitizing her sensory experience, the work is to appreciatively support her to re-sensate through breath work and somatic awareness. If she retires an outdated introject, she may have to articulate a new introject that is adaptive to her current world. If she undoes a projection, she may have to examine which aspects of herself she was disowning and what it means to own that aspect. If she was holding back behavior, and that retroflective pattern no longer serves her, she has to practice with the risky rewards of being more bold and active. If her use of deflection interferes with her effectiveness, her work is to learn to focus until task completion. If she overused confluence, where she lost her voice and vitality, then learning how to engage in differentiation is the needed self-work.

Doing the work of uncovering and reshaping our resistances in order to be adaptive to the needs of life and work demands commitment, courage, strength, and an appreciation for one's vulnerabilities. We do not engage our swamp work solely through an act of will. We must engage with our awareness, and with acceptance of what we are aware of, while being also willing to engage with our umwelt, our alienated parts, and the multiple realities of others, which can test our perspective(s). On the path of this awareness work, change begins.

CHAPTER 5
Presence and Use of Self

We convince by our presence.
—WALT WHITMAN

... the intervener becomes the embodiment of theory. The nature of this integration and how it is accomplished determines the quality and power of the presence.
—EDWIN C. NEVIS

Presence as a concept is elusive and somewhat mysterious. Over the past decade or so, as the search results for the term will tell you, the concept of presence—particularly in the fields of organizational leadership, coaching, and organizational development—has become a hot topic. As often as the term has been descriptively defined, the diversity of definitions makes the quality of presence harder to articulate. In part, the challenge of articulating what presence is may stem from the very richness of these multidimensional approaches, which range "from phenomenological and experiential viewpoints to philosophical and scientific ideas."[1] But while a definitive definition is hard to come by, the phenomenon appears to tap into a deeper knowledge, since there *is* an intuitive and visceral recognition of presence: Presence is immediately recognizable when we encounter another person who "has it."

Perhaps especially within the world of Gestalt practitioners, presence can be "something [like] the 'sacred cow' of Gestalt theory," despite (or because of) a pervasive lack of conceptual clarity.[2] I intend here to explore the mystery, the power, and the practicality of the development and application of presence for coaches, specifically with regards to "use of self," the related concept of presence that significantly impacts the practice of Gestalt coaching. Coaches benefit by differentiating between the terms "presence" and "use of self." Presence captures qualities related to our identity and distinctive way of being in the world; use of self refers to utilizing the awareness that comes from presence to create interventions with the intent to influence an outcome. Presence is the integrated totality of what we have developed and worked to become; use of self is how one leverages one's presence to impact and to strategically provoke client work.

Acknowledging its significant role in the coaching encounter, the International Coach Federation (ICF) has designated *coaching presence* as one of its 11 core competencies to master. They define presence as the "[a]bility to be fully conscious and create spontaneous relationship with the client, employing a style that is open, flexible and confident."[3] *Relationship* here explicitly reminds us that presence is experienced only in interpersonal and social exchanges, in the company of others—coaching always involves a relational component.[4] Coaching presence may be the most important of the ICF core competencies because it is an integrative state of being that holds all we know as well as our capacity to respond adaptively. The Gestalt coach's primary work is to inspire clients' capacity to access their courage, energy, hope, and perseverance on their journey toward new possibilities. The coach's presence, and the impact her presence has on clients' perceptions of her, influences whether clients trust their coach to guide them safely through volatile, uncertain, complex, and ambiguous situations that require resolution. Terrence Maltbia and his colleagues assert that when a coaching encounter begins with the client's positive experience of the coach's presence, a stronger personal bond is forged that allows both coach and client to better "navigate the vulnerability, sense of risk, and personal reliance often associated with seeking help from others."[5]

One's presence fuses a way of being with a way of presenting the self to others. Presence is always intrinsically evocative because just showing up to others evokes a response. Clients are often either immediately attracted to or discouraged from working with a coach based on what is evoked when in the coach's presence. The first test of presence, then, is whether the client does or does not feel chemistry with the coach. Thus coaches need to learn what their presence evokes and what that may mean for the work. Richard Strozzi-Heckler, a leadership coach with Gestalt roots, says that presence is communicated to and impacts others not primarily through intention but subtly and very powerfully through the embodied self (e.g., speech patterns, spine straight or curved, breathing deep or shallow).[6] *Embodiment* is a recent term to move us beyond the Cartesian split of the mind and the body toward the integral nature of human experience that is manifested in a somatic manner that other people can sense. Strozzi-Heckler's descriptions of the physical manifestations of presence echo a Gestalt perspective first articulated as "aspects of presence" by William Warner in 1975, and later amplified by Ed Nevis (Figure 5.1).

Figure 5.1 Aspects of Presence

FACTOR	EXAMPLES OF HOW MANIFESTED
appearance	*Physical characteristics:* size, body type, hair, color of skin *Facial characteristics:* beard or clean shaven, eye and lip shapes *Posture:* carriage, quality of movement, gestures *Age:* actual vs. apparent, "congruence" of age and behavior *Dress:* casual or formal, bland or colorful
manner	*Where and how the self is placed in relation to others:* one of the people or a leader; "small town boy/girl" or "city sophisticate"; eloquent or earthy; hard or soft; public or intimate; informal or businesslike *Behavior at first meeting:* shy or outgoing, enigmatic or definitive
voice	*Sound quality:* loud or soft, thin or resonant *Pitch:* high or low *Modulation:* even or varied, limited or broad range
language/ speech	*Language use:* rich or barren; use of metaphor, imagery, simile or highly concrete; colloquial or academic speech patterns *Flow:* reticent or effusive, measured or spontaneous
mood state	Even-tempered or manic or depressed Serious or humorous Emotionally available or "poker-faced" Optimistic or pessimistic—sets the conditions for encounters
role/title	*Professional role definition:* expert, consultant, advisor; minister, priest, rabbi; healer, medicine man; mentor, guru *General role definition:* father, mother, brother, sister, grandparent *Name-dropping:* use of names, importance and nature of reputations (before and after contact) *Use of formal titles:* Doctor, Mister, Miss, Mrs., Ms.
values	*Explicitly stated* attitudes and values *Implicit or inferred* from behavior
sexuality	*Energy:* how expressed and radiated *Emphasis of same-sex* characteristics or *Acceptance of opposite-sex* characteristics *Androgyny*
uniqueness (style)	*Distinguishing qualities* that color how factors are integrated: active/passive, flamboyant/serene, clear/ambiguous, microscopic/macroscopic, orderly/bumbling, inward-looking/outward-looking

As outlined in the Aspects of Presence chart, physical attributes—appearance, voice, sexuality—tend to be the most immediately visible. The idea that one's somatic stances and cues influence what gets evoked in others and impacts relational effectiveness is getting increased recognition.[7] However, although physical cues are powerful, they are not the only factors at work, as Warner's chart offers.[8] We encounter people every day who attract and hold our attention but who do not visually stand out in any notable way. Other qualities—mood state, language use, manner—may evoke our interest in such people. But compelling presence depends much more on a coherent and consistent presentation of self. The underlying and intangible structure of presence is congruence between body, mind, and spirit, which evokes resonance in others. Such congruence occurs when "our speech, facial expressions, postures, and movements align," and this "internal convergence . . . is palpable and resonant [and] makes us compelling. We are no longer fighting ourselves; we are being ourselves."[9]

The particular gestalt of a congruent integration of all aspects of presence is a kind of aesthetic uniqueness that evokes resonance in others. Mary Ann Rainey Tolbert and Jonno Hanafin remind us that "everyone possesses presence, regardless of the level of awareness of the impact of that presence." But in coaching, the coach's presence is meant to transform "personal appearance, manner, values, knowledge, reputation, and other characteristics into interest and impact. . . . In this sense, presence can be understood as 'practitioner DNA,' a composite of unique qualities."[10] The skill and art of coaching intervention is enriched by being aware of how we leverage our presence for interest and impact, where use of self unites "who I am" with "what I do" to provoke and serve client learning.

Qualities of Presence

While Bill Warner offered interesting aspects of presence, and I have written on differentiating presence from use of self,[11] it is now essential to understand the "being" qualities that comprise presence. Following the groundbreaking work of Grant Soosalu, who unites perennial wisdom with somatic and evolutionary neuroscience, and the energetic intelligence typology of Jayne Warrilow,[12] I offer seven qualities of presence that are the focus of self-work: 1) the energy of being connected to and **embodying one's values**; 2) the energy of **creativity**; 3) the energy of **emotions and emotional range**; 4) the energy of **heart-based relations** with others and care for oneself; 5) the energy of **communication and voice**; 6) the energy of **intuition**; and 7) the energy of **scanning and field sensitivity**. These are qualities that are available to each of us, but we are responsible for developing, embodying, and accessing them (Figure 5.2). A brief review of what each quality offers follows.

Figure 5.2 Qualities of Presence

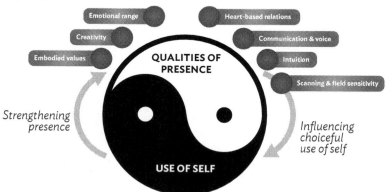

Embodied Values

Values can be broadly defined as preferences concerning appropriate, even ethical courses of action or outcomes. Values reflect a person's sense of what is right and wrong and of what "ought to be." Personal values "provide an internal reference for what is good, beneficial, important, useful, beautiful, desirable and constructive. Values generate behavior and influence the choices made by an individual."[13] When a person is aware of and in alignment with his values, a higher level of self-trust is generated that translates into greater interpersonal trust. Feeling clear about one's values serves to strengthen one's sense of self, one's purpose in the world, and one's identity. When we are connected with our values, such connection serves to orient perception and behavior.

In 1982, seven people in Chicago died after ingesting Tylenol Extra-Strength capsules that had been poisoned with cyanide by an unknown suspect. Johnson & Johnson, the maker of Tylenol, was faced with a devastating crisis involving both public reputation and market profit. The response of Johnson & Johnson's Chairman at the time, James Burke, is an example of acting from a stance of embodied values. Burke immediately formed a strategy team, whose guidelines were "first, 'How do we protect the people?' and second, 'How do we save this product?'"[14] Within a comparatively short period of time, Burke oversaw the following steps: The company used the media to alert consumers not to consume any more Tylenol, temporarily ceased production and advertising of the product, ordered a nationwide withdrawal of the product from all commercial venues, and eventually became the first company "in the industry to use . . . new tamper resistant packaging . . . ."[15] Burke's ability to move forward quickly and adaptively demonstrates not only the practicality but also the humanity of embodying one's values.[16]

Creativity

Creativity is connected to the capacity for adaptability, resilience, and innovation. Creativity is an integrated function of knowledge, curiosity, imagination, and openness. The greater one's knowledge base and level of curiosity, the more ideas and patterns—and combinations of both—can be perceived and achieved, which leads to creating innovative products and services. Creativity requires self-discipline to learn the horizontal tasks associated with one's particular professional focus. A measure of professional excellence is learning the basics that are required to understand what the standards of that professional practice should be. Those tasks that are basic to any profession follow along the horizontal line of development. But when originality, divergence, and conceptual flexibility are called for, we are then following a vertical line of development, which embraces awareness in action.

Creativity can be thought of as "the tendency to generate or recognize ideas, alternatives, or possibilities that may be useful in solving problems, communicating with others, and entertaining ourselves and others."[17] But there is also a distinctive playful energy about creativity, as the capacity for play allows for a relaxed state that can embrace multiple perspectives and that can see novel configurations and possibilities. Neuroscience has revealed that "creativity does not involve a single brain region or even a single side of the brain, as the 'right brain' myth of creativity suggests; instead, it draws on the whole brain."[18] Leadership scholar David Slocum observes that current examples of business creativity are often drawn from the "technology-driven" sectors. But he stresses that "creative leadership today is not simply about technological wizardry. At Apple, [Steve] Jobs' creative genius was to envision and market new horizons for emerging technologies and existing industries alike . . . ."[19] As coaches to those in leadership positions, one important question regarding presence is: What is my capacity to support my clients to see, communicate, and act on new possibilities and new ways of being in their leadership roles?

Steve Jobs is often mentioned as a modern-day exemplar of the "creative mind." Although he was not responsible for the conception or the text, Jobs is remembered for overseeing and introducing his ambitious Apple ad campaigns of 1984, when the Macintosh—the first accessible personal computer—was introduced, and for 1997's "Think Different" campaign, when he was seeking to reinvigorate his company's sales.[20] Those campaigns were unlike anything anyone had seen before on network TV, and they were both wildly successful in their own ways. Despite dismal marketing research scores, Apple went ahead with the 1984 ad, which aired only once during that year's Super Bowl: "Mesmerized by the ad's state-of-the-art cinematography and alluring message about the promise of technology, consumers flooded electronics stores across the country when the Macintosh debuted the following Tuesday. Those consumers would go on to purchase $155 million worth of Macintoshes in the three months after the Super Bowl."[21] Similarly, while the "Think Different" ad did not have the same scale of sales results, it managed to turn around Apple's damaged image slump during the 1990s. Steve Jobs is said to have remarked: "It only took 15 . . . 30 . . . maybe 60 seconds to re-establish Apple's counter-culture image that it had lost during the 90s."[22] Jobs had specifically wanted a "brand image campaign . . . . designed to celebrate not what computers could do, but what creative people could do with computers."[23] This may be the reason that the name Steve Jobs is so synonymous with the concept of creativity: he understood how to apply creativity as acts of innovation.[24]

Emotional Range

Emotions can be defined as "short-lived psychological-physiological phenomena that represent efficient modes of adaptation to changing environmental demands."[25] Emotions have an immediate physiological response, but are also associated with expressive behavior and subjective meaning-making. While emotions can "show considerable variation across individuals, groups, and cultures," seven universal, invariant emotions have been identified that can be discerned in very brief, or micro-, expressions of the face: anger, fear, sadness, disgust, contempt, surprise, and happiness.[26]

A great deal has been written about understanding emotions as a form of intelligence as important as analytical intelligence. Emotional intelligence (EI) is defined as the ability to recognize, understand, and manage one's own emotions while also recognizing, understanding, and influencing the emotions of others.[27] Being aware of one's emotions and of their positive or negative impact suggests a critical "self skill"—the capacity to manage one's emotions. Recent advances in neuroscience have made clear the importance of executive and higher order cognitive functioning in relation to hyper-emotional, reactive responses that can emerge, which play a role in what is known as an "amygdala hijack."[28] David Rock's neuroscience-based SCARF model, discussed in Chapter 3, shows us, for example, how easily the emotion of fear can trigger a panicked response through perceived threats to one's status, one's sense of certainty, one's need for autonomy, one's sense of relatedness to others, and one's sense of fairness in relation to others. The value of the SCARF model is to assist us in understanding the various conditions that can lead any of us to being emotionally hijacked. Understanding the pervasive implications of the SCARF model allows us to understand and have compassion for how easily we can be emotionally triggered.

The importance of EI to one's personal presence continues to be articulated. The person who has access to her emotional repertoire and responsibly manages what serves the moment is the person who brings possibility to herself and to others. Whether coach or leader, the person who can manage emotions to avoid being hijacked into negative expressions is a person who has achieved emotional self-discipline. Averting potential amygdala hijackings requires managing one's emotional reactivity and relaxing into the higher order functioning of the neocortex. This is the self-discipline—and the gift—of meditation and mindful practices.[29] It is the embodiment of the wisdom of *shugyo*, the Japanese description of self-mastery, discussed later in this chapter. When coaches or leaders cannot access and apply their emotions in the needed moment, to validate or to connect with others or to manage negative emotions, they lose a sense of personal presence. The capacity to feel with and for others is the power of empathy and compassion. The capacity to care for oneself, without undue narcissism, constitutes good health. The capacity to care for others is what holds the power of intimacy and enduring relationships.

EI is important for all professionals in relationship to success, as it means that one can manage one's own emotions and, in recognizing other people's emotions, understand how to respond to and interact with others in constructive ways. Positive examples of EI are evident when people show empathy or compassion for, or give recognition or support to, another in a time that matters deeply to the person. An example is the CEO who hears about an employee losing an important bid who then meets with that employee with both validation of the effort he put into the project and encouragement for the next project. Insufficient EI is evident in many stories of career derailment or demotivation. Examples include the physician who cannot manage her fear of making a diagnostic error and allays those fears by chastising her patients; or the team member who avoids the discomfort of having a sensitive conversation with a colleague, who then fails in an important effort because she did not have the necessary information.

Research on emotional intelligence has suggested that when IQ is compared, the person with higher EI is the one with stronger leadership capacity. EI is a quality of presence in that it allows one to quickly sense and make meaning of the gestalt of an important relational situation, similar to the quality of intuition, discussed below. Paying attention to our "gut wisdom" is a key attribute of use of self, but we must first have the capacity to be present and stay centered across a myriad of emotions, our own and others'. Strong emotional intelligence provides for a strong personal presence that resonates with and impacts others. EI is now recognized as a challenge to be developed and integrated into coaching practices and organizational leadership. The application of an EI model to leadership development contains a powerful assessment of the self and social awareness of one's environment and field with regard to self- and relational management.[30] A wisdom from Viktor Frankl could stand as a definition of the capacity that EI fulfills: "Between stimulus and response there is a space. In that space is our power to choose our response. In our response lies our growth and our freedom."[31] Frankl continues to be a presence who inspires others, as he articulated his insight from the unimaginable experiences of a Holocaust survivor of the Auschwitz concentration camp. His wisdom embodies the concept of choiceful response over instinctive reaction. In our fast-paced world, the discipline of non-reactivity is the discipline of managing one's emotions.

Heart-Based Relations

Empathy, compassion, friendship, charity, passion, and courage are the emotional expressions of heart-based relations, with oneself and with others. The HeartMath Institute has been researching the power of the heart across four primary physiological dimensions: 1) neurological communication, through the nervous system; 2) biochemical communication, through the hormones; 3) biophysical communication, through pulse waves; and 4) energetic communication, through electromagnetic fields. All of these factors "significantly [affect] the brain's activity. Moreover, our research shows that messages the heart sends to the brain also can affect performance."[32] For example, the researchers discovered that the cardiac field can be detected at a distance of some feet from the body, but more interestingly, when we touch each other or are close enough to hold a conversation, "the heartbeat signals are registered in the other's brainwaves."[33] Additionally, the research showed that the heart communicates with the brain through shared neurotransmitters. This communication "can influence our cognitive processes such as how we make decisions and how we perceive reality."[34] Thus the organ that most of us consider simply a biological pump turns out to be much more, and is now sometimes referred to as the "heart brain."

This research showing the range of roles the heart plays, and the idea of the "heart brain," has also resulted in the concept of "heart intelligence," defined as

> the flow of awareness, understanding and intuition we experience when the mind and emotions are brought into coherent alignment with the heart. It can be activated through self-initiated practice, and the more we pay attention when we sense the heart is speaking to us or guiding us, the greater our ability to access this intelligence and guidance more frequently. Heart intelligence underlies cellular organization and guides and evolves organisms toward increased order, awareness and coherence of their bodies' systems.[35]

Clearly, this is relevant to the development of one's personal presence, and there are HeartMath activities, offered through the HeartMath Institute, that support heart-brain entrainment for greater connection with oneself and resonance with others.

Perhaps no one that I know was as masterful in describing the power of heart intelligence—or "heart energy," as she called it—as the late Angeles Arrien, a Basque cultural anthropologist. Arrien described the guiding mantra of heart-based wisdom as "follow what has heart and meaning." In her model, the Fourfold Way, the archetypal task of paying attention to what has heart and meaning bears the fruits of vibrancy, health, and healing. So critical is heart energy to one's personal presence that it is best expressed through actions that maintain personal health and support the welfare of others and of our environment. For Arrien, the energy of the heart is made obvious by what we care enough to stand for, and in this way, heart energy supports values. The power of the heart is displayed in how vulnerable one allows oneself to be, which is why leaders can touch so many people when they make visible what they most care about.

One of the greatest examples of the power of heart-based relations occurred in Lawrence, Massachusetts in 1995. When the Malden Mills textile factory burned to the ground that winter, Aaron Feuerstein, the third-generation owner and manager, chose to spend millions of his own money rebuilding on the same spot and paying his now-idle employees full salary, with benefits, for a number of months until they could return to work at the new mill. According to Feuerstein, "I have a responsibility to the worker, both blue-collar and white-collar. I have an equal responsibility to the community. It would have been unconscionable to put 3,000 people on the streets . . . ."[36] Feuerstein became a media hero following his decision to support his workers and their families, and he received numerous civic, social, and business awards. But his response to all this positive attention is noteworthy: "I got a lot of publicity. And I don't think that speaks well for our times. . . . At the time in America of the greatest prosperity, the god of money has taken over to an extreme."[37] Feuerstein's choices made visible what it looks like to care for others and to have the courage to apply one's values for oneself and for others.

Communication and Voice

The importance of being able to communicate a message, in language that is vocal or somatic, is a critical aspect of coaching presence and use of self as instrument. In Chapter 8, we introduce the concept of "direct communication" as one of ICF's core coaching competencies. The essence of this competency is being able to be clear and direct in one's communications with others. This competency is also clearly linked to leadership skills. A senior VP client of mine revealed his ambivalence about being regarded for a promotion to CEO. After some inquiry, he stated that he wished to remain "under the radar"—less visible to others. Being in a position to influence others, whether as coach or as leader, means being accountable for how we are visible when we use our voice. What emerged for my client was that he was tired of the heavy obligations of leadership and chose to plateau himself rather than accept more challenge. The capacity to communicate to others and to use one's voice to articulate what is needed or missing in the client system is a skill, an art, and a responsibility. But the words must be imbued with values and with the emotional and heart-based energy that has the capacity to touch others, in both hearts and minds.

Albert Mehrabian found that in face-to-face communication, presence is largely a somatic, embodied influence: visual cues account for 55% of the impact, tone of voice 38%, and words only 7%.[38] However, for the communication to be effective, all three elements—body language, voice tone, and the words themselves—need to be congruent. Confusion or disconnection may occur when one element is out of sync with the others. However warm or supportive one may wish to be, for example, a lack of eye contact, words delivered in monotone, or incorrect words can sabotage one's intentions. Voice is an important attribute of presence. The late Margaret Thatcher, British Prime Minister in the 1980s, was advised to take vocal lessons to overcome what was perceived to be an off-putting delivery. In a way, Shakespeare was right that in terms of presence, we are our entrances and exits, and we all play many different roles. Paying attention to the tone of our voice, the quality of our words, and the congruence of our body language as we speak affects the impact we make.

Recorded history gives us many examples of great leaders whose words have sifted our consciousness and consciences and ignited new possibilities of perception and behavior. One example is John F. Kennedy's 1963 speech, "Ich bin ein Berliner" [I am a Berliner], given "against the geopolitical backdrop of the Berlin Wall," which had been erected in 1961 and had escalated Cold War tensions.[39] Addressing the nation after the Wall had gone up, Kennedy described Berlin as "the great testing place of Western courage and will," and spoke before the city hall of West Berlin, seeking to express American commonality with the German people, who had been bitter enemies just 20 years before. In his speech, Kennedy delivered "a series of devastating critiques of life under communism" and expressed democratic faith in an eternal human yearning for "liberty and self-government." He voiced political solidarity with and emotional empathy for the citizens of Germany, East and West, closing his speech with: "All free men, wherever they may live, are citizens of Berlin, and therefore, as a free man, I take pride in the words *Ich bin ein Berliner.*" These spoken words were considered courageous, most especially as spoken by the leader of another country.

Intuition

Much interest in leadership literature has been focused on the value of intuition. In everyday usage, intuition is understood to be a natural ability or power that makes it possible to know something without any proof or evidence, or a feeling that guides a person to act a certain way without fully understanding why.[40]

That instinctual or "gut feeling," as we often think of it, keeps being relevant because information so attained can be absolutely right, even though it came without rational processing. The word *intuition* is from the Latin ("to look at, consider") but came into English originally as a theological term denoting "insight, direct or immediate cognition, [or] spiritual perception."[41] Organizational management scientist Herbert Simon, however, defined intuition as "subconscious pattern recognition" and something "not associated with magic and mysticism."[42]

While controversy remains over the role and validity of intuition in our everyday and institutional lives, these definitions point to the need for a different kind of sensing and listening in order to hear what intuition is communicating. In our fast-moving world, where there usually isn't time for extensive information gathering, intuition can assist us in responding quickly and effectively to an emerging or critical situation. Business management people have become interested in intuition as a way of being more responsive more quickly, and with viable information. Perhaps "thin slicing" can help intuition be more precisely studied and assessed within organizational environments as the subconscious pattern recognition that Simon proposed. Thin-slicing refers to drawing "inference[s] about others from brief glimpses or 'thin slices' of behavior. Thin slices of expressive behavior are random samples of the behavioral stream, less than 5 min[utes] in length, that provide information regarding personality, affect, and interpersonal relations."[43] John Gottman, a psychologist focusing on relationships, uses thin-slicing as a guide for divorce prediction. Gottman videotapes interviews with couples who come for marriage counseling and analyzes the interactions captured on film. Over the years, he and his colleagues discovered that "if they looked at only *three minutes* of a couple talking, they could still predict with fairly impressive accuracy who was going to get divorced and who was going to make it."[44]

Research on developing one's intuitive capacity suggests that meditation is one route to developing greater intuition. Four relevant states of consciousness are identified:

> Beta is a normal level of consciousness. Alpha is relaxed awareness, theta is a state of meditative trance, and delta is a state of transcendental experience. Of these four mental states, alpha is the level that helps you learn, memorize, interact, and read the thoughts and emotions of others and yourself. The alpha state of the brain also relates to meditation. A daily meditation practice helps you control this alpha state, and therefore control the intuitive process.[45]

And mindful practice helps us here, as well, to listen to the message rather than to the cognitive ego.[46] Intuition deserves to be recognized as a quality of presence because it has been described through the ages as a way of perceiving important moments—sometimes life-or-death moments—and new opportunities. As a measure of coaching mastery, the ICF introduces the relevance of intuition into the competency of active listening at the MCC level. The coach at this level "recognizes both hers and the client's ability of intuitive and energetic perception that is felt when the client speaks of important things, when new growth is occurring for the client, and when the client is finding a more powerful sense of self."[47]

As a quality of presence, intuition offers needed information when data is not available. As a measure of excellence and accountability, it is nevertheless relevant to discern when analytic evidence is needed to secure accountability. The discipline of deliberate practice—what has been called the "10,000 hour rule"—is a commitment to horizontal development, which assists the awareness moment best when integrated with a recognition of thin-slicing, an aspect of vertical development.[48] Coaching mastery occurs when we can use our flexible abilities for evidence-based data where possible while also being able to listen to our thin-slicing where needed.

Scanning and Field Sensitivity

We presented scanning as part of the Cycle of Experience in Chapter 3. Our full discussion of field appears in Chapter 7, but for now we briefly summarize it as the "intimate interconnections between events and the settings or situations in which these events take place."[49] Scanning and field sensitivity refer to the capacity to recognize what is important as it is still emerging, almost unformed, in the purview of one's experience. Perhaps the best voice for this competency is that of Otto Scharmer and his model of Theory U, introduced in Chapter 1. The book that introduced this theory is subtitled "leading from the future as it emerges: the social technology of presencing." The ability to recognize something new and significant "as it emerges" is in part a function of "presencing," which is a portmanteau word combining *presence* and *sensing*.[50]

One fine example of scanning and field sensitivity for offering what is needed or missing even before it is clearly recognized was the 2009 business strategy of American-based Hyundai Motors, headed by Rick Case. During the 2009 economic downturn, while other auto dealers in the industry faced severe losses, Hyundai USA increased their sales by 60% by allowing U.S. buyers to return cars without penalty if they lost their job and covering three payments after a job loss if the buyer chose to keep the vehicle.[51] Case's capacity to link an emerging need with a new sales strategy illustrates the capacity to read what was needed in his field to both lead the industry and act humanely in a crisis situation.

Another example of one who is astutely scanning and anticipating emerging needs in the field is Nicolas Berggruen, a 55-year-old investment billionaire who is pledging millions of his own money to endow the Berggruen Institute, a think tank whose mission is "to develop foundational ideas and, through them, shape political and social institutions for the 21st Century," contending that "[i]n the age of technology and globalization, as our traditions are challenged, new social orders are emerging and political institutions falter—critical analysis of our most fundamental beliefs and the systems founded on them is required."[52] The Institute's primary projects are the 21st Century Council, the Council for the Future of Europe, and the Think Long Committee for California, which invite renowned scholars, thinkers, and government and industry leaders to meet and work together. Among other global activities, the Institute has offered a $1 million cash Berggruen Philosophy Prize to "honor a living thinker whose ideas are of basic importance for contemporary and future life" and, in partnership with the *Huffington Post,* a publication called *The WorldPost,* "an online global publication gathering top editors and first person contributors from all corners of the planet."[53]

The inside-out learning that comes from one's presence is based on "reflection, awareness-raising and personal insight. It requires a deeper self-examination that can lead to changes in perspective, often an enlarged perspective."[54] In considering the qualities of presence, we need to remember that all of us view the world through the filters of our own values, our creative capacities, our emotional states and relational concerns, and our current environments. There are also moments when we are informed by an intuition "in the field" of our awareness—information that moves us to go beyond quantitative or cognitive data to pay attention to something emerging that is vital to respond to. Being present in the moment means being able to pay attention through the lens of our unique identity. The qualities of presence—our values, creativity, emotional range, capacity to care, use of communication and voice, acceptance of intuition, and ability to scan and be sensitive to the field—are the gifts of our presence that is our challenge to develop.

Yet the coach's presence is not only a self-reflective and self-identifying construct immediately sensed "evocatively" by the client, but is also an intentional, deliberative instrument designed to sense awareness of what is needed or missing for the client. The person who sees the coach as having a grounded stance in relation to values, availability of creativity, access to emotions, authentic caring, capacity for critical conversation, intuitive knowing, and ability to recognize what is occurring in the field may immediately become aware of needing these qualities in his own life. Gestalt theory has all along made such presence a significant integrative construct in either therapeutic or organizational contexts. Whatever we call it—self-generative presence, signature presence, or executive presence—Gestalt coaching has made specific and powerful contributions to understanding the processes needed to discover one's presence and, from there, to make aware decisions about how best to use and leverage one's presence in the service of client work and coaching practice.[55]

The Use of Presence in the Coaching Encounter: Use of Self

One can think of presence as a sort of "being" intervention—it's accomplished evocatively without the coach taking any deliberate action. The way a person is embodied communicates a message to others. Use of self, or self as provocateur, does involve deliberate action, and is a "doing" intervention.

Use of self moves the coach beyond witnessing to acting and provoking with intention (Figure 5.3).

Figure 5.3 Presence and Use of Self

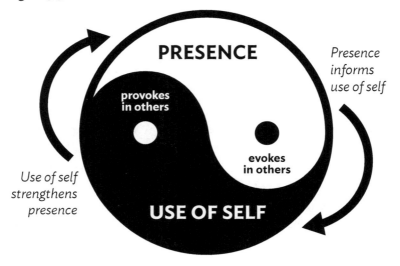

The primary goal of any Gestalt intervention is to heighten awareness in the client, as this positions the client with increased capacity for choice. Use of self is therefore innately provocative, though selectively applied and designed around the values and ethics embedded in one's presence.[56] So, for example, if a strong client resists acknowledging what seems obvious, the coach might more persistently offer data that helps the client see what she's missing; on the other hand, if the client is fragile or anxiously resistant, the coach may heighten awareness by offering more support and appreciation. This skill, integral to the safe emergency of Gestalt practice, is a key skill for effective use of self. The coach needs to determine the best use of herself in the moment to assist the client's own mobilization of energy toward meeting a desired goal. There is, as well, an element of artfulness in use of self, as so many variables must be addressed in the moment of choosing to intervene.

For coaches, presence means that we show up with full accountability for what gets evoked in clients and for how we use our presence to provoke the necessary awareness that will move clients' work forward. This requires the ability to assess clients' needs and the use-of-self skills to heighten clients' awareness and energy around what is needed. Use of self is a conscious and strategic dimension of coaching presence. Use of self leverages the coach's intentional presence through skilled and artful practices. Blurring the difference between the powers of being and doing reduces coaching competency because presence and use of self are distinct but symbiotic aspects of coaching mastery. One's presence may do some of the coaching work by evoking clients' attentiveness and curiosity as well as by opening them to potential learning opportunities. Use of self purposefully draws from the qualities and resources of one's presence to influence and provoke clients to do the work they would not, or could not, do on their own.

Gestalt-trained coaches understand that presence is a cultivated component of their practice that is continually worked on. Presence isn't "a permanent, transcendent mode of being.... It is a moment-to-moment phenomenon."[57] The embodied, integrative presentation of self that characterizes a compelling presence serves to positively impact and influence clients. But such "effortless" embodiment does not come naturally—it is created and shaped through experience over time and through deliberate practice. A number of dynamics contribute to one's "practitioner DNA," the uniqueness of one's presence, so a high degree of aware self-work is necessary to develop and enhance one's presence in the coaching encounter in order to appropriately and effectively leverage that presence in the service of clients.

Adapting wisdom from the martial art of Aikido, Strozzi-Heckler offers the concept of *shugyo*, which concerns the disciplined use of one's gifts (while being also accountable for one's limitations) in the service of others. The striving for shugyo is revealed by ongoing practices of self-mastery "for the sake of a larger commitment."[58] We posit that those who are striving for shugyo are in fact working to develop their use of self for the purpose of better serving others. If each of us has "original medicine" for vision and healing, as Native American folklore expresses, then our commitment to self-work is a crucial factor for achieving both personal and professional mastery.

Self-work is the work of getting centered in our strengths, to be aware of and responsible for our limitations, and to access the distilled wisdom of embodied life lessons. Clients' responses to our presence provide the initial barometer of impact. This may be disconcerting, since we must take responsibility for evoking a negative response. Clients' negative responses to coaches can be influenced by covert or unarticulated factors.[59] Our physical appearance and non-verbal or verbal behaviors could remind clients of others they know or knew, or clients could be responding to conditioned responses to certain types or groups of people. People project what gets evoked in them—from their history, memories, or other externally cued interpretations of the person, the environment, and the moment. Context also plays a significant role in what is evoked in clients. We often hear the statement, "You remind me of _____." When the reminder is negative, clients may find it difficult to separate their evoked response from the coach's evocative presence. Young women in the workplace may evoke projections from male coworkers of a desired or a lost girlfriend; older women in the workplace may evoke projections from unfinished business around mothers or issues of female authority. Younger men may evoke uncomfortable projections in older men of competitive challenge or obsolescence, while older men may experience "father figure" and associated authoritarian projections from younger male coworkers. These projections may have nothing to do with the people who evoke them: the young woman may be happily married and strongly career oriented, the older woman may wield little power, and both young and older men may be struggling with a professional sense of powerlessness.

Coaches benefit from being prepared to expect that they *will* evoke something in the client, and to be sensitive to that fact before undertaking any intervention to provoke a new possibility. When the coaching involves intimate and important work with the client, we are called on to control what has been called our Personal Weirdness Index (PWI), which is explained as the degree of "difference" in relation to the client that the coach brings to the coaching encounter, and knowing how to strategically meet the client with enough familiarity so that he feels safe but also with enough difference so that he is interested.[60] If the coach is too similar to the client, she may be too safe to evoke the client's interest. If the coach is too different from the client, she may be perceived as scary or "weird." One of the integrative tasks of self-work for coaching presence and use of self is attending to personal strengths, values, and intentions for influence. The art is in knowing how to manage one's PWI, and that comes from the practices of shugyo, which is where the discipline of self-work requires both horizontal and vertical integration. The commitment to all that we have learned must be sensed in the moment of awareness.

Early in my professional life, often within the first few hours of entering a group, I would receive a great deal of feedback about how "intense" I was. At the time, I was an immigrant with an Eastern European background from a French Canadian culture. I made very direct and extended eye contact, which caused some discomfort, particularly within the American group. And, as is more customary in the French Canadian culture, I tended to stand closer to people than most Americans would, again causing discomfort. Both habits were interpreted in America as intensity or what some might call "premature intimacy." It took me several years to become more conscious about my habitual physical interactions—I learned to stand a bit farther apart from others, to speak more slowly, and to explain my longer-than-usual eye contact as a manifestation of my style of learning by watching. It also took some time to learn that showing up with the gifts and strengths I brought to clients was a powerful, evocative gesture in itself. That required heightened self-awareness and self-support. In essence, I learned that by supporting myself, I supported others to be with me. In doing so, I adjusted my actions to suit the context and the clients in ways that would tune my presence in to a more resonant frequency for the coaching encounter. When I suggest that self-work is required to consolidate the sense of one's presence, I mean that each of us has to find the coordinates of cultural distance, eye-contact interactions, and other interpersonal cues that affect our impact upon others. This calibration is, of course, also a bottom-line business imperative that may influence whether the client hires you.

We are evocative from the start, before we even speak or act. Absorbing the informational data from my early coaching endeavors and learning how to recalibrate my approach to each coaching engagement required vigilant, self-disciplined awareness of self and context. Through the experience of living and aging, we change over time; moreover, the coaching contexts we enter constantly change as well. Everything is in flux. Much of the information we need to hold and call upon from our awareness—cognitive, emotional, visceral, spiritual—is complex and subtle because so much of what is important remains nonverbal (sensed, intuitive) and not easily articulated.

While we can't control clients' initial, visceral response, if we become aware of actual or potential negative responses, we can take action to address this through personal or environmental changes. These instances signal a crucial need to be contextually aware of what our embodied presence evokes in our clients. In all cases, but particularly when what's evoked is not accurate, we need to know how to meet the consequential projections purposefully and non-defensively. These challenges, while subtle, can have a dramatic effect.

We move from evocation to provocation, from presence to the leveraging of presence, which is use of self, the intentional commitment to provoke the client's learning and awareness through use of self skills. Frequently, the client consciously presents the verbal content of his issue, i.e., the "story" and his interpretation of it. But what is more revealing may actually show up in the nonverbal process of the telling. Creative and masterful use of self requires that the coach stay curious and vigilant about this dance between content and process, and be prepared to heighten the necessary awareness in the client through skillful use of observations, aware projections, feedback, or inquiry (Figure 5.4).

Figure 5.4 Qualities of Presence and Use of Self Skills

When the coach is fully present in her presence and attuned to the existential reality of the moment, she is further assisted by the power of the Cycle of Experience information as data to offer the client. The COE teaches coaches to attend to internal and external awarenesses, and to track the ways clients do or do not pay attention to their needs or wants, or the habitual behavioral patterns that interfere (what we understand as resistance) with satisfying their needs, wants, or goals. The COE supports the coach to be more aware of, and therefore more responsible for, her use of self: her behavioral observations of the client, her aware projections, or her curiosity about emergent figures that she can offer as questions.

The COE is also used to track and assess the impact of our own presence as coach. When we feel disoriented, like we are "not all there," or we behave in a manner that suggests we aren't aware of the available resources, the client inevitably senses this disjunction, and trust and confidence in the work will decrease. Our responsibility as coach is to recognize when we've been derailed in relation to our own presence and, once recognized, to re-center to our grounded self-awareness that is in alignment with our "who am I" working identity and narrative.

For example, while my professional identity is a master certified coach, there are distinct cultural differences between teaching in Toronto and teaching in Istanbul. Both contexts support excellence in learning, but the Toronto environment asks for me to offer a cognitive rationale for experiential activities before beginning while the Istanbul environment allows me to begin with experiential activities. The similarities between the environments are substantial and familiar, but the cultural differences are important to understand in terms of using presence to inspire and maintain trust. Even in Istanbul, however, the context may change and there may be a need to begin in a more rationalistic manner. Being sensitive to context—what Gestaltists call "the field"—is required of the coach.[61]

Having a grounded presence provides others with an invitation to trust. Gaining trust requires sincerity of expression (verbal and non-verbal), confidence in one's presence, and consistency in the values we espouse. Powerful use of self occurs in any situation or environment when we act on our values and strategically engage our resources to support clients to move forward on what is needed, wanted, or missing within the field of possibility.

Use of self is where strategically useful coaching competencies become visible. In offering clients data guided by the COE, aware projections, feedback on their behaviors, and powerful questions about their observed behaviors, the coach works to raise clients' awareness of and interest in new possibilities. The coach's present-moment awarenesses serve as the ground from which, through choice, to move to effective use of self. A grounded presence creates energy evocatively, but use of self provokes impact through the intentional interventions just described. One critical aspect of use of self is the ability to offer observations as data and projections with accountability. Masterful use of self requires knowing the difference between feedback and projections as well as knowing when to provoke awareness with the power of inquiry. Presence requires self-work and the ability to be centered and able to re-center as needed. Masterful use of self requires being able to access the competencies to provoke learning since it takes skill to offer observations, aware projections, feedback, or inquiry.

Presence as Vertical Development

In the coaching encounter, a coach's presence is an influential tool. Using Nick Petrie's distinction between horizontal and vertical leadership development, presence is knowledge that lies along the vertical pathway of leadership development.[62] Horizontal and vertical leadership development models manifest complementary but different mindsets. Both are useful and productive, but the emphasis on horizontal development at the expense of vertical development has proven problematic. Skills, tools, techniques, and the right information are essential for successfully executing well-defined purposes and tasks. But in a VUCA-driven world, we need to also train and support leaders who have emotional intelligence, are able to learn from failure, and are capable of discerning emerging possibilities within the seeming appearance of chaos: "If horizontal development is about transferring *information* to the leader, Vertical Development is about *transformation* of the leader."[63]

What is stimulating about this distinction between horizontal and vertical development has to do with the variable of presence as an influence beyond the technical tools and techniques used to forward learning. The prejudice toward equipping people with new skills and behaviors suggests that these will always translate into improved competency. Yet while "core skills, informational content, and technical expertise" are important, the reality is that they are not sufficient.[64] Presence as a vertical development construct involves not only knowledge and specific skills, but also social and emotional intelligence, experiential learning, and a commitment to cognitive, emotional, and spiritual experimentation. Research has shown that what we do concertedly and with intentional effort changes not only our own brain patterns but also directly influences those with whom we interact: "[C]ertain things leaders do—specifically exhibit empathy and become attuned to others' moods—literally affect both their own brain chemistry and that of their followers. Indeed, researchers have found that the leader-follower dynamic is not a case of two (or more) independent brains reacting consciously or unconsciously to each other. . . . [G]reat leaders are those whose behavior powerfully leverages the system of brain interconnectedness."[65] Recent neuroscientific findings support placing presence within the frame of vertical development—assisting coaches and clients to think in more complex, systemic, strategic, and interdependent ways. Grossly simplified, horizontal development is more a matter of rote memorization and repeated application. Presence, however, evinces the vertical challenge of critical thinking in diverse and unexpected circumstances, and requires an active commitment to its development.

To adequately serve their clients, coaches need the integration of vertical and horizontal developmental competencies. The coach's use of self becomes a significant factor in guiding and influencing the coaching encounter. The embrace and acceptance of an openness to change must be as true for the coach as it is for the client. Gestalt coaching emphasizes ongoing self-work as key to coaching effectiveness. Presence—how you show up to clients and how that impacts their trust in you and their willingness to work with you—is not rooted solely in the horizontal accumulation of knowledge of theories and methods or toolkits of specific instruments and strategies. The self-awareness needed for compelling presence—congruent, resonant, impactful—includes:

- Owning the values that are important to you, and acting in congruence with those values
- Having a generative and creative narrative that allows you to be compassionate and caring about your developmental edges
- Knowing where failure can be transformed into new wisdom through both emotional and mental reflection
- Acknowledging and integrating your strengths and gifts, with compassion, in ways that serve others and are therefore compelling without being "self-advertising" or affectedly charismatic

- Being mindful about what you evoke in others while remaining non-judgmental and compassionate
- Recognizing what is within your agency, and accepting and adapting to what is outside your control
- Constantly practicing and honing your observation skills, your capacity to give aware projections, and the clarity of your feedback and inquiry
- Embodying your presence in ways that integrate physical, cognitive, emotional, and spiritual strengths

Coaches are compelling when they have done their self-work: the vertical development, which inspires a generative narrative that invites the capacity for new perspectives and new choices. Coaching presence is compelling where the coach demonstrates congruence and integration between outward manifestations and inward values and core convictions through speech and behaviors. The vital learning skill today is the capacity to respond productively in the midst of uncertainty and ambiguity. The greater the coach's capacity to model this responsiveness—by being centered in her presence and able to effectively respond through use of self—the greater her mastery in coaching others.

Skill Development for Use of Self

The aim of any coach is to cultivate a presence that evokes trust in and energy for the coaching work. Then one's presence can be leveraged to serve clients' awareness and learning in a manner that allows them to best coach themselves. This involves self-identifying perceptual and behavioral patterns that are no longer useful, experimenting safely with alternative perceptual and behavioral patterns, making meaning of and situating themselves within their multiple contexts and realities, and determining their best choices for success. Gestalt coaches serve primarily as awareness agents, able to provoke more specific or enhanced self-awareness in the client. Awareness is contingent upon what exists in the environment and what is important in the moment. Awareness includes the energetic capacity to regulate our interaction with our environment, to creatively adjust to given circumstances to get what we want or to avoid what we do not want. Awareness is the key component that feeds embodied presence, purposeful use of self, and the recognition of emergent, aware choices.

The Gestalt Cycle of Experience is the conceptual tool that teaches coaches to attend to their internal and external awarenesses. This awareness-tracking tool assists both cultivation of presence and intentional use of self, as it illuminates the range of self-awareness and patterns of behavior that block awareness of alternative possibilities. Using the Cycle, the coach is better able to offer in-the-moment observations about clients' behavior as well as the coach's own internal experience, which get evoked by being in the client's presence. Our presence creates impact through its evocative energy, but our use of self has a provocative impact through our intentional interventions. The coach's masterful use of self is best and most powerfully revealed when she is able to:

- Differentiate between observations, projections, feedback, and inquiry
- Skillfully use what gets evoked to make constructive and aware projections that assist client awareness
- Provoke what is needed or missing in the client system
- Create interventions and experiments that are sensitive to timing and choice points specific to the client's goals[66]
- Identify and intervene at the system boundaries where the work resides[67]

- Attend to client cues to shape the safe emergency of the client's work, maintaining just enough risk to sustain interest and engagement

The coach works to maintain contact with self and client, to identify key figures, and to work at the correct level of system by using the Cycle to track client awareness through offering observations, projections, feedback, and inquiry. Use of self is involved in effectively being able to intervene in the moment to assist the client in moving toward what is needed, wanted, or missing. In Figure 5.5, we have collected the coaching use of self competencies which influence effective use of self in the moment.

Figure 5.5 Coaching Use of Self Competencies

Process Skill Data
- Attend to my experience and selectively share feelings, sensations, and thoughts.
- Observe and selectively share observations.
- Track and identify themes.
- Encourage client's mobilization of energy.
- Support and facilitate meaningful contact.
- Support client's closure and meaning-making.

When the coach is leveraging the resources of her presence intentionally as use of self, she moves to integrate the Unit of Work, discussed fully in Chapter 6, with the COE (Figure 5.6). Unit of

Work is a tool to assist the client through experimentation to gain new possibilities and to mobilize energy toward goal attainment. Unit of Work is a learning process that is invited by the coach. When using Unit of Work, one aspect of coaching mastery is how ably the coach can access a broad range of resources to creatively serve the client's work through experimentation.[68] The coach is required to be sensitively collaborative while also being strategically bold. The collaborative invitation to engage in a learning experiment is always met by clients' acknowledgment of what they wish to learn. The coach, in being an awareness agent, recognizes the power of offering data, observations, aware projections, feedback, and inquiry. We will further explore Unit of Work in the next chapter but now wish to distinguish the strategic aspects of Unit of Work, which require deliberate and skillful use of self.

Figure 5.6 Unit of Work and Cycle of Experience

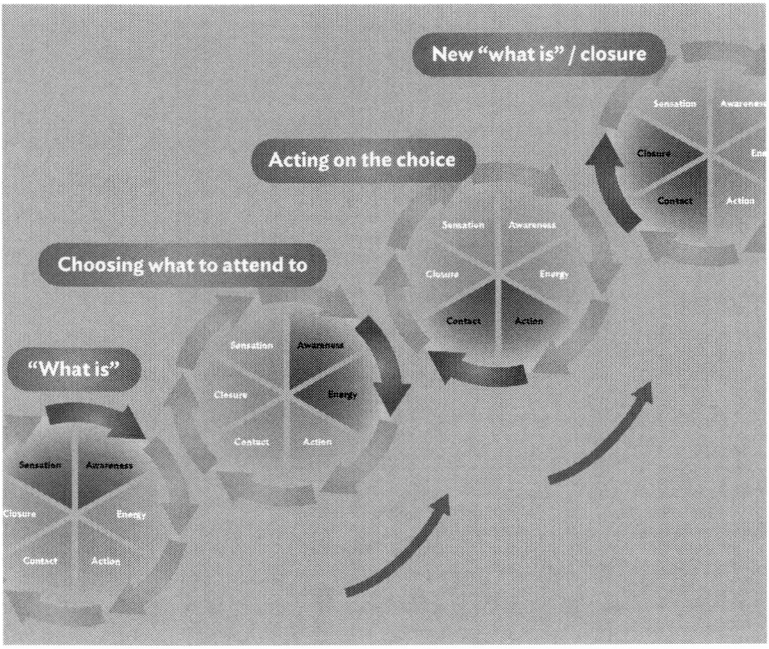

Strategizing one's presence may be more difficult for coaches who subscribe to stricter definitions of "personal authenticity" that don't allow for environmentally adaptive tweaking of one's self-presentation (the "I just have to be me, no matter what" school of thought, for example). Because presence can, in fact, change over time through experimental and experiential learning—both outside and within the coaching practice—authenticity is an issue of being clear about one's strengths, mindful of the skills we have to offer, and leveraging both in service of the clients. The more successful and effective the coach is at leveraging her presence and use of self, the greater the clients' trust in their working relationship. Once competence has established credibility, "the intervener is then able to launch ways of interacting that challenge, provoke, and unsettle the system."[69] The creation of trust and credibility allows the coach to bring in more creativity that was being managed by her PWI. Some creative invitations can appear weird to the client (e.g., some somatic exercises). But the creation of trust and perceived competence is what lets coaches introduce innovative learning experiences.

For Gestalt coaching practices, then, the most important questions revolve around "how well [coaches] understand their presence and what it evokes in others, to what extent it is grounded and integrated, and whether the coach can bring flexibility and intentionality to it."[70] One aspect of Gestalt psychology and a Gestalt approach that is now part of mainstream social science thinking is that *subjectivity drives perception*. Who we are drives what we perceive, and what we perceive reinforces who we are and the meaning we make of the world—a necessary understanding that tells us that presence is powerful but malleable. Presence can be developed and enriched. Use of self can be practiced and enhanced in effectiveness. Coaching mastery reveals itself through both self-development of presence and through practice of use of self: knowing how to access our strengths and manage our limitations to best serve our clients.

Therefore, what you evoke and what you are able to provoke are critical to the coaching encounter. When coaches are aligned with their strengths and with their wisdoms, and attuned to the client and to the context of the moment, they are able to access what the client needs—this is when use of self is in synchrony with presence and creates the effortless "flow" that Csíkszentmihályi has described as the zone of optimal performance.

CHAPTER 6
The Power of Experiment(s) in Unit of Work

Wisdom begins in wonder.
—Socrates

Many professional programs that offer focused learning exercises aimed at horizontal development are well-planned and organized vehicles for achieving a specific and expected outcome. Such programs offer exercises which may ask the client to enact a predetermined behavioral process or to use specific language in order to improve an identified professional or personal weakness or flaw. Gestalt experiments, however, are not learning exercises—they demand much more from both the coach and the client. A Gestalt experiment invites risk-taking in learning, and the outcomes are unknown because they depend on what the client has yet to become aware of.

Nick Petrie's work on vertical development suggests that experiment is a process to assist the client in integrating and making sense of perspectives and experiences from the different stages of awareness needed to understand new perspectives, worldviews, or behaviors. He describes a disruption process, where the familiar approach no longer works and there is a moment of disorientation that invites the innovative power of experiment. This is the essence of the Gestalt approach.

For the Gestalt approach is experimental, experiential, and existential and has a distinctive strength in its experimental stance. More than any other approach, Gestalt coaching uses this principle of experiment to develop the vertical skills that drive our capacity to use our awareness in expanded ways. These are experiments that illuminate a potential shift in perception, worldview, or behavior in order to learn something new about oneself. Gestalt experimentation is a practice of evoking unexpected creativity and innovation that neither the coach nor the client could have predicted.

In the experiment, the coach invites the client to enter into unexplored territory, which requires a strong commitment to being curious and to keeping an open mind and heart. Whatever is discovered during the experiment, acceptance of the outcome is key, even if the outcome feels unclear or is perceived to be a failure—learning that emerges from experimentation can come equally from a sense of success or failure. Success is when a new possibility is realized, and failure is when an old pattern emerges that continues to obstruct new possibilities. Both are opportunities for learning. If the experiment provokes a sense of stuckness and old, familiar patterns, then the ensuing exploration with the client should encourage awareness of what is familiar in that stuckness and the cost of staying in that pattern.

The parameters of a Gestalt experiment are co-created by both coach and client. The client is invited to explore the dynamic between a desire for change and a resistance to that change. Gestalt experiments involve serious and difficult work that demand that clients take steps into their discomfort zones, which are associated with new perceptions and new behaviors. For this reason, Gestalt experiments are presented as "safe emergencies" where the identified issue that is significant to the client, requiring a significant change in thought, perception, or behavior, is done in an environment where the client knows that no damaging consequences (to career or professional position) will ensue.

Two Types of Experiments: Awareness and Thematic

When a client comes for coaching, we orient them to the experiential, experimental, and existential quality of our approach and we offer observations for their attention. When clients present their issue, the Gestalt coach may notice something figural—an expression, a gesture, or a mood—and become curious as to how that figure of behavior may be affecting the client in relation to the presenting issue. The coach offers awareness of this figure of interest to the client while also tracking what the client herself is attending to as a relevant figure. For example, a client may present an issue of a subordinate complaining about lack of supervision; as coach, however, I notice that she is smiling when she relays this issue. When I share my observation that she is smiling, the client admits that she really does not take seriously whatever this subordinate says. So the work begins with the acknowledgement by the client that she actively discounts any negative feedback received from subordinates, and that this dismissal may have contributed to the poor rating she received on her 360-degree feedback surveys.

By using our Cycle of Experience (COE), Gestalt coaches are paying attention to cues that are being played out in our field of awareness. We will notice when a figure becomes interesting to a client, and we offer the client an invitation to focus on that figure for a few seconds or a few minutes. Again, the figure of interest may be an expression, a gesture, or a mood. In whatever instance, the coach has used the COE as the vehicle of intervention for clients to experience something about themselves that may be obvious to others but invisible to them—something that is part of their pattern, what we identify as the "what is" of their experience (like the client who discounted feedback from her subordinates by her dismissive smile). When we invite clients to engage in awareness of what they have ignored or missed, we are offering them an opportunity to have an awareness experiment.

Awareness experiments are the Gestalt version of "mindful practice": attending to a microcosmic moment that carries a core truth, often concealed in a narrative. When the coach notices a habit that the client is not aware of, the client's lack of awareness suggests an "alienated part" of him that once served some personal or professional imperative but that may no longer respond to current demands. But this alienated awareness needs to be owned so that new choices can emerge. When clients receive observations that get their attention, the coach can invite them to further experience that given observation. Clients who are not aware of how low their voice is when they talk might be invited to speak again, with a slight exaggeration of the low pitch, so that they can become more aware of their voice. Clients who use their hands when they talk might be encouraged to speak again and exaggerate their hand movements.

These invitations to become more aware of a small behavior reveal the greater power of awareness experiments, which usually take clients by surprise because they may be offered even at the beginning of new work when the coach doesn't have a great deal of the client's history or relationship with the client. However, the trained Gestalt coach can see already a "biography" of physical gestures and bearing, along with facial and verbal expressions, that display a living gestalt that clients may not know they are presenting to the world. When a client engages in an awareness observation offered by the coach, she will make contact with a part of herself that may be influencing the very issue she has presented. The client who came to coaching after getting negative evaluations on her

360-degree feedback survey was asked to "experience" her exaggerated smile as she talked about the concern she had regarding her evaluation; and, in experiencing that smile, she acknowledged a sense of inauthenticity. This client voiced surprise that her smiling, which she felt was a good presentation, actually felt insincere. This pivotal awareness began the coaching work.

Such small awareness moments, coming out of an awareness experiment, are almost always both surprising and illuminating to the client. Often the contact with this new or recovered awareness unleashes increased energy, born both of recognition and acknowledgement of oneself and of the possibilities of further choice. Awareness experiments, which use the COE to guide the intervention, can be offered at any time in the work, but are particularly useful in beginning work to identify what is habitual, and therefore thematic, which will generate what we call a Unit of Work.

As an example: Charlotte, an executive client, tells me that she has received feedback that she is often perceived as aloof or difficult to approach. In experiencing how this client presents herself, I notice that her posture appears stiff and I see her expression as a frown. I offer her this awareness, and I ask her to exaggerate her posture and facial expression. Charlotte then has an "aha" experience by making contact with her habitual manner of self-presentation that she says she wasn't aware of until this awareness experiment. This "aha" moment at first holds some surprise (and perhaps dismay), but it is followed by an excited energy that comes from recognizing and reclaiming one's alienated aspect of the self. Charlotte made contact with the disowned awareness that she was in fact presenting herself with stiffness and disapproval, a manner that she disliked in others. The realization was surprising, but the awareness about what she was alienating gave her increased power over a choice for change.

This awareness experiment reveals the immense power of even small moments of awareness. The experiment asked the client to fully inhabit her habitual way of being, as the paradoxical theory of change requires. And when this client became aware of that unaware behavior, she could then choose to liberate herself from that prison of habitual behaviors and invite in new possibilities. The client had denied feedback about her abrasive interaction style; having accepted the feedback's reality, she stated she now wished to present herself in a less arrogant manner. This awareness experiment provided a dramatic learning moment for the client: she recognized her habitual pattern, she acknowledged the cost of that pattern, and she expressed her desire for other options.

The COE is the vehicle of intervention for heightening awareness. Continuing with our case example, the coach used the COE as process tool by inviting Charlotte to pay attention, across all the points of the COE, to her posture and facial expression through exaggeration. Charlotte voiced surprise about how unaware she was of her habitual frown, and was even a bit disturbed by the unexpected recognition that she embodied a way of being that she disliked in others. She reported that while her intentions were to look stronger than she felt and to become an emotionally intelligent leader to inspire people, she recognized that she felt stiff and punishing in her interactions with others and feared intimacy in the work situation. These were several figures that came to her awareness, and she was invited to choose a figure to explore. Because she worried that she was not growing as a leader, she chose to explore how her aloofness was interfering with exploring new possibilities. This exploration revealed her introjected "should" that she needed to be strong to be an effective leader.

While she was determined to be a more emotionally sensitive leader, Charlotte's old introjections revealed deep-seated connections to authority figures. A series of awareness experiments followed that allowed her to explore these behavioral patterns. We took only 15 to 20 minutes exaggerating her habitual postures; then, with coaching intervention, I asked her to speak to her awareness of how she experienced this behavior. She reported that she experienced this behavior as being arrogant and irritating, but that she had never had good models that she could trust and was terrified of not being able to manage people if she was too kind. As a result, she had emulated an arrogant style that she had seen in business leaders who had succeeded. She became aware now that she had never felt comfortable with this style or felt self-trust. This awareness provided a major moment of contact, signaled by an energetic shift when she realized that this style was foreign to her and not as effective as she had hoped. Her closure from this awareness experiment was to contract to start the next session by exploring more emotionally responsive options that would allow her to be the leader she desired to become.

Thematic experiments are created around a chronic pattern of thwarted or frustrated goals. As in awareness experiments, the coaching aim is to help clients recognize some aspect of themselves, outside their awareness, that persistently stops them from achieving their goals. A thematic experiment invites clients to be curious about their familiar patterns of behavior, and then offers a collaboratively designed experience to provide learning about those patterns that may impact the achievement of their stated goals. The thematic experiment requires that the coach act as a collaborative guide and invited intervener to support client understanding of outdated patterns and/or possibly to experiment with other choices that will serve the client's current interests. A thematic experiment typically builds from an awareness experiment by defining the uppermost figure in the client's awareness, and then working with the client to support an articulation of a discerned need or desire that chronically has been frustrated or unsatisfied.

In a thematic experiment, the coach works with the client to identify a pattern of what the client may be needing or is resisting—or the polarity between the two—as a basis from which to begin the experiment. There is often an intimate quality to this moment, as the client is invited to get interested in a core pattern so deeply embedded that the coach can offer support that ensures a safe exploration of this chronic issue.

In the awareness experiment, the coach uses the COE as the vehicle of description and analysis, what gets referred to, in simple terms, as the "what is." The COE is the phenomenological description of what is occurring, as well as where there may be interruptions to awareness and the action across the different parts of the COE. In the thematic experiment, the Gestalt coach first uses the COE to assess clients' processes of identifying what is wanting and where they may have a pattern of being stuck. The Unit of Work (UOW) is the next integrated action: the energetic, defined structure that intentionally orchestrates client learning and change. A UOW is shaped in the following way (Figure 6.1).

Figure 6.1 Unit(ing) of Work

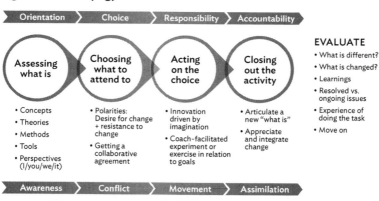

THE DRIVER OF CHANGE is The Paradoxical Theory of Change

In working collaboratively with the client to create the UOW, there are four distinct steps:

UOW Step One: **The "what is" process analysis.** This is where the figure of interest for the client is recognized as a phenomenon that is either observed by the coach or identified by the client. The coach offers attentive scanning and supports the client's awareness, using the COE to bring to light a figure that is interesting to the client and is named the "what is." For example, in our first meeting with Harry, an executive client, he presents himself as wanting to implement a succession plan for the company that has been under his leadership for the past ten years. As coach, you notice that he talks quickly and appears to be breathing rapidly. You offer this awareness to the client. He laughs and affirms that he is familiar with his fast pace.

UOW Step Two: **Engaging in the choice.** This is the place for the coach to support clients in their choice of what they wish to attend to, and to identify a pattern that thwarts the want or desired goal as expressed in Step One. The work in this second part of the UOW is to decide what to pay attention to and then to explore by means of a learning experiment. The coach works as a guide to assist the client in choosing what to pay attention to, whether this be the uppermost figure (the desired goal), the obstruction or resistance to the goal, or the interplay between them. If the client wishes to pay attention to the goal which seems to be the uppermost figure of interest, the coach will recognize this by the client's verbal expressions of "I want" or "I need." If there seems to be obstruction to a desired want or need, and the obstruction manifests as a behavior that frustrates (resists fulfilling) the goal, then the pattern of resistance may be more figural for the client than the want or need itself—it is familiar and therefore thematic. Thus, one direction for the work may be to explore the chronic resistance pattern. Another option for client exploration may be the relationship between the desired goal and the pattern of resistance.

The client has an active role in choosing what to work on. The coach is there to support the client's choice by engaging, clarifying, and asking powerful questions that assist the client in choosing what to attend to. Our questions for Harry, our client example from Step One, could be: "So, what is most interesting to you to explore? Your succession plan itself? How your fast pace affects your succession plan? Or the relationship between your fast pace and its effect on your succession plan?" Harry could explore any one of these three options. Harry asked to look at how the pace of his work affected the succession planning and his hopefulness about the future.

UOW Step Three: Acting on the choice. The third stage of the UOW, called "acting on the choice," is where the thematic experiment is implemented. Here, the coach offers an experiment to work the issue chosen by the client in Step Two. The experiment is collaboratively designed between the coach and client, with the coach inviting the client's curiosity to determine how to explore the issue and shape the experiment.

Proceeding confidently into unknown areas of the self—the essential learning of a Gestalt experiment—requires both a sense of safety and a sense of risk. A core belief regarding learning is that emotion is a signal of learning. So if we see too much calmness, it suggests no emotional risk and, therefore, no learning. If we see too much emotion for the client to manage, this suggests that fear has supplanted curiosity about the unknown. As coaches, our responsibility is to support the client and to bolster client learning by using ourselves as a kind of barometer to discern our client's tolerance for vulnerability and for risk. As coaches, we keep inviting clients to explore learning connected to their areas of discomfort and vulnerability while also keeping clients from falling into fear or derailment.

Our executive client Harry suggested that he wished to look at how the pace of his work interfered with the implementation of the plan for succession, which in turn affected his hopefulness about the future. The experiment the coach co-designed with Harry was for him to engage in a brainstorming activity regarding the succession plan: One version required him to name all the critical activities that needed to be addressed, one-by-one and quickly; a second version asked him to list the conditions of the succession plan one-by-one, but in detail. Harry agreed to the experiment. He engaged quickly in articulating the activities that needed to be addressed and started laughing at how easily a manic quality of energy got evoked. When he was invited to switch to speaking slowly about the activities involved in the succession plan, however, he was surprised at the emotion that got provoked and the issues connected to the phenomenon of his legacy.

UOW Step Four: **New gestalt–New "what is."** This is the step where the energy is focused on supporting clients to integrate new learning. One way of closing the experiment is to ask the client to name resultant learnings and to invite reflection on new insights and new possibilities in relation to his goals. This is the closure part of the UOW, the culmination of experiential learning that feels like an energetic "shift" or an "aha" moment in awareness of new choices. For Harry, our executive client—who engaged in both a more common, frenetic rendition of his succession plan and then a more unusual, deliberate presentation of it, one allowing for breath and physical expansion—the learning outcomes were dramatic. Harry reported a painful familiarity with the seduction of speed, and how moving too quickly through the succession plan was already meeting with familiar failure. He then spoke to the emotional vulnerability he was aware of when, in going slower, he experienced a sense of his own vulnerability that was attached to issues of legacy. In his new "what is," Harry reported wishing to take more deliberate meetings with his executive team to review the succession plan itself and to provide a way to interview invited candidates in order to address ongoing important initiatives. He was more hopeful as he elaborated on his new "what is," which held more emotional and imaginative possibilities than the original.

Not surprisingly, Harry was surprised by the power of his Gestalt experiment, which explored his chronic pattern of speediness and how that was an old pattern of resistance against emotional sensitivity that actually weakened his leadership power. Such is the invisible and powerful magic of the UOW—moving through seemingly "simple" steps holds transformative possibilities of learning and change.

Let's look at one more example involving an awareness experiment leading to a thematic experiment using the UOW. This example involves Maria, a highly successful general manager. Maria sought leadership development coaching because she had received feedback that her direct reports found her highly reactive and difficult to work with. The coach's awareness was caught by the upward tilt of Maria's chin and by the appearance of her lips, which were tightly compressed in a thin line. The coach shared this observation, and Maria responded that she was often not aware of how her expression appeared to others and that she had already received feedback about how stern she could appear. She reported being interested in learning about what made her react sharply to stressful news and about ways that she could be better grounded and more resourceful in her interactions. Maria expressed interest in learning how to attain greater calmness, but she also stated she didn't think she could do that. The coach asked her to alternate between being reactive (to thrust her chin up and press her lips tightly together) and then being in her imagined state of calm leadership and centeredness.

As she alternated between the somatic experiences of reactiveness and groundedness, however, she expressed her inner doubt that she could be trusting of, and therefore calm with, subordinates or business associates when there was any perceived threat from them. What then emerged was her secret trauma about how her entrepreneurial father had been bankrupted by colleagues he had trusted. She expressed both deep sadness and a feeling of shame about this that she always tried to conceal. The shame stemmed from what she had lived through with her father, but she also feared she would be as guileless and vulnerable as her father if she allowed herself to be trusting and open. This awareness-thematic experiment revealed to the client that her reactivity served as a preemptive strategy to forestall any kind of threat. The new "what is" revealed in working through a UOW was her awareness that she really wished that her leadership development would provide better tactics for managing a workforce that wanted to be respected and involved in meaningful work.

What evolved from the thematic experiment with Maria was far more powerful and unexpected than could be achieved through any pre-scripted learning exercise. Thematic experiments are like an anthropological dig, where what gets unearthed and discovered may not be exactly what is being sought but has deep value and relevance to the individual client. The surprises that are revealed to the client from thematic experiments confirm that a process of growth and development is the work of reclaiming what has been alienated and outside of awareness. This is why the coach must have a stance of "creative indifference," having no vested interest in any particular outcome in the client's experiment. This stance supports the client's ability to face the existential uncertainty of the experiment, while the attitude of creative indifference allows the coach to "embrace the practice of genuine interest combined with an equally genuine lack of investment in any particular result. The [coach] is willing to accept whatever 'is and becomes.'"[1]

As can be seen, the UOW is a powerful structure that invites the client into a learning sequence first brought into awareness through skillful use of the COE. The COE supports client awareness of any figure of interest, in the here-and-now, that emerges from the ground of all that is possible for the client. The UOW is the energetic structure whereby the client is collaboratively invited into deeper work on a chosen issue. Because with the UOW there is a process that needs orchestration through four distinct steps, the coach must have clear intentionality around supporting the client's work. While we describe the coach's stance as being embedded in creative indifference, paradoxically there is also a quality of "playing God with a small g," since the coach also acts deliberatively to invite the client across distinct and distinctly risk-taking steps (in particular, a learning experience in Step Three that is intended to assist the client to move into a discomfort zone in order to deal with what has been alienated and needs new consideration).

The coach has a vital role in being a supportive guide and encouraging the client to the edge of tolerable discomfort in order to generate the heat of new learning.[2] A client may become more aware of her disapproving expressions through an awareness experiment, but offering a UOW created out of her interests and challenges and envisioning a doable experiment is what will engage that client to successfully explore her issues. However, the coach must also be prepared for rejections to those invitations to move through the sequence of the UOW yet still remain committed to offering a more tolerable, doable UOW to the client—this is what it means to "play God with a small g."

The Power of Experiment(s) in Unit of Work | 157

This is the challenge for the coach, to dynamically use all the concepts that are involved in coaching. The coach has to recognize when there has been enough issue identification to shape a doable piece of work. Then the coach is required to be competent in using her COE to skillfully track the processes of the client, in the here-and-now, while being dialogically collaborative and engaging the client interactively. There is an artful quality to being able to use the COE and UOW. When the COE and UOW are synchronized, multiple interactions occur across the UOW steps. The coach uses the COE to discern when to move through the steps of the UOW, as indicated in Figure 6.2.

Figure 6.2 COE and UOW Synchronized

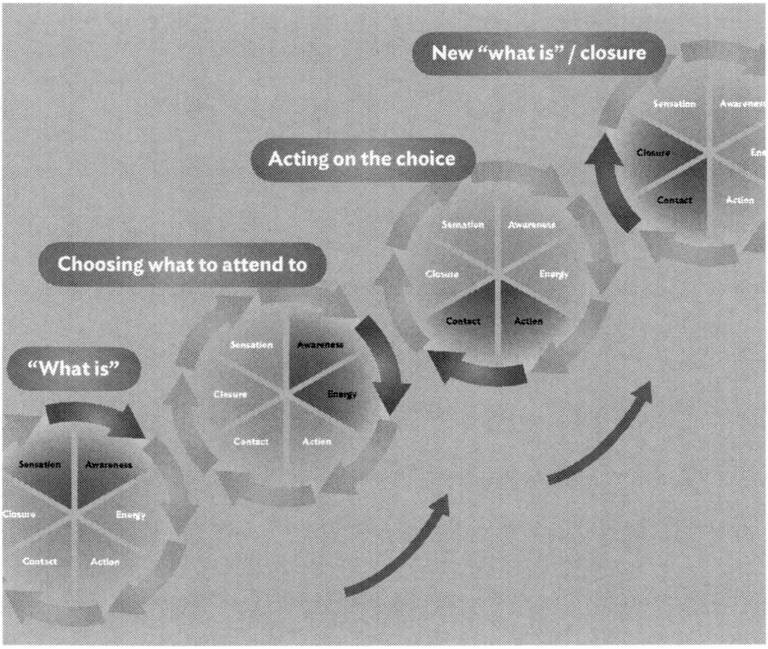

The coach uses the tracking data of the COE to identify and invite the client into the next steps of the UOW. Too much focusing on Step One can become distracting and too divergent to proceed into Step Two, which can deter from the client's choosing what to really attend to as the focal issue. In Step Two, too much careful preciseness about asking the client to confirm the focal issue of choice can create fragmented energy and prevent progressing into Step Three, where the work is to actively move into an experiment. Too much staying in the experiment can drain the energy the client needs to step into the last and assimilative stage of the UOW, Step Four, where the client is invited to focus on his new learning—this step being the desired outcome of the UOW. This is the art of managing the UOW, and the challenge for the coach is to practice being supportive around the next learning possibilities without taking over the work for the client.

Time management is important in guiding the UOW, and it is imperative for the coach to assist the client in choosing an issue that can be scaled to the time available for the work. As an example, the client desiring a career shift could be encouraged to explore smaller issues embedded in career shifts, whether it is what is possible or what has been considered. There can be multiple UOWs in a coaching session, or a UOW can start at the beginning of a session and take the entire session to complete. It is useful to gauge the time available and to scale the work so that the steps of the UOW can be completed, allowing for closure and learning integration to take place. If a UOW does not get completed in the session because the client could not or would not move forward to completion, it is important to name what is unfinished and invite the client's interest in what she feels needs to be finished. This allows the client to continue to reflect on an issue with an appreciation that something is still waiting to be understood and/or learned.

Gestalt Experiments

Albert Einstein said, "Imagination is more important than knowledge. For knowledge is limited, whereas imagination embraces the entire world, stimulating progress, giving birth to evolution." And Joseph Zinker, in his seminal *Creative Process in Gestalt Therapy*, identified the core of his work as focused on experiment, which he defined in part as "a move or series of moves with an unknown outcome."[3] Zinker highlighted that Gestalt practice was particularly strong in being able to bring the creative process of experiment as a power that could invite new possibilities. This is seen in the capacity of the Gestalt approach to offer experiments with the client.

Gestalt coaches, in learning their craft, must manage the dance between horizontal and vertical development. The horizontal skill is to learn the structure of experiments and the vertical skill is to discern what design is best for the client. Horizontal learning in Gestalt practice involves knowing the types of experiments categorized by Erving and Miriam Polster: 1) Enactment, 2) Directed behavior, 3) Fantasy, 4) Dreams/Dreamwork, and 5) Homework.[4]

Enactment Experiment. This involves dramatization of some event from the client's experience, which: 1) May be unfinished and hold a great deal of energy for the client; 2) May be a current issue where the client feels stuck; or 3) Is an enactment of a desired or undesired characteristic.

In enactment experiments, the coach is paying attention to the client's figure, which is encouraged to be "fattened" through awareness experiments by first inviting the client to try on the noticed behavior. It can begin with a gesture or expression from the client that is relevant to the presenting issues. As an example, one client who voiced alarm over the poor feedback report she received on her performance review revealed a gesture of turning her eyes away and holding her jaw. When she was invited to experience this, she responded that she had learned to never ask about "bad feedback" but to keep moving forward no matter how it felt, and that this was how she felt about this bad feedback. Now she wished she could understand what was going on, since the feedback was so important to success. The coach asked her whether she was more interested in how she stops herself from asking or how she could experiment with asking. She chose to get interested in how she stops herself from asking.

The enactment experiment that she was offered was to "be" all the aspects of how she held herself back. She was invited to exaggerate holding her jaw and looking away and to exaggerate other ways that she held herself back. She was also asked to speak to what was familiar about this pattern. She identified her introject of "I should not ask" and the price that she paid for such a restricting resistance. Having confronted the shoulds of her introjects, she voiced self-compassion in that she had subjected herself to relentless ambition, no matter the impact of her actions, and that moving on, despite all the feedback, had often left her feeling alone rather than supported by others. She then began to voice different choices, and another UOW emerged for further work.

There is an open-ended quality to enactment, where through engagement with specific behaviors the client discovers or "uncovers aspects of himself which in turn generate further discoveries."[5]

Directed Behavior Experiment. This experiment invites the client to practice behaviors he may be avoiding or be unaware of. Directed behavior experiments are not intended to make a person do what he is not interested in doing or learning about. They are intended to offer clients the opportunity to practice specific behaviors, with support from the coach. The coach supports the client in engaging in specific behaviors as opposed to the open-ended quality of enactment experiments.

One example of directed behavior involved a client who had been promoted to a leadership position but who felt inadequate in the role since she was uncomfortable delegating tasks to her subordinates, who were older than she was. She asked for help in learning how to speak with older subordinates and was invited to speak to the coach (who was herself older) as if the coach were her direct report. The client, Abby, was asked to speak with a stronger tone and to make requests with clarity about what was being asked. When she spoke, she was also invited to make eye contact, to breathe more deeply, and to thank the subordinate for following through on the requests. After several minutes of engaging in this directive experiment, Abby was asked to pay attention to how it felt. She reported that it was not as weird as she had imagined, maybe "even helpful," as she had previously avoided the kind of clarity that she herself would have found useful. What was easily witnessed was that Abby developed an understanding for the wisdom of talking more directly and with clarity. A directive experiment can be a safe space to try on important and new behaviors.

Fantasy Experiment. "Fantasy is an expansive force in a person's life—it reaches and stretches beyond the immediate people, environment or event which may otherwise contain him . . . . [S]ometimes these extensions can gather such great force and poignancy that they achieve a presence which is more compelling than some real life situations."[6] Much has been written on the power of imagery and imagination to ignite creative, unimagined possibilities, and fantasy work can offer space for them. Experiments that invite the client to engage in fantasy are actually inviting the client's power of creativity and innovation.

Polster and Polster suggest that we can invite clients into fantasy work by having them make contact with what is desired or with what may be resisted or never attempted. Fantasy work may feel like enactment, but the major difference is that whereas enactment takes its form from some past event, the work that gets created from fantasy comes out of a client's imagined possibility. Fantasy work has great power as the fiction a person creates for himself, either as a nightmare or as desired reality, which when processed as experiment can help the person discover new possibilities in the non-fiction of his lived experience.

Dreams/Dreamwork Experiment. Dreamwork offers the client the opportunity to have a dream form the basis of the experiment where the aim is to bring the message of the dream to full awareness. The Jungian writer Marion Woodman described dreamwork as the picture of one's life taken from the perspective of one's unconscious. The Gestalt method of working with dreams is to have the client tell the dream in the present tense to bring immediacy and power to the dream. The dream elements are projections of the dreamer's alienated aspects of self. In working a dream, clients are invited to become an aspect of the dream and, by doing so, to make contact with and reclaim their alienated part(s).

For example, a person tells a dream about a fast-looking new model car, driving to a new city. In establishing the dream experiment, he is invited to play the part of the new car and to speak as if he is the car. He speaks of himself as young and vibrant and admired by everyone. He voices pride over his innovative features, which allow him great speed. He is invited to speak about the new city. In speaking as the new city, he reveals that he has stopped asking for directions. He was invited to consider what he learned from being the car, and he spoke to the strengths available to him in the new job offer he was considering. When invited to speak to how he also was the new place he was traveling to, he spoke of his desire to create a new brand in his company that would yield great benefit if successful but that carried risk in implementation. When asked how he felt as he talked about these possibilities, he noted the feeling of more energy, more excitement in himself, and less of the fear that typically restricted his consideration of these options. As coach, I remember giving him feedback about how he looked different, with more color in his face and a different tone to his voice. Polster and Polster describe the ownership qualities available to the dreamer:

> [I]n acknowledging kinship with many aspects of the dream, [the client] is extending his sense of diversity, broadening his experience of self and centering himself in his world, instead of arbitrarily fractioning it into the world-out-there and me-out-there. This new extended sense of self generates the energy for a dynamic alignment of a whole range of fresh intrapersonal material. Instead of [a] stagnant self-image, where contradictory characteristics seemed to require denial, he becomes free to seek integrations of his own multiplexity.[7]

Dreamwork can be worked effectively in a coaching group by having the dream holder describe her dream and then asking her to assign dream components to group members. The important meaning-making of the dream rests with the dream holder. The coach tracks the engagement the dream holder is making with each role, and the coach supports the dream holder in paying attention to what she is becoming aware of and reclaiming from previous alienation.

Homework Experiment. This is a recommended form of experiment for real life application of new behavior that requires accountability and ongoing support. While there is support when in the coaching environment, self-responsibility and accountability outside of this environment measure the real success for the client. The Polsters suggest that homework must be "[customized] to the particular conflict of the [client]."[8] Homework must be collaboratively created for the client to try, and the range of possibilities is only limited by the imagination of the coach and client. When the client has completed a UOW in the coaching session that yields new understanding about a goal, the coach can then follow up with, "So what would be a practice that allows you to continue working on this after this session?" One executive client who had a demanding presentation to give to her executive board was invited to practice her speech every morning in front of a mirror. At the end of each rehearsal, she was invited to identify what she said well. She was also invited to give herself a grade that ranged from good to excellent. What became clear when she returned for more coaching was that the practice had provided her with the needed self-support for her presentation.

To recapitulate, the sequence of experiments has been described as:[9]

1. Identifying the figure
2. Suggesting an experiment
3. Grading the experiment for risk and challenge
4. Developing the experiment
5. Completing the work
6. Assimilating and integrating the learning (Figure 6.3)

The Unit of Work in relation to experiment is summarized as follows:

Step One is where the figure of interest for the client emerges.

Step Two is the place for the coach to support the client in choosing which figure of interest he wishes to attend to, the resistance pattern that holds him back from his goals, or the interplay between his resistance and a desired new possibility. The coach offers an experiment for the client to explore.

Figure 6.3 Gestalt Experiment

	An intentional, organized behavioral event intended to explore, define, clarify, and illuminate an issue important to the client
PURPOSE	• See the price of old perceptions and behaviors • Explore new possibilities in a safe setting with graded and acceptable risk • Experiment with new goals or habits of resistance, or the interplay between them • Experience and accept support from the environment for new possibilities
PRINCIPLES	• Stress doing over talking • Create "safe emergencies" • Focus on the present • Aim for closure
GRADING	• GRADE UP = **RAISE THE RISK** *or* **LOWER THE SUPPORT** • GRADE DOWN = **LOWER THE RISK** *or* **RAISE THE SUPPORT**
STEPS	• Secure agreement—establish grounding and contact • Achieve clarity of intention • Grade the intervention to a degree you and the client can handle • Adjust the experiment to the client—creativity serves learning • Support the client's experience and learning • Provide closure—be unattached to the outcome

Step Three involves the client acting on what has been chosen. The coach acts to support the client in choosing and engaging in an experiment.

Step Four is the energetic space to support the client in integrating her new learning by revisiting what she chose to attend to and assimilating her learning from her original "what is" picture into a newly defined "what is" that incorporates the learning derived from the experiment. This is the experiential learning culmination, the shift of awareness into new possibilities.

The use of experiment and the management of Unit of Work speak to the power of the Gestalt process and the intervention skills of the coach. The coach is required to assist clients in a collaborative manner by maintaining her creative indifference, which is based on not being attached to any specific outcome while still being available to offer observation and inquiry that can serve the client. This is the marriage of the learned horizontal skills of the experiment with the vertical development that ensures that the coach knows the appropriate application and timing of her place in the encounter. "It is trust in the healthiness of [client] self-regulation and in the deeper wisdom that lies within us. Most of all, it is trust that if we as [coaches] provide the proper conditions in the process of [coaching] the client will choose his own right direction."[10]

We provide that the Unit of Work is the organizing structure that holds the experiment and provides an organized way of orchestrating the process for a coherent learning experience. The UOW asks the coach to work with intent on behalf of the client, using thematic issues as pathways into an invitation to experiment and unleash new possibilities. Being able to co-design, support, and guide a client through UOWs is a powerful aspect of Gestalt coaching that also benefits from both horizontal and vertical development. The more a coach can support clients to engage in their UOW, the more the coach learns how to invoke and harness her own wisdom and how to shape creative experiments inside the UOW. The power in the UOW is that it provides a safe place to confront habitual patterns with new experimental possibilities that can generate new outcomes—a process and result that often gets experienced as the magic of Gestalt.

CHAPTER 7
Group and Team Coaching

*If you want to go fast, go alone. If you want to go far,
go together.*
—African proverb

In the 21st century, competition has brought about greater demands for performance goals and achievable outcomes. This has focused attention on groups and teams at all organizational levels as critical strategic resources for overall financial success.[1] This shift to promoting groups is a signal to the coaching community that our fundamental toolkit needs to include ways to intervene effectively at the group level and to facilitate learning by using the power of groups.

Group participation is an organic feature of human social life. Belonging to a group satisfies multiple needs: survival needs (safety and sustenance), psychological needs (intimacy and status), informational needs (environmental knowledge and evaluative criteria), and identity needs (providing a collective basis for beliefs and values).[2] Though groups are comprised of individuals, they exist as separate entities and have a collective power that can make the whole greater than the sum of its parts.

Systems Theory: Awareness and Applications

A system is a group of related interacting and interdependent elements that work together toward a common purpose or goal. For this primer, we are talking about *living* systems, which means people who share the capacity for learning, development, and evolution. More specifically, we are talking about organizational groups, which could be thought of as living subsystems of the organization. System thinking principles give us several concepts that make systems theory a vital component of the Gestalt approach for group coaching. These principles are the lens through which the coach sees the group, offering a view that allows the group to become more aware of itself as a group and accountable for determining how to meet group goals and for its own improvement.

These central system principles are:

Holism: This principle states that the whole is different from (greater than) the sum of its parts, a concept firmly aligned with the Gestalt perspective.[3] The group is a systemic whole whose needs and functional values may differ from individual members' needs or values. The principle of holism requires the coach to give equal regard to both parts of the group and the whole of the group, depending on what serves its development best. Sport teams are often used to describe holism in groups, where the group is seen as a different entity from its individual star players. A memorable example of a group being more powerful than a star player alone was when Michael Jordan, the great basketball star, began to consider the needs of the group as a whole rather than his capacity alone to play the game. That perspective shift is what resulted in team championships.

Open/Closed System: Information exchange and emotional contact occur across various group boundaries, i.e., between each individual and the group as a whole, between one individual and another, and between the subgroups. The more "closed" the group is, the more rigidly drawn the various boundaries are; the more "open" the group is, the less filtering or screening takes place. Contact boundaries are specific relationships within the group that hold emotional or psychological energy and that offer the coach choice points for intervention. In the development of identity and a sense of "we-ness," strong group boundaries promote more cohesion. But for the ongoing vibrancy of a group, boundaries need to be permeable enough to allow information exchange.

Entropy/Negentropy: These terms describe the energy configuration of the group. Lack of or disruption of information creates entropy. Those groups that block interpersonal exchanges starve the group as a whole of needed information and energy. Sharing information creates negentropy (the opposite of entropy). Group members' willingness to share awarenesses (e.g., expressions of anger or vulnerability) helps create new figures for the group's exploration and the opportunity for new possibilities to emerge. This dovetails with the experience of contact, which is embedded in boundary management. A sign of diminished energy can often be traced back to a group not being aware of the conditions of its entropy. A way of decreasing entropy in a group is to call for more interpersonal exchange within the group.

Self-regulation: The ability to self-regulate (manage) assures system integrity regarding group purpose and identity. Stability engenders a sense of trust and is the required ground from which new possibilities can be recognized. Groups self-regulate by assigning specific roles to members and by developing powerful (often implicit) norms that govern behaviors. Norms support safety within the group, whether it is confidentiality or fairness in distribution of resources, and support self-regulation by giving a structure that allows self-assessment. The principle of self-regulation assists a group to be self-responsible while also feeling liberated to be so.

Feedback: For the system to contend with an ongoing influx of information and energy from the environment, it must have a capacity to maintain its status quo but also be able to adapt to conditions requiring change. In a group situation, feedback is information received from others that can provide guidance that helps the group as a whole assess whether it is "on track" with its goal or task or needs to redefine or reorganize to achieve that goal or task. Feedback is an active ingredient of self-regulation and reduction of entropy.

Equifinality: There are many ways to achieve a goal or desired outcome. One viable approach doesn't necessarily exclude others, which may be equally valuable or productive. The energy that embodies holding a stance of equifinality is to be able to offer appreciation for any perspective. This principle supports coaches in acknowledging multiple perspectives, honoring the group's strengths and diverse resources. Criticism and judgment, even when given with the best intention, reduce the application of equifinality.

Suboptimization: In the group context, this denotes a highly effective strategy to enhance group performance. When an individual or subgroup demonstrates superior skills in a particular critical area, allowing this individual or subgroup to "take charge" increases every group member's opportunity for success. Suboptimization assures that the entire group benefits from *each* individual's skills and knowledge. It may not be easy to achieve, as it requires the active use of retroflection, i.e., people holding back so that other people in the group may be more active in offering their particular competencies. The strength of suboptimization lies in dynamically supporting different choices for group achievement. Self-regulation can be used in service of suboptimization.

Using these system principles, Gestalt group coaches have an appreciative way to understand the properties of the group that allows them to determine if the group is "doing the best it can" at any given moment. It also lets coaches identify where certain boundaries are interfering with the group's ability to achieve its goals. When Gestalt group coaches apply these principles, group members become more strategically involved in both their individual development and as a group.

While these principles are relevant for group and team coaching, we also suggest that they can be used for individual coaching. For the first 20 years of coaching, most practitioners considered coaching to be "individual" coaching. We offer that coaching, particularly of an executive client, requires thinking with system principles. All clients are, in some way, part of a system, and these principles are as relevant to individual coaching as they are to group coaching.

Field Theory: Awareness and Applications

Since the advent of general systems theory, a number of refinements and reformulations have arisen.[4] Field theory—also called field dynamics—is "a set of principles, an outlook, and [a] way of thinking that relates to intimate interconnections between events and the settings or situations in which these events take place."[5] These interconnections can be visible and observable (e.g., spoken dialogue or eye contact), more subtle and intuitive (e.g., body language or breathing patterns), or barely perceptible at all yet something we viscerally feel. When applied to organizational change efforts and leadership development, the field theory framework extends the relevant focal elements in systems theory into 21st-century "knowledge era" challenges. Gestalt coaches must develop effective strategies and tools to manage both systems and field elements.[6]

Environmental influences on the group easily multiply and become entangled, and have a major impact on organizational (and therefore, executive or leadership) health. Our organizational clients are pressured to be able to work comfortably within highly turbulent complex systems, which, like all postmodern paradigms, requires both coach and client alike to have the adaptive VUCA competencies of Vision, Understanding, Clarity, and Agility.[7] Although systems theory and principles continue to inform and guide, field theory/dynamics more directly addresses the modern chaos of new and unpredictable events, rapid change, and murky boundaries. The **system** holds reliable understanding of levels and boundaries and their interactions. The **field** holds opportunities for innovation, growth, and sustainable learning.

Gestalt theory and practice have always acknowledged that individuals exist in a complex web of influences, ranging from the immediate to the remote: from the individual, to the family, to the community, to the organization, to the culture to which the individual belongs. Complex organizational environments can impact individuals' interior life in positive and negative ways. The challenge is to invite individual identity and group identity to join in a purposeful and productive partnership. The individual is strengthened by belonging to a vibrant group whose purpose and practice strengthen individual efforts. The group is strengthened by individuals who bring needed resources to add to the identity and development of the group.

Group Work: The Gestalt Perspective

In the Gestalt model, first articulated by Kurt Lewin in field dynamics and later by Elaine Kepner in her seminal article "Gestalt Group Process," the principles and practices of Gestalt therapy merge with those of group dynamics. In Kepner's words, the group facilitator "wears bifocal lenses, paying attention to the development of the individuals in the group and to the development of the group as a social system." Kepner lays out three system levels (intrapersonal [self], interpersonal, and group-as-a-whole) and establishes a three-stage temporal developmental process (identity and dependence, influence and counterdependence, and intimacy and interdependence).[8]

In 1992, Mary Ann Huckabay provided an expanded review of Gestalt group work and the three major theoretical frameworks (Systems, Field, and Gestalt theory) that "provide[s] the why, the what, and the how of effective work with small groups": general systems theory answers the why—"the explanatory undergirdings" of group behavior; field theory answers the what—"the focal elements to be observed and monitored" in a group; and classical Gestalt psychology answers the how—"a way to focus awareness on what is occurring in groups." Huckabay identifies four stages of group development: inclusion, identity, and dependence; influence, autonomy, and counter-dependence; intimacy and affection; and interdependence. She offers four approaches regarding the design and implementation of group leader interventions: the goals of the group work, stage-related interventions, level-related interventions, and regulatory system interventions.[9] Understanding these dynamics supports the Gestalt group coach to determine appropriate, effective interventions.

Few Gestalt practitioners writing on group work draw any clear distinctions between systems theory and field theory because there is extensive theoretical overlap between these theories and both serve the Gestalt coach.[10] I would like to draw a somewhat nuanced distinction for Gestalt coaching, however, with an eye to illustrating the incredibly complex demands of the organizational environments our executive and leadership clients inhabit today, and therefore the equally complex demands placed on the coaches who serve these clients. Coaches must use themselves as a kind of barometer to gauge the development of the group. Conducting group and team work, then, isn't a question of understanding *complicated* systems but of understanding *complex* systems.[11] Yet the crucial skills are those that Gestalt practitioners are already attuned to: integrating awareness processes with context sensitivity to offer observations and to create resonant interventions. When there are multiple boundaries and phenomena to attend to, awareness itself can become fragmented and confused. Being able to stay present and use the Cycle of Experience to differentiate the relevant figures is where leadership and practitioner mastery is revealed.

Integrating systems and field principles, for the Gestalt coach, is the relevant skill of knowing when to apply the dynamic strengths of one or the other in specific conditions. These "two paradigms—linear predictability [systems] and chaos adaptation [field]—are not mutually exclusive" but are more like complementary forms of meaning-making to be chosen depending on an assessment of the situation.[12] For example, in instances where the problem being addressed is "simple"—limited in scope and influence, and clearly defined—a systems approach will offer the most effective intervention choice points, e.g., who holds the issue that is being discussed, which may be located at a particular level of system. However, when the problem is unique, open-ended, and the parameters "fuzzy" (unseen variables may be involved), a field approach may inspire more innovative intervention choice points.[13] Here we may welcome people to focus inward and outward (scan the environment) and speak to what they are aware of, which may reveal phenomena that are not obvious, in fact, until people speak of them.

Today's organizational environments may require improvised teams with revolving membership, and expectations that these teams "perform complex, urgent, and often highly consequential tasks."[14]

What may best allow such unconventional teams to succeed is a melding of systems-based hierarchical structures and the open-form processes associated with field dynamics: "Bureaucratic structures provide sufficient order, clarity, and stability that organizational members may engage in flexibility-enhancing processes without devolving into chaos or conflict. Flexibility-enhancing processes permit sufficient autonomy and adaptability that organizational members may accept bureaucratic structures without giving into inertia, rigidity, or unresponsiveness in the face of changing situational contingencies."[15] The same sort of supple paradigmatic blend of system theory and field dynamics is a developed skill for the Gestalt coach working with groups or teams.

Group Characteristics and Stages of Development

Any group, anywhere, contends over time with similar concerns in the process of "becoming" a group. Even though organizational groups "tend to be organized, task focused, and formal," they will follow predictable sequential processes and behavioral patterns, and they will encounter predictable emotional or psychological challenges, since "any behavior that an individual can perform alone can also be performed in a group context."[16] Group stage development theory is, therefore, about normative developmental sequences and their correlated behaviors. The issues and concerns inherent to each developmental stage need to be successfully worked through before moving on to the next stage, although challenges and disruptions may take a group back to an earlier stage.

While not every researcher agrees on the number of stages or what to name them, most agree on three core facets that control group development.

1. **Group Purpose/Goal and Outcome:** Groups come together for a common purpose to achieve a common

goal. The specificity of the group's reason for existence serves as the framework for any coaching observation or intervention. Organizational groups have particular needs in terms of purpose, but they must also have a need to: inculcate a spirit of inquiry and experimentation; expand members' awareness around emerging opportunities and alternative action choices; increase the range, diversity, and capacity for collaborative (even cross-cultural) work; and encourage self-awareness and self-developmental work.

2. **Norms:** These are the rules of "expected behavior," whether physical (e.g., body language, physical proximity) or verbal (e.g., communication styles, expressions of intense emotions). Often tacit and unspoken, norms are very powerful rules that govern what is and what is not acceptable behavior in interactions between group members and in external organizational settings as well. Norms are the principal means by which the group self-regulates. An example of an impactful democratic norm is whether group members feel free to openly contest established norms that have become irrelevant or even dysfunctional relative to the group's goals and growth. Like unrecognized habitual patterns that obstruct individual growth, a group norm that no longer serves the group's goal or intended outcome needs to be called into awareness and re-examined.

3. **Roles:** Whether formally defined from the outset or emerging over time, an assigned role defines an individual member's participation and function in the group. When roles are made explicit, they're more easily changed or re-assigned. Nevertheless, when roles emerge from group dynamics, over time their breadth and diversity are only constrained by the range of possibilities imagined by the

group itself. Various members will fulfill various roles to meet group needs as the group evolves (e.g., someone may need to play the role of "task-master" while someone else may need to play the role of "devil's advocate"). Some roles may gradually become obsolete, and group roles that no longer serve the group's goal or intended outcome also need to be called into awareness and re-examined.

These three foundations of group existence are embedded in the ongoing life of the group and are the framework for the many competing models of group development (Figure 7.1). This chart allows us, as practitioners, to view the similarities of group development in relation to the group's temporal stage of development, and how the stage affects norms, expectations, and behaviors.

Group and team coaching has become the next wave of competency development in the field of executive coaching.[17] It is important for practitioners to recognize stages of group development since each stage calls for different needs and behaviors. We typically see the following three basic stages of group development:

Beginning (Orientation): Inclusion, Identity, and Dependence This stage is characterized by orientation issues of self-identity and boundary definitions of role and commitment: Why am I in this group? How should I behave? Who's "in" and who's "out"? Who can be trusted? How much should I commit to this group and its goal? Individual and group energy is spent seeking to establish norms, and the group coach needs to provide enough leadership facilitation to support the group answering the orientation questions so that the group can move to the middle stage of development.

Middle: Influence, Autonomy, Differentiation, and Counter-dependence This stage is characterized by group members testing authority and status. This can lead to the types of conflict that occur when the

Figure 7.1 Group Development Theories: Some Comparisons

Theorists	[New Groups] Beginning/Orientation	[Ongoing Groups] Middle/Conflict	[Established Groups] End/Cohesion	[High Performing Groups] Exit/Termination
Bales & Strodtbeck[1]	Orientation	Evaluation	Control	[N/A]
Bennis & Shepard[2]	Dependence	Counter-dependence	Resolution	[N/A]
Caple[3]	Orientation	Conflict	Integration	Achievement
Huckabay[4]	Inclusion (dependence)	Influence (counter-dependence)	Intimacy	Interdependence
Schutz[5]	Inclusion	Control	Affection	[N/A]
Srivastva, Obert & Neilsen[6]	Inclusion	Influence	Intimacy	Interdependence
Tuckman & Jensen[7]	Forming	Storming	Norming	Performing/Adjournment

[1] Bales, R. F., and F. L. Strodtbeck, "Phases in Group Problem Solving," *Journal of Abnormal Social Psychology* 46 (1951): 485–495.

[2] Bennis, W. G., and H. A. Shepard, "A Theory of Group Development," *Human Relations* 9 (1956): 415–437.

[3] Caple, R. B. "The Sequential Stages of Group Development," *Small Group Behavior* 9, no. 4 (1978): 470–476.

[4] Huckabay, Mary Ann, "An Overview of the Theory and Practice of Gestalt Group Process," in *Gestalt Therapy: Perspectives and Applications*, ed. Edwin C. Nevis (Cambridge, MA: GestaltPress, 2000), 303–330.

[5] Schutz, W. C., *FIRO: A Three-Dimensional Theory of Interpersonal Behavior* (New York: Holt, Rinehart, 1958).

[6] Srivastva, S., S. L. Obert, and E. H. Neilsen, "Organizational Analysis through Group Processes: A Theoretical Perspective for Organization Development," in *Organizational Development in the UK and USA: A Joint Evaluation* (London: McMillan Press, 1977), 83–111.

[7] Tuckman, B. W., and M. A. C. Jensen, "States in Small Group Development Revisited," *Group and Organizational Studies* 2, no. 4 (1977), 419–427.

politeness of orientation moves into differentiation. When orientation needs are satisfied, group members can move into experimentation for control and leadership, which can result in conflict. Cliques or subgroups may emerge, and questions of how much to use or be used by others arise. As boundaries around the work to be done are more clearly defined and conflict is effectively negotiated and managed, group identity is deepened, trust is enhanced, and exchanges between participants increase in number and depth. The key focus of the group coach is directed toward supporting the group in their assigned goal by using the middle stage of development to encourage task leadership. This is the energy of participants working to influence the task. Group development, and what it offers to task enrichment, is supported by participants being able to use the innovation linked to differentiation. When the diversity of multiple perspectives can be accessed and applied, the group has had a successful development that allows it to move forward to its closing stage.

End: Intimacy, Cohesion, and Interdependence This stage, at its best, is characterized by a heightened awareness of interpersonal relationships, highly developed integration and differentiation, greater tolerance and support for collaboration and intimacy, and open acknowledgment and acceptance of conflict as an avenue to new possibilities. In the orientation stage, participants' language is dominated by an "I" perspective; in the end stage, participants' language is dominated by a "we" perspective. In the orientation stage, no participant is an obvious leader; in the end stage, leadership roles are recognized and change based on participants' skill or expertise. Decisions in the end stage are taken with the consensus of the group, which would be hard to achieve in the orientation stage.

Because organizational environments are increasingly pressured to manage multiple outcomes in a limited time, they often establish groups that have no long-standing membership. As a result, many groups never reach this end stage of development. Nevertheless, these groups can have extraordinary moments of connection and cohesion where there is not only a sense of accomplishment but also a sense of breakthrough to new potentials and possibilities. Whether there is just a "puff of cohesion" (as the late Don Keller, a colleague, used to say) or an experience of cohesion so deep that it reignites the energy of the group, this sense of connection between individual and group identity is what inspires a group to collectively recommit itself to ongoing work that can become excellent. The foremost task of the group coach here is to assist the group in recognizing and celebrating their accomplishments.

While some fundamental themes are present in the group at all times, at particular stages certain issues take on greater emotional charge and salience—that is, they become figural. Group coaching requires that the members fulfill the purpose of satisfying the goal of the group as well as the processes of the group—how the members fulfill the purpose and move toward the goal.

To see where the group is at any given moment, we watch for behaviors that indicate group stage development. Throughout, the Gestalt coach uses the Cycle of Experience to track awareness and energy around particular stage-related behaviors at all levels of the system (LOS). When there is a collaborative choice about the work required, we invite the client into Units of Work. If we want to know where to intervene, we use LOS as the intervention guide. Let us introduce LOS, which is a powerful tool for the group coach.

Levels of System: Boundaries and Intervention Choice Points

A system is primarily defined by its purpose, and this purpose determines what or who is included in or excluded from that system. When we are referring to the experience of inclusion or exclusion, boundaries become the determining variable affecting the degree of openness. Because these boundaries are permeable to varying degrees—in terms of information, resources, and energy—some degree of exchange with the environment is always going on to ensure the continued existence and integrity of the system. These system boundaries provide distinct leverage points for group coaches to assess the group's behaviors as well as to effectively intervene in order to support group work and move the group forward in its development. The important questions are which boundaries are most relevant in relation to the work in the system, when to engage those boundaries, and how to recognize an error in LOS.

A wisdom from Gestalt theory is the mantra that "contact happens at the boundary." This means that to satisfy what needs attention or change, the focus for group work effectiveness is often driven by identifying the geography of the work—at which level of system the work is located: individual, dyad (two-person), subgroup, or organization. Knowing how to work at and with the different levels is what allows the richness of group work to emerge. This knowledge is intricately connected to understanding and to recognizing how to use boundaries, which are embedded in the LOS.

Boundaries help identify the nature of the work, where narratives describe who we are or transactions are needed to support the narrative of who we are (Figure 7.2).

Figure 7.2 LOS Boundaries

Nature of the Work: *What is the work?* Boundaries define the task and component	Driver of the Work: *What information is needed?* Boundaries benefit from transactions
INDIVIDUAL DYAD SUBGROUP GROUP	SYSTEM TO SYSTEM SUBSYSTEM TO SUBSYSTEM SELF TO SELF
• Supports self-narrative and self/system narratives • Brings the self/system into greater alignment with its own qualities, values, ethics, and vision	• Activity is between systems and subsystems • Focus is on activity to integrate alienated aspects of self, system, or environment

When a person, a subgroup, or a group is questioning itself in relation to identity, vision, or purpose, we can think of those questions as self-definition. The focus of the work or inquiry is within the boundary that is being defined. For example, a person in the group talks about being confused about an issue. His lack of clarity suggests he cannot articulate what is important in the moment, and an intervention is to invite him to take a breath and check his feelings with the question, "What do I want?" This question is definitional since it asks him to check within himself. When individuals, subgroups, or the group need more information in relation to any challenge, they need to undergo more exchange with group members. For example, two group members appear to have different figures regarding the group task. They are invited to ask each other for more clarification. In inviting them to ask each other, they are being directed to have an exchange intervention because they are speaking to each other across their personal boundaries. Key questions for the group coach are: 1) What is the figural work, the issue that needs to be addressed?; 2) Is the work within the boundary and therefore about self-definition, or external to the boundary and therefore needing exchange of information?; 3) Where should the work be done, at what level of system?; and 4) How does level of system drive the work?

The four primary levels of system that coaches need to understand and be able to address are: self, or individual; self and other, or interpersonal; subgroup, or two (dyad) or more people; and group, as a whole.

Self, or Individual Level

Work at the individual group member level focuses on the individual's relationship to her own experience of response and interaction. The goal is to heighten the individual's awareness and regulation of sensory input, meaning-making, mobilization of energy, and closure to empower the individual to make desired changes in her management of self.

Assessment at this level remains personal; that is, attention is paid to an interaction only in terms of how that interaction affects the individual in question. But work at the individual level often benefits the group as a whole. For example, the group coach might use the conflict embodied at the individual level as a way to examine group dynamics at the interpersonal level. Or, an individual's perceptions regarding other group members may in turn express an issue or a theme that needs resolution at the group level. As well, it is a sign of group coaching mastery to recognize how to finish work at the individual level before moving to another level. The primary issues at this level can embrace organizational priorities but will be manifested through self-scenarios.

Self and Other, or Interpersonal Level

At the interpersonal level of system, boundaries are drawn between pairs: individual to individual, individual to subgroup, and individual to group. The goal of work at this level is to clarify the nature of the boundary, i.e., to define how often and with whom interaction takes place as well as how exchanges of influence and information occur across that boundary. Examples are communication between partners, among colleagues or co-workers, or between boss and subordinate.

An interpersonal intervention might highlight differences, similarities, or perspectives that each hold but neither are aware of. Often, differences are identified to make discernable the contribution each individual brings to the exchanges. For example, two individuals could explore the differences in their styles of speech and the implication of those differences for their interactions. Alternatively, an individual could request feedback from each member of the group and reply to that feedback. An example of an individual intervention becoming an interpersonal intervention by mistake is when the coach may ask the client to start speaking to the coach instead of directing the client to stay engaged with herself. When this happens, it is an example of coaching mastery to be able to say, "Wait a minute, let's go back to you" or "Do you wish to speak with me?" in order to give the power of choice to the client. The primary contribution of the interpersonal intervention is to bring participants into contact with multiple perspectives and new information.

Subgroup (Two or More Individuals) Level

The subgroup level of system involves interaction between two (dyad), three, or more people. Work at this level focuses on the subgroup as an independently functioning system in itself. The goal for the subgroup is to develop awareness that it has a life of its own, and the emphasis of intervention is on identifying and articulating the jointly created characteristics that define the nature of this functional whole. These characteristics may be short term (temporary), in mutual response to a current problem, or the characteristics may be long term (chronic). The coaching intervention may be when two or more people share some particular characteristics and it would support them to become aware of those characteristics. Examples are: participants who may have been identified as high talent; participants who have been relocated; participants who are the only men or women in the groups, or those of a certain work generation, or those who share important values; and so on. Calling on the subgroup to highlight these characteristics is important to the vibrancy of the entire group, but may remain hidden unless the group coach is able to help the subgroup appreciate the strength of those shared characteristics.

Within a dyad, the group coach can intervene by approaching the pair from either the interpersonal or the subgroup level, depending on the coach's judgment regarding the nature of the relationship and on personal skills. For example, if each individual in the pair is highly differentiated and in conflict with the other, the group coach may prefer to emphasize the subgroup boundary, focusing attention on how each individual contributes to the creation of a subsystem with distinctive traits to heighten the cohesiveness of the subgroup. In a two-person subgroup where inequality or passive agreement is problematic, the coach may choose to intervene at the interpersonal level, emphasizing differentiation and supporting the development of each individual's boundaries. It takes coaching mastery to be clear about the difference between working at the interpersonal or the subgroup boundary. When two or more individuals share characteristics that evoke vulnerability, it strengthens those individuals to be joined in a subgroup where they experience a sense of "we-ness."

Group Level

The defining boundary of a group is set by the purpose of the group as well as by the membership, including the group coach.[18] As with the subgroup level, the goal is to heighten awareness that the group has a life of its own and is a whole whose sum is different from its parts. The group is a system in which all members play a role, in which any individual may display the symptoms of the entire group's problem, and in which individual members are always responding personally to the group experience. However, the focus of intervention at this level is on perceiving and assessing the group as a whole.

Something that is true about the group may not be true of each individual member, or not true all the time. The group speaks through its interactive behavior, through the nature and quality of the interplay among the members. The group coach may notice that the group is avoiding the inclusion/exclusion issue by forming two distinct subgroups, or that all but one member agrees to membership requirements, or that work in the group primarily gets done through two-person encounters. Such observations call for intervention strategies that draw members' attention to the fact that they are functioning within a higher level of system, not just as separate entities.

The Practice of Group Intervention: A Coaching Toolkit

General systems theory emphasizes an organism's holistic interactions with multiple environments. Because systems theory thinking about levels, boundaries, and system integrity gives order and predictability to group work, it lends itself especially well to determining where—at which level of system—to offer our interventions. For the Gestalt coach working with organizational clients, the systems approach supports strategic intervention across levels of system(s), which serves to focus client awareness work at multiple levels. For example: One person in the group may raise a question regarding the nature of the group's purpose. Although the question presumably involves the entire group, the coach can choose to address an initial intervention directly to the individual who raised the question (i.e., at the individual level). But that individual intervention can be followed with a group-level intervention to focus, confirm, and validate the issue of group purpose at both levels. So, for example, if Suzette, a group member, asks about the group's purpose, an individual intervention to her could be: "Suzette, can you give your answer for what the group's purpose is?" After Suzette gives her answer, as a way of honoring that question, the coach invites the group to address the same issue of purpose with a group level intervention: "Could each of you speak to this question of purpose?" The power of a group addressing what initially looks like an individual concern reveals the contribution of diversity that enriches everyone.

While each system level is a conceptual construct with distinct boundaries, changes at one level of system will affect all the other levels. To maximize performance and growth for each level, some work has to happen at all levels. There are no prescriptive rules to determine the most effective level of system at which to intervene. The choice of level depends as much on the coach's strengths and preferences as on any presumably "objective" measure. Awareness of critical group factors will also influence the effective coach's choices, among these: the stage of a group's development; the existence (or lack) of a shared sense of purpose; the extent of trust and familiarity between coach and system; and the extent to which one level has been developed at the expense of another. The coach must recognize that while working at one level precludes working at a different, perhaps just as relevant level, phenomena continue to occur at all levels simultaneously. The group coach needs to be able to perceive and differentiate between system levels but also be able to easily shift attention to whichever level is figural for the work.

Awareness of the ongoing interplay between system levels allows the group coach to better assess how the group as a whole is interacting and what work is necessary. It's important, then, to keep in mind that "[e]quifinality operates here as in all social system phenomena: There are many paths to the same end, and groups move toward increasing awareness, choicefulness, and contact, in short, toward system self-regulation, via a bewildering array of behavioral innovations at various levels."[19]

Paradoxically, it is often easier to understand the group as a whole from the conceptual vantage point of one particular level. Using such a lens allows the group coach to pay attention to specific kinds of interactions and to identify several distinct intervention strategies. From a Gestalt perspective, deciding where and when to intervene in group work is informed by Gestalt theory and principles of group stage development as well as by systems and field thinking. Throughout all interventions, Gestalt coaches apply the awareness process model of the Cycle of Experience integrated with specific stage-related interventions at the appropriate level of system (Figure 7.3).

Figure 7.3 Coach/Leader Interventions at Stages of Group Development

Issues & Phenomena	BEGINNING: ORIENTATION	
	Interventions	Coach/Leader Examples
Inclusion/membership Norm clarification Trust development Leadership—followership Purpose/goals *Data-collection* *"Polite" interactions* *Social posturing for influence* *Goal articulation*	Work at individual and interpersonal levels is dominant INTENT * Elicit multiple perspectives and responses to purpose/goals * Experience the possibilities and potential of the group as a whole * Weave together threads of commonality and differences * Forge connections between members * Demonstrate and embody supportive behaviors * Establish ongoing current and relevant information	**Individual Inquiry:** Ask each member to speak to what they want from the group. **Interpersonal Interaction:** Ask members to direct questions and feedback directly to one another. **Pacing:** Slow down risky or charged exchanges and invite members to talk about how they are experiencing themselves and others. **Modeling:** Set standards of appreciative curiosity, responding directly to individuals, inviting expression, articulating faith in the group's competencies. **Check-Ins:** Frequently invite members to share with the group any changes in personal information.

MIDDLE: DIFFERENTIATION, CONFLICT, INNOVATION

Issues & Phenomena	Interventions	Coach/Leader Examples
Manage differences and conflict Acknowledge and accept conflict Confront and talk through conflict *Activities are driven by more assertive individuals or quiet members who feel strongly about an issue* *Conflict acknowledges tension around agreement over ideas and positions* *Members recognize that conflict is valuable for energy and innovation* *The group verbally addresses conflict without moving to premature conclusions* *The group finds creative, flexible means for managing conflict*	Work at the interpersonal and subgroup level is dominant Work to get completed units of work that inspire more trust INTENT * Demonstrate that conflict potentially inspires new possibilities and innovative resolutions for group challenges * Build ground and support * Model the message that conflict, rightly managed, can harness energy and information	**Highlight differentiation:** Invite two participants who are in conflict to speak directly to each other in the group. **Use Unit of Work:** Complete a UOW at the two-person and group levels to build trust and model conflict management.

END: COHESION, INTEGRATION, INTIMACY

Issues & Phenomena	Interventions	Coach/Leader Examples
Self-responsibility Expression of feelings Connection between members Use of full resources Clarity of purpose Conflict managed without "blame" Norms maintained, negotiated, and perpetuated *Members take responsibility through "I" and "We" statements* *Understanding and care of one another* *No single individual is accountable for the success/failure of the group* *Clarity for all is required* *Conflict and "opposition" are accepted and constructively managed* *Decisions are made on a consensus model* *Strong and flexible norms ensure group resilience* *Greater confidence in the group*	Work at the sub-group and group levels is dominant INTENT * Unfinished business is work that needs to be carried forward, either individually or for the group as a whole * Address the human need to assess our experience—what was learned, what remains unlearned (unfinished)	**Use the Cycle of Experience "withdrawal" phase:** Ask members what they are aware of that's unfinished or unclear for them. **Use Unit of Work closure:** Ask members what the new "what is" is, how this relates to the group's work over time, and what's next.

The factors that shape intervention choices and design include:
- The temporal situation of the group: beginning (orienting), middle (in process), or end (nearing goal accomplishment and identifying as high performing).
- A plan that takes into account group development and what is needed to move the group forward toward stated purpose and goals.
- Strategies to deal with conflict: Multiple perspectives are a powerful aspect of group life, as all activities become enriched by a diversity of viewpoints. Yet this very diversity also evokes conflict since members can always potentially disagree about which viewpoint is better. Working in groups makes conflict management a necessary coaching competency.

There is always a beginning, a middle, and an end to every group meeting. Therefore, every meeting has orientation needs, energy management needs, and closure needs. All elements of these needs are always present but are influenced by group longevity. The focus of what a group needs is affected by the developmental strength of that group in relation to their capacity to manage their orientation, their needs for differentiation, and the relational strengths that come with long-term self-management.

Stage Guide for Coach/Leader Intervention

Beginning: Discerning Group Purpose and Orientation Needs

When a group is new and requests assistance, one important task for the group coach is identifying the group's purpose. Supporting the group to identify their purpose or goal helps ground the group in the basic, beginning energy that enables members to connect with each other and do the work of orientation. The coach ensures that purpose is articulated, either through individual inquiry or through an in-the-moment intervention, such as by asking: "How would you define your purpose for being together? What is it that you wish to accomplish?" Emphasizing connection and other orientation work varies depending on whether the group is newly formed or already established, but it can also be differently expressed at all stages of group life.

Beginning groups need to establish connections and create trust. One basic intervention at this stage is to invite each member to make a personal statement that allows others to know them. When all members have made their statements, the outcome is that everyone can now experience the possibilities and potential of the group as a whole. During the personal statements, it's the natural tendency of group members to begin to notice commonalities and differences. The group coach supports weaving these threads together by encouraging participants to relate their observations directly to each other—by telling the other person what they've noticed about him or what they've learned about him, and how they might relate to him based on this knowledge. The coach encourages expressing these awarenesses in a non-judgmental manner.

Sharing personal information can be the emotional risk-taking that serves to support connection and opportunities for interpersonal exchange. In addition, asking that members speak directly to each other rather than about each other supports immediate interpersonal transactions regarding similarities and differences. If a personal disclosure is sensed as being far from the safe politeness that characterizes all beginnings, the coach uses her skills to slow the pace of the exchange and invite people to speak to how they are experiencing themselves and others. This simple intervention is an organic way for the members of the group to begin to connect with one another and to experience themselves as having greater potential as a group than any individual member could offer.

The coach's work is to model desired behaviors, which can include: encouraging an attitude of appreciative curiosity; setting a standard of speaking directly to individual group members and offering non-judgmental responses; inviting members to express their expectations; articulating a sense of faith that the group has all the needed competencies to move forward and to accomplish their goals.

While trust development is particularly critical at the beginning of a group, it needs to be monitored and nourished throughout all stages of development. If a group has already been in process for some time, the coach should still encourage orientation check-ins that enable participants to update any personal information that may have changed and affect their contribution to the group. Even long-term, ongoing groups need such "orientation work" to sustain the shared sense of connection. Using such a check-in as a consistent opening intervention elicits current and relevant information for the group.

Middle: Differentiation and Conflict

As a group moves through orientation and begins to have a sense of each other and the purpose of the group, the polite energy of orientation and checking in moves on to the need for greater momentum and the necessary, less polite work of differentiation. Where the beginning of a group invites individual-level activities aimed foremost at establishing commonalities, the second stage of development highlights differentiation and its inevitable conflicts. This stage is the optimal time for the group coach to invite and work with interpersonal exchanges and to model and guide safe ways of addressing the ambivalent energy of differences.

The group coach needs to be aware of the group's need for differentiation, which means that the coach must be skilled in the management of conflict. Conflict has to do with the attention given to different figures and interpretations. In the group, the different figures that people perceive are identified as multiple realities and versions of the "truth." Acting from a ground of difference and conflict stirs strong feelings, ranging from anger and resentment to fear and sadness. The necessary work of differentiation has the potential to be dysfunctional or destructive, but multiple realities also have the potential to inspire new possibilities and innovative ways of attending to group challenges. Conflict that occurs in differentiation provokes a variety of responses among group members. But if the group coach is aware of the triggers within the group and manages her own emotional intelligence in relation to the social intelligence of the group, this middle stage of group development can be skillfully facilitated, where the diversity of the group assists greater resourcefulness for the group task.

One effective intervention strategy at this stage is to invite two participants who are in conflict over a certain issue to speak directly to one another before the group, allowing the entire group to observe and hear how the two people address their differences. This exchange can be tracked through the Cycle of Experience (awareness statements) and framed as a Unit of Work (intentional learning toward some shared goal). Once the interaction is completed, a follow-up invitation can be made to the group as a whole about assumptions regarding group norms and personal projections around speaking issues. In this way, the entire group benefits from the two-person work by engaging the central issue of differentiation at the group level of system.

In working with the differentiation stage of group development, clear definitional statements need to be elicited from group members, such as: What is important for us? What do we want? Who are we as a group? Interpersonal conflict has two facets: expression of self-identity and perceived degree of influence—Who am I? How can I influence others? Influence is often experienced as a form of control, so other people may respond with oppositional energy—"digging in" even deeper into their own beliefs or viewpoints. The degree to which people experience other people's reality as a form of personal assault can be problematic. In group settings, an individual member's inability to accept another person's perception could compromise group integrity and integration.

The group coach needs to be attentive to the behavioral signals that participants reveal regarding acceptance or rejection of differences and must skillfully design interventions that effectually address conflict management. When a group appears to need more connection and personal safety, conflict can be deferred until there is more ground and support, or it can be redirected to another figure of shared interest. The appropriate time to enhance differentiation and conflict is that moment in the life of the group when safety and conformity lower the energy ignited by differences, and the work loses a sense of vitality. What proves most useful for group coaches is to model the message that conflict, rightly managed, can serve as a powerful opportunity to harness energy and information to accomplish innovative solutions.

End: Cohesion, Integration, Intimacy

The effective group coach is just as interested in good closure as in strong beginnings and strong middles. It is in the end stage that true learning occurs. As previously noted, there is a strong human need to "end well," even when things have not gone well during the group meeting. The need to end well drives the desire to articulate what was learned and what remains unfinished.

When time constraints require that we end a group through "withdrawal," we can use the COE to ask: "As we're ending, what are you aware of that is unfinished for you?" Withdrawal with unfinished business indicates work that needs to be carried forward, either individually or for the group as a whole. When we seek to end the group with appreciation for what has been learned, we can use the COE as well; but if we have done specific units of work with the group, we ask more specific closure questions: "What is the 'new what is'? How does that relate to the work of the group over time?"

COE and Interruptions to Contact at the Group Level

We looked at the Cycle of Experience at the individual level in Chapter 3, and now review how the Cycle model continues to guide coaches at larger levels of system. The COE offers coaches a way of recognizing behavioral phenomena at all levels of system. The group coach uses her own Cycle to identify and assess the relevant figures that can support or detract from group development. The questions that the COE can assist in answering concern what people are attending to and what is interfering with contact and change at the different levels of the group system—intrapersonal, interpersonal, subgroup, group, or organization. The COE powerfully reminds coaches that phenomena are always occurring in the group system, even when there is an absence of observable behavior. Some kind of self-narrative is always being constructed within people, and some kind of influence is always happening through information exchanged between people.

Just as many cycles can be going on regarding our individual wants and needs, multiple interactive cycles can be occurring simultaneously at different intensities at different levels of a system. The group coach is wise to remember that energy is always present within and across these cycles. The coach's task, then, is to determine where the energy is at the system level that is most relevant for catalyzing movement toward a desired group goal. The COE provides the phenomenological base from which to understand and differentiate between the similar Cycle steps of individual and group:

- At the individual level, we begin with sensory experience (sensation); at the group level, we begin with the activity

of scanning, both internally and externally, in order to distinguish an emergent figure of need or disruption.
- At the individual level, awareness is the articulation of the uppermost figure of what is needed or wanted; at the group level, this awareness is conceptualized as the shared figure of a goal.
- At the individual level, energy is experienced as either anxiety or excitement in response to the uppermost figure; at the group level, discussion mobilizes energy toward the identified shared figure.
- At the individual level, action refers to what is done to satisfy the uppermost need or want; at the group level, action refers to collaborative strategizing as to how to realize the shared figure goal.
- At the individual level, contact results in a perceived change that occurs when the uppermost need or want has been satisfied; at the group level, contact is experienced as change in terms of agreed-upon strategies toward shared-figure resolution.
- At the individual level, closure is the assimilation of learning around and celebration of a met need or want; at the group level, closure involves an assessment of how learning or change has occurred.

In facilitating groups, the coach uses the COE to assess the available energy for the task at hand and to ascertain what obstructs the completion of the task. Use of the COE enables coaches to shift their focus across system levels in order to situate the necessary work at the optimal level of system. When work is done at the wrong LOS, the power of the work is reduced or becomes ineffective. The data generated by using the COE as such an assessment model allows coaches to meet group-level clients at the boundaries within the group, where the relevant work exists.

In using the COE at the group level, coaches are also reminded that each system level is impacted by productive and non-productive use of resistance. The COE helps group coaches to: a) identify client needs and wants; b) recognize adaptive and non-adaptive uses of resistance; c) use phenomenological data to help bring resistances into clients' awareness; d) ask the relevant questions regarding the coach's own stance toward resistances; and e) see how resistances manifest at the organizational level. We outline Gestalt's six classic resistances (discussed in depth in Chapter 4) to illustrate these COE applications at the group level (Figure 7.4).

Figure 7.4 Six Classic Gestalt Resistances at the Group Level

Desensitization

Numbing the sensory experience of excitement, energy, or arousal; avoiding physical, psychological, or emotional pain

As a positive force	Protecting oneself from getting hurt (physically, psychically, emotionally); preventing over-stimulation; maintaining personal boundaries
As a negative force (out of awareness)	Turning aside from anticipated pain, frustration, or arousal; dissociating oneself from the immediate situation; refusing to engage with others
Phenomenological data	Talking quickly and bluntly with no discernible emotion or commitment; emphasizing logic and reason ("all head, no heart"); refusing, dismissing, or marginalizing personal experience, knowledge, or emotional investment
Questions for coaches	How does desensitizing *serve* your work? Alternately, how do you support you and your client staying in sensation? Has desensitizing ever gotten in the way of your work (e.g., if a difficult "what is" emerges, do you move clients quickly beyond their sensory experience)?
At the group level	Avoidance of information, change; leads to little or no scanning of internal or external environments

Introjection

Uncritically accepting the values, behavior, ideas, etc., of another without regard to personal meaning or resonance

As a positive force	Identifying with positive role models or mentors; following rules that ensure safety; accepting the policies of a new job
As a negative force (out of awareness)	Over-trusting, naïve, gullible; giving personal power away to authority figures; not thinking for oneself
Phenomenological data	Speaking in a "lecturing" or "righteous" tone; using language that emphasizes "should, must"; acting like a parent rather than a colleague; lack of critical examination of the advocacy for one approach over another
Questions for coaches	Do you have "shoulds" about managing the work (e.g., what good work *should* look like)? How do you manage your discomfort or the client's discomfort?
At the group level	Avoidance of work, assimilation, integration; leads to the unquestioning incorporation of all proposals, the conservation of energy, the evasion of real change

Projection

Attributing one's own feelings, thoughts, or actions to another

As a positive force	Using empathy to understand another; using imagination to explore an unknown
As a negative force (out of awareness)	Not taking self-responsibility, blaming others for one's own feelings or actions
Phenomenological data	Shaking one's head in "disgust" or smirking but remaining silent; using "they/us" language rather than "I" language; possibly aggressive language and moods
Questions for coaches	Do you use your own experience as a barometer of the client's experience? Do you allow your own experience to guide the work (e.g., staying with your own experience rather than using it to explore what is happening with your client)?
At the group level	Avoidance of seeing the self or the environment clearly or fully; leads to maintenance of the status quo, a steady state where blind spots are kept out of awareness

Retroflection

Holding back from requesting something from others or the environment

As a positive force	Allowing oneself time to think a situation through; avoiding spontaneous reactions that one may later regret
As a negative force (out of awareness)	Suppressing intense emotions to avoid conflict; not acknowledging and meeting one's own needs
Phenomenological data	Constraining energy, not taking action; remaining silent, avoiding eye contact; a "pained" facial expression, a "tight" or rigid posture
Questions for coaches	Do you hold back opinions, feelings, knowledge, or wants/needs selectively and with awareness? Has such "holding back" ever compromised your work as a coach?
At the group level	Avoidance of contact with the environment, conflict; leads to defensiveness, preemptive actions

Deflection

Diverting awareness or attention away from a difficult or problematic issue

As a positive force	Cooling down heated circumstances to allow for reasoned discussion; keeping discussion focused on the issue at hand
As a negative force (out of awareness)	Diverting awareness inappropriately; refusing to acknowledge the importance of others' wants/needs
Phenomenological data	Avoiding *doing* things or completing work; changing the topic abruptly, changing the focus from self to other; interrupting discussions and process, taking off on tangents; using inappropriate humor to ease perceived tension
Questions for coaches	How do you use interruption and distraction to *serve* your coaching work? Do you have creative ways for managing a client's evasion of work? Does unaware deflection ever get in the way of your coaching (e.g., when clients are in conflict, do you divert attention to another issue)?
At the group level	Avoidance of clarity, loss of control; leads to a state of confusion

Confluence

Agreement for the sake of minimizing or eliminating tension or for gaining acceptance from another or others

As a positive force	Creating a safe environment for everyone; "choosing one's battles"; channeling energy toward a mutual goal
As a negative force (out of awareness)	Agreeing with others or with whatever "is" in order to avoid conflict; going along with others in order not to be different or to avoid the risk of rejection
Phenomenological data	Retreating quickly from any position that arouses "push back"; putting out little or no physical or intellectual energy; using a soft voice, offering lots of smiles and head-nodding; striving to be agreeable and "likable" in all situations
Questions for coaches	In what ways do you use "going along with what is" to *support* the client's sense of stability or safety? Do you ever avoid conflict by becoming confluent/non-differentiating with the client (e.g., by *not* asking powerful, differentiating questions)?
At the group level	Avoidance of differences, disagreements; leads to little or no conflict, a state of complacency

Leadership in Group and Team Coaching

A key focus for leadership effectiveness in group and team coaching is the awareness of one's presence and management of use of self. Coaches as group or team leaders are required to appreciate their presence at the personal level, at the group level, and at any larger organizational level. A core competency of self-awareness is the ability to own and to embody one's strengths so that self-trust exists in the capacity to discriminate among observations, interpretations, and judgments. Use of self as a group leader requires adherence to core values while being able to respond to cues that call for taking action to support what is needed or what is missing. The coach as group leader needs to be able to re-center in the face of threats of derailment, which can be catalyzed by poor self-care, misalignment with one's values or one's vision, or poor boundary management regarding the identification of where the work of the system is located. The coach as group leader needs to be vigilant around ungrounded assumptions in data, judgments that are negative, and projections that lack personal accountability. At the group level, the coach as leader can use the COE to recognize multiple figures as well as blockages around those figures that may be holding energy the group needs to advance.

A significant strength of the coach as group leader is the ability to honor multiple perspectives and to recognize the multiple levels within the group. The coach needs to be able to facilitate meaning-making across multiple perspectives and to use the COE to support the group in finding shared meaning. An important coaching competency in this regard is awareness of emerging leadership as the group develops rather than "deifying" one's own leadership, which can ultimately impede group development. A natural evolution in group development is for different leadership to emerge, and the coach who hangs on too tightly to the leadership role will make herself the target of opposition instead of a force for support and facilitation. As a team develops, a natural stance for the coach is to step back and share leadership with the emerging leaders. Many years ago, a project group called me for a consultation. The formal leader could tolerate no informal leadership, and all innovation had stalled. A necessary intervention and UOW was to support the group in talking to the formal leader about the need to rotate some leadership roles. This "simple" intervention served to allow the group to succeed in its goals.

Where there is "stuckness" in group development, the coach as leader benefits from the capacity to use LOS interventions to move the group forward by choosing a level of system that seems to be more available. So, for example, if a group member seems reticent to discuss a provocative issue for the team, the coach can go to a subgroup or group level intervention and ask, "Who here can speak to this concern?" At the organizational level, the coach as leader empowers the group by supporting the members to use their relational boundaries to encourage greater exchanges and new choices. The key intervention in undoing stuckness is to increase information exchange across boundaries, which is a critical ingredient of innovation and change.

The skill involved in facilitating groups across the needs to orient, differentiate, and close reminds us of the coach's need for masterful use of self. A group coach must be able to own and embody her values and knowledge across different levels of system. She must be able to re-center from derailment, blockages to the work, and outdated introjections in herself and others. We have often found that facilitating groups is an excellent developmental experience for the skills required for effective use of self, which is always tested by the ability to adaptively respond to various group phenomena (Figure 7.5).

One reason group and team coaching has become the next wave in the field of coaching is that team dynamics offer exponential learning power and capacity for change. We close this chapter by reiterating how crucial it is for the coach as group/team facilitator or leader to commit to the self-work necessary to remain grounded and aware of her presence across the different levels of system. Being a group/team coach requires consistently honing one's presence and use of self across the many different dimensions in process. Working in groups is really a test of one's competencies, but it is also one of the most exciting places to find out just how aware and effective we can be in using ourselves as an instrument and supporting the embedded wisdom of a group or a team in becoming more resourceful, creative, and accountable for its choices.

Figure 7.5 Model of Coaching and Consulting Presence

MODEL OF COACHING AND CONSULTING PRESENCE		
	Own and embody . . .	**Re-center from . . .**
PERSONAL PRESENCE	Tuned in and trusting internal and external sensory clues	Derailment: • Poor self-care • Disconnection from values and vision • Poor boundary management • Outdated "shoulds"
	Capacity to discriminate among observations, interpretations, and judgments in the moment	• Disowned projections • Ungrounded assumptions • Negative judgments
	Values and the capacity to add value Trust in "use of self" data	• Unaware resistances without understanding or energy • Threats of S.C.A.R.F.
GROUP PRESENCE	Able to track multiple figures	Blockages that hold energy
	Able to honor multiple perspectives and multiple levels within the group	Lack of choice *(there is always a choice to made in groups)*
	Able to facilitate shared meaning	Being the only leader *(leadership can be shared)*
ORGANIZATIONAL PRESENCE	Able to see the organization as a system and as a whole Able to see which boundaries need attention for the work	Outdated "shoulds" in relation to organizational processes and policies
	Able to provide a new perspective and different choices across the system	Boundaries that reduce exchange

CHAPTER 8
Universal Coaching Competencies—International Coach Federation and Gestalt Coaching

Primum non nocere—First, do no harm.
—Hippocratic Oath

A growing body of literature has been devoted to defining what coaching is and is not.[1] The Gestalt Center for Coaching has aligned itself with the wisdom and guidance of the International Coach Federation (ICF). We adhere to the core definition of coaching that ICF offers the field: "Coaching [is] partnering with clients in a thought-provoking and creative process that inspires them to maximize their personal and professional potential."[2] There are no legal requirements to presenting oneself as a coach, but the ICF has noted that coaches without training or verifiable credentials are perceived to be a significant obstacle to the advancement of the professional coaching field.[3] While a number of excellent executive coaches have never taken coach-specific training or earned coach certification from a credible organization, yet are known for their ongoing commitment to learning and cutting-edge practices, an increasing demand for such accreditation exists to ensure client confidence. A program accredited by the ICF has gone through a review process that demonstrates that its curriculum aligns with ICF's definition of coaching, its proposed coaching competencies, and its code of ethics.

Ethics are the foundation of coaching and shape all coaching encounters. The Hippocratic Oath—"first, do no harm"—informs the ethical practice of coaching. Coaches are privy to a stunning array of self-disclosures. Effective coaching that supports learning and change invites clients to open themselves to experiment with new possibilities in the coaching encounter, and this requires a degree of vulnerability in the service of learning. Therefore, coaching agreements need a client-directed focus that will guide the work, as well as ethical guidelines that protect the client and that differentiate coaching from psychological work (therapy) or from work that is within the realm of directive consulting. Founded in 1995, the ICF has most visibly presented the role of ethical practice and is the largest coach credentialing body serving to define and support professional coaching. The ICF's organizational vision states the intent to "advance the art, science, and practice of professional coaching" around the world.[4] To that end, the ICF provides credentialization to individual practitioners and program accreditation to organizations that define themselves as coach trainer providers.

When I introduced Gestalt coach training programs starting in 1996, my colleagues and I chose to align ourselves with the ICF's vision and purpose, as these were completely congruent with how we were defining and developing our Gestalt coach training workshops and programs. As a testament to ICF's dedication to supporting a diverse range of coaching approaches that meet its high standards, my inaugural program, the International Gestalt Coaching Program, was the first Gestalt-based coach training program world-wide to achieve ICF accreditation. Where Gestalt practice had been viewed as too idiosyncratic in application to be amenable to the types of standardized assessments involved in professional credentialing systems, the ICF agreed that Gestalt theory, methodology, and processes provided for robust, effective, and exceptional professional coaching and coach training.[5]

In terms of 21st-century professional development needs, we are most interested in determining what coaches need as specific competencies that will lead to coaching excellence. With a broad diversity of coaching approaches, there is an agreement to use core competencies as benchmark requirements common to all coach training certifications. The ICF has developed 11 core coaching competencies to define the fundamental interventions of greatest benefit to any coaching encounter. These core competencies are:

A. *Setting the Foundation*
 1. Meeting Ethical Guidelines and Professional Standards
 2. Establishing the Coaching Agreement

B. *Co-creating the Relationship*
 3. Establishing Trust and Intimacy with the Client
 4. Coaching Presence

C. *Communicating Effectively*
 5. Active Listening
 6. Powerful Questioning
 7. Direct Communication

D. *Facilitating Learning and Results*
 8. Creating Awareness
 9. Designing Actions
 10. Planning and Goal Setting
 11. Managing Progress and Accountability

The basic structures of coach-related knowledge emphasize horizontal development as the primary means of supporting verification of coaching professionalism. As detailed previously, there is a continued prominence of horizontal knowledge in leadership development trainings as various coach accreditation and certification organizations proliferate. Horizontal knowledge assures current and specific coach knowledge and skills. Nick Petrie, however, has championed insightful distinctions between horizontal development (content, tools, techniques) and vertical development (what I identify as Awareness IQ, use of self, and presence). Both are needed, by both coach and client, to achieve coaching excellence. It bears remembering that "effective coaching requires an emphasis on both task and relationship."[6] While acknowledging the need for horizontal development, Gestalt coaching has always attended to vertical development, perhaps more than other coaching approaches. Gestalt coaching calls for an integration of vertical development into its processes: knowledge of and working with such factors as emotional intelligence, context awareness, and multiple realities.

Along with the ICF's definition of coaching as a creative partnership between coach and client, participants in ICF-approved coaching curricula learn the 11 core competencies and must demonstrate their proficiency in them during the ICF credentialing process. For Gestalt coaches and trainees, what's striking about the ICF core competencies is how well they synchronize with standard core Gestalt values and practices. What follows are the basic ICF definitions regarding the core coaching competencies, followed by the Gestalt Center for Coaching's understanding and application of those competencies in our coach training programs.[7]

A. Setting the Foundation

1. Meeting Ethical Guidelines and Professional Standards *The ICF defines this core competency as: "Understanding of coaching ethics and standards and ability to apply them appropriately in all coaching situations."*

At its most basic level, an ethical stance in virtually every professional practice is to ensure that clients are protected from harm, in whatever form harm might be defined. The field of professional coaching likewise demands that its practitioners abide by a code of ethics. The ICF almost immediately made ethical behavior a central component of its certification requirements, first issuing an "Ethics Pledge" in 1997 (revised in 2000) that "included sections on the philosophy and definition of coaching, an ethics pledge, and 18 standards of conduct" as well as "a set of core competencies that included compliance with ethical standards." The ICF's current Code of Ethics addresses standards of ethical conduct in four broad areas: professional conduct at large, conflict of interest, professional conduct with clients, and confidentiality/privacy.[8]

Published standards of ethical conduct "make the moral dimension of the practice more visible and, when enforced by oversight agencies, differentiate those with credentials from providers who do not subscribe to such a code."[9] Ethical practice in coaching is essential for building trust in the coaching encounter. When coaches adhere to a code of ethics, they become more keenly aware of borderline ethical practices, and they accept greater accountability for their duty to protect their clients. The ICF's Code of Ethics, which asks all who apply for coach certification or recertification to adopt, is promoted in the Gestalt Center for Coaching's coach training programs.

To Gestalt coaches, the code of ethics extends to not only the visible but also to the invisible boundaries that need to be respected in our work with clients. While not directly addressing or speaking of or for Gestalt practitioners, H. C. Law writes:

> Ethical thinking and its principles are . . . embedded in many professional bodies in the form of self-regulation . . . the main aim is to protect clients and the public from dangerous practice with the objectives to: benefit clients; ensure safety; protect clients; manage boundaries; and manage conflict.[10]

Law's astute inclusion of boundary and conflict management references our 21st-century global reach and increasing workplace diversity, which challenge us to acknowledge differing values and powerful (often invisible) cultural boundaries.

There has been a call in the coaching field to unbundle coaching from either therapy or organizational consulting. Gestalt coaching undoubtedly uses insights and techniques drawn from Gestalt psychotherapy, as does Gestalt organizational consulting (which went through a similar challenge to its uniqueness when introduced in the 1980s). The Gestalt foundations remain the same, but their practical usage highlights the distinctions between Gestalt therapy, consulting, and coaching. Each has different assumptions about relationships, perceptions of expertise, and ethical responsibilities (Figure 8.1).

Figure 8.1 Therapy, Consulting, and Coaching: Similarities and Differences[11]

SIMILARITIES		
Therapy	**Consulting**	**Coaching**
Uses a diagnostic interview and history to lay the foundation for work	Uses an entry and contracting agreement to determine process and outcome and lay the foundation for work	Uses an interview to determine a work agreement, design a coaching relationship, and lay the foundation for work
Uses many techniques similar to coaching skills	May use some therapy or coaching skills	Uses many skills similar to therapy skills
Works with the client's whole life	Client's whole life sometimes brought in	Works with the client's whole life
Often works with emotional material	May address topics such as emotional intelligence	May work with emotional material
Some modalities (solution-based) include an action focus	Defines and develops the work around desired outcomes	Forwards client action while deepening the learning around specific goals or desired outcomes

DIFFERENCES		
Therapy	**Consulting**	**Coaching**
Primary focus is on healing and potential	Primary focus is on change, learning, alignment, and results	Primary focus is on evolving and manifesting
Emphasis is on past and present	Emphasis is on future organizational impact	Emphasis is on present, past, and future
Insight oriented	Action oriented	Action and being oriented
Problem oriented	Solution oriented regarding the organizational task at hand	Solution oriented regarding personal learning and growth
Explore the genesis of problems that create low self-esteem	Explore how to work with esteem issues in relation to organization/leadership	Explore actions and behaviors that manifest high self-esteem

Analyze and treat origins or address historical roots of negative self-beliefs	Attempt to shift negative beliefs to a positive focus (through Appreciative Inquiry, for example)	Coach negative self-beliefs as temporary obstacles to new possibilities
Coach and client consider: "From where"	Consultant often advises on "what's next"	Coach and client ask "why," "what's next," and "what now"
Works mainly with internal phenomena	Works mainly with external phenomena	Works equally with internal and external phenomena
Works with/encourages transference as a tool	May or may not recognize transference	Discourages transference as an inappropriate tool
Accountability of either therapist or client is less expected	Clarifies exactly who is accountable for what	Accountability and "homework," including between sessions, is central
Contact between sessions is expected	Ongoing contact (e.g., email or phone calls), as agreed	Contact between sessions for accountability and "wins" regarding emerging processes

With the application of Gestalt principles and concepts to multiple types of intervention, Gestalt coaches need to be able to differentiate coaching from therapy and consulting, as well as from training and teaching, to assist them in understanding the scope of their professional competencies and boundaries. One ethical imperative in coaching is for the coach to be able to clearly articulate these differences. Gestalt practice has always valued collaborative practitioner-client co-creation, which invites considerable leeway for following clients' experiential pathways. However, a client's experiential interpretation of a coaching exchange can at any time confuse the boundaries around the different practices, and such confusion is especially likely when the coach herself is unclear about the distinctions between them. We believe that coaching ethics, such as those defined by the ICF, have highlighted our responsibility to clarify boundaries that suggest any conflict of interest, and to thereby enhance the protection of clients' confidentiality.

2. Establishing the Coaching Agreement *The ICF defines this core competency as: "Ability to understand what is required in the specific coaching interaction and to come to agreement with the prospective and new client about the coaching process and relationship."*

Gestalt coaching embraces the wisdom of arriving early at a coaching agreement that collaboratively shapes and identifies the work. Previous research into unsatisfying coaching results strongly suggests that one of the key elements missing was the coach's failure to arrive at a shared agreement with the client as to the central figure(s) of the work.[12] Because Gestalt practice presupposes the client's total engagement with the learning process, and believes that genuine "change comes from within,"[13] the coach works jointly with the client to generate the specific terms of the coaching agreement. Key to a successful coaching agreement is the clarity of agreed-upon goals and outcomes as well of a plan for how these might be achieved.[14]

"A professional coaching relationship exists," the ICF Code of Ethics states, "when coaching includes a business agreement or contract that defines the responsibilities of each party."[15] Organizational settings add another layer of complexity to the coaching relationship. In organizational environments, the roles of those involved almost always require further clarification. It's usually necessary, for example, to distinguish between the "client," the person(s) being coached, and the "sponsor," the entity (including its representatives) arranging and paying for the coaching. When an individual arranges and pays for his own coaching, he is both client and sponsor, and is therefore referred to simply as "the client." But when an organization contracts and pays for the coaching of one or more employees, the organization is the sponsor. In drawing up the coaching agreement, the distinction is crucial for establishing clear boundaries among coach, client, and sponsor, and for ensuring that both coach and client are protected by a confidentiality clause.

B. Co-Creating the Relationship

3. Establishing Trust and Intimacy with the Client *The ICF defines this core competency as: "Ability to create a safe, supportive environment that produces ongoing mutual respect and trust."*

The Gestalt coach provides a trustworthy presence in the coaching encounter by adhering to the ICF's requirements that the coach be honest and sincere, present clear agreements and keep promises, and show respect for the client's perceptions and learning style. Gestalt coaches commit to inviting the client into new behaviors or actions, but also to the wisdom of asking the client's permission to coach her in sensitive or unfamiliar areas that hold the risk of failure but also the potential for new learnings.

4. Coaching Presence *The ICF defines this core competency as: "Ability to be fully conscious and create spontaneous relationship with the client, employing a style that is open, flexible and confident."*

The ICF's full description of coaching presence might almost serve as a remarkably similar checklist for the Gestalt conception of presence and its central role in Gestalt coaching, as we learned in Chapter 5. However, integrating coaching presence with Gestalt coaching's concept of active use of self appreciably expands coaches' repertoire for developing planned strategies to move forward and to deepen the client's work. Developing competency in both coaching presence and use of self is an excellent example of Gestalt coaching's embrace of Petrie's conception of vertical leadership development. We see the competency of coaching presence as the meta-level integrative proficiency of all coaching strengths.

C. Communicating Effectively

5. Active Listening *The ICF defines this core competency as: "Ability to focus completely on what the client is saying and is not saying, to understand the meaning of what is said in the context of the client's desires, and to support client self-expression."*

Listening to other people implies the capacity to understand, at a deep level, what is being said not only verbally, but also somatically and emotionally, and even unintentionally. In the Gestalt coaching encounter, active listening captures a range of skills that includes what people are saying somatically but may not be aware of, what they are saying emotionally but are not cognitively aware of, and what they are saying as an adopted concept but may not clearly understand. As Solomon Asch has said, the ability to hear what a person is saying is one way of affirming that person's reality.[16]

As a measure of coaching mastery, the ICF introduces the relevance of intuition into the competency of active listening at the MCC level. The coach at this level "recognizes both hers and the client's ability of intuitive and energetic perception that is felt when the client speaks of important things, when new growth is occurring for the client, and when the client is finding a more powerful sense of self."[17] We believe that the capacity for intuition needs to be recognized and cultivated through reflective practice so that it is not confused with one's personal agenda or ego issues, and so that the practitioner is able to state her intuitions clearly and in relation to the client's agenda.

6. Powerful Questioning *The ICF defines this core competency as: "Ability to ask questions that reveal the information needed for maximum benefit to the coaching relationship and the client."*

Powerful questioning in Gestalt coaching supports clients' self-inquiry process by inviting them to delve into their inner knowing to discover and construct meaning. Such inquiry invites clients to engage in an inductive discovery process, moving from the inside out rather than from the outside in (taking in the expertise of others). As recent neuroscience research has shown, powerful questions serve to interrupt habituated thought processes, thereby encouraging self-discovery through the emergence of different ideas and energizing new associations for new possibilities. This is the force of powerful questions, which through disruptive inquiry evoke surprising new thoughts and unleash the energy of unexpected ideas. Powerful questions act to take the client immediately to a new possibility while letting go of narrative and lengthy explanations.

7. Direct Communication *The ICF defines this core competency as: "Ability to communicate effectively during coaching sessions, and to use language that has the greatest positive impact on the client."*

The Gestalt coach's competency in using words precisely and in tapping the metaphorical richness of language, without being directive or herself becoming a focus of attention, is both skill and art. Concision and clarity in the coach's communication are desired, as this has the greatest support for assisting clients' learning and self-discovery of alternative ways of thinking or acting.

D. Facilitating Learning and Results

8. Creating Awareness *The ICF defines this core competency as: "Ability to integrate and accurately evaluate multiple sources of information and to make interpretations that help the client to gain awareness and thereby achieve agreed-upon results."*

This ICF competency is in direct alignment with the central teaching of Gestalt coaching (discussed in depth in Chapter 2), where attending to and heightening awareness supports clients' learning and developed ability to self-identify and track their habitual perceptual or behavioral processes, patterns of satisfaction and dissatisfaction, and functional and dysfunctional resistance patterns. Implicit in the ICF definition, that awareness catalyzes agreed-upon results, is the Gestalt concept of paradoxical change, which makes awareness the first step in the change process.

9. Designing Actions *The ICF defines this core competency as: "Ability to create with the client opportunities for ongoing learning, during coaching and in work/life situations, and for taking new actions that will most effectively lead to agreed-upon coaching results."*

The Gestalt coach and client co-create opportunities for ongoing learning, both in the coaching encounter and in external work/life situations. In promoting a stance of experimentation, the coach works collaboratively with the client to design activities that can be practiced during and following the coaching session. The coach assists clients in exploring the behaviors that support or derail desired wants or needs, co-creating the conditions that might lead, in turn, to agreed-upon coaching results. For further appreciation of the role of experiment in Gestalt coaching, see Chapter 6.

10. Planning and Goal Setting *The ICF defines this core competency as: "Ability to develop and maintain an effective coaching plan with the client."*

The Gestalt coach co-develops and sustains a coaching plan that addresses clients' desired areas for learning and development, determined to be attainable, measurable, and time-sensitive. Resources for learning are considered and incorporated where possible. Clients' successful steps toward goal attainment are recognized and celebrated as important motivational incentives.

11. Managing Progress and Accountability *The ICF defines this core competency as: "Ability to hold attention on what is important for the client, and to leave responsibility with the client to take action."*

The Gestalt coach works to support clients' accountability for actions taken toward stated goals. This competency reminds clients, as Gestalt coaching agrees, that they are the agents of their own success. The more clients can hold themselves accountable for attaining their desired goals, the greater their motivation and willingness to experience sustainable learning, satisfaction, and success. The competency of accountability most distinguishes the resourceful capacity of coaching clients as differentiated from therapy clients. Accountability for sustaining the desired coaching goals is also understood as the client's return on investment in the coaching endeavor. Managing one's ongoing progress requires a level of engagement that the coach can assist the client in activating. The client needs to feel both engaged in the work and that there are activities that can sustain his success.

In the Gestalt Center for Coaching programs, we take into account the effectiveness of introducing these competencies at different stages of the training. We require students to demonstrate the coaching competencies in supervised practicums and in the final oral examination process, which involves coaching a client. Successfully completing our or any ICF-approved coach training program is only the first step toward becoming an ICF-certified coach, but it is where aspiring coaches gain critical knowledge and hone the skills of professional coaching.[18] ICF competencies are standards established as "core" to coaching practice, and are fully supported by the Gestalt Center for Coaching. What the Gestalt-based approach adds to the ICF core competencies is a strategic dimension of the implementation of presence, which is identified as "use of self." As described in Chapter 5, use of self is when the coach acts skillfully to apply intentional interventions designed to support clients' learning and change. We see use of self, the active side of coaching presence, as a central integrating competency that effectively guides the masterful art and practice of coaching. Use of self has a key position in activating all other competencies (Figure 8.2).

Universal Coaching Competencies | 219

Figure 8.2 The Integration of Horizontal and Vertical Development

A. Setting the Foundation
1. Meeting Ethical Guidelines and Professional Standards
2. Establishing Coaching Agreement

B. Co-Creating the Relationship
3. Establishing trust and intimacy with the client
4. Coaching presence

C. Communicating Effectively
5. Active listening
6. Powerful questioning
7. Direct communication

D. Facilitating Learning and Results
8. Creating awareness
9. Designing actions
10. Planning and goal setting
11. Managing progress and accountability

Choiceful Use of Self Awareness IQ

Coachability

The professional coaching field has established: 1) foundational universal coaching competencies; 2) professional codes of ethics, which support and protect client, coach, and coaching activities; and 3) a base of shared knowledge to sufficiently recognize when a client's presenting issues necessitate referral to a different professional practice. Because professional coaching in private or organizational settings can catalyze emotional, cognitive, somatic, or spiritual responses in clients, coaches need to stay aware of relevant boundaries distinguishing coaching from therapy or counseling, consulting or advising, and teaching or mentoring. That awareness is imperative to fulfilling and sustaining any ethical coaching relationship.

"Coachability" is a fairly recent descriptive term that helps coaches define practice boundaries and determine effective ways of satisfying clients' goals and assessing successful coaching outcomes. The Lore International Institute developed a seven-level coachability scale that ranges from "C0: Not Coachable at Present" to "C6: Excellent Coachability" and provides brief descriptive behavioral or attitudinal checklists to help coaches determine whether the potential client is a viable candidate for coaching (Figure 8.3). The scale makes clear one further reason that coaches need to be able to distinguish coaching from other support functions: attempting to coach clients who exhibit "red flag" psychological problems—such as active mental illness (clinical depression or schizophrenia, for example) or chronic substance abuse—is beyond the boundaries of professional coaching. These individuals' behavior, which is understood as dysfunctional, renders them "not coachable at present," and they should be referred to a qualified therapist or psychiatrist.[19]

Figure 8.3 Seven Levels of Coachability[20]

Level	Description
C0 Not coachable at present	Identified psychological or medical problem that is beyond the scope of a coaching intervention in the workplace.
C1 Extreme low coachability	Narcissistic personality. Arrogant. Sees no need to change.
C2 Very low coachability	Resists or deflects feedback. Rationalizes negative perceptions. Is openly negative toward the coaching, saying that it is not helpful.
C3 Fair coachability	Is complacent and unmotivated to change. Pays lip service to change, but is not really committed to it.
C4 Good coachability	Demonstrates some resistance to the coaching process, but has a growing awareness of the need for change.
C5 Very good coachability	Accepts feedback and shows an earnest desire to improve.
C6 Excellent coachability	Has an intrinsic need to grow. Is a lifelong learner. Has a realistic sense of self.

Other situations that indicate dysfunction that may require psychotherapeutic intervention and prohibit coaching might include:

- You are unable to align with the client regarding goals or roles, and the client seems unable to bring in the relevant data (i.e., feedback from others experiencing disruptive difficulty with the client).
- There is an irresolvable power imbalance that compromises the ability of either party to be fully present and expressive, or prevents the coaching relationship from existing in a safe space.

The coachability scale's descriptive behavioral/attitudinal checklists may also indicate where some clients might reasonably benefit more from referral to another type of support model, either from consulting to coaching or from coaching to consulting, for example. Some instances might include:

May indicate a referral from consulting to coaching:
- The client repeatedly projects issues onto others with no willingness or ability to consider aspects of her personal ownership.
- The client has personal characteristics that cause you to doubt the possibility of creating and realizing a successful consulting partnership (i.e., the client is unlikely to accomplish his stated goals without significant heightening of personal awareness—similar to an inability to align on goals or roles or a power imbalance, as described above).

May indicate a referral from coaching to consulting:
- Following the contracting discussion, you find yourself wondering if this coaching request could lead to a hidden or unconscious desire to "fix" this person in response to a more complex array of organizational dynamics.
- Designing the coaching relationship is impeded by organizational/system dynamics that cause you to wonder about: a) the limits of your competency, or b) how the coaching constructs (i.e., how you as coach wish to deliver the work) could be limited in this situation.
- The work, as described, calls for expertise you don't currently possess, such as: a) group or leadership development; b) conflict management or trust building; c) large system alignment or strategic planning; d) diversity or cultural change; or e) business management or technical expertise.

Some instances constitute "gray areas," where the accumulation of horizontal tool and technique development will not serve, but rather the wisdom derived through vertical development will be necessary. Years ago, I was coaching Mark, a high-level executive. After giving me his list of issues to work on, Mark said in a matter-of-fact tone, "I remarried after a bad divorce, and I have estrangement issues with my kids. But I never want to discuss this." I responded that his message was received and we would focus only on what had been declared to be affecting his work goals. He said he appreciated that we could manage this boundary. Several months into our work, we met after he had returned from a corporate retreat. When asked about it, he reported that it had been "a total failure." In the course of discussing what had made it a failure, Mark said that during the retreat, the executive clients were asked to state what they were most proud about. Everyone at Mark's table identified their greatest source of happiness to be their relationship with their children. When this exercise came around to my client, he was unable to speak, as he felt shamed by his poor relationship with his children. At that point of his narration, I suggested that perhaps we could explore his other possibilities. He defiantly stated, "You said you understood that I don't want to discuss personal issues. Why bring it in now?" I invited Mark to consider how his personal issues were affecting his presentation of self to his colleagues, which led him to agree to take it on. We then collaborated on identifying areas for work with regard to reestablishing a satisfying relationship with his children. This new agreement served his leadership agenda of having more personal balance.

I find it poignant to reflect on the happiness this small piece of work brought my client. This work was not therapeutic in the sense of working with emotionally fraught material. Rather, it was an assessment and evaluation of the power Mark himself possessed, and steps he could take, to end the alienation and isolation he experienced around his relationship with his children, as this impacted his presentation and use of self in the work environment as well. The work was difficult for him, but he discovered it was as important to him as any issue more directly linked to his career.

The most valuable learning lesson, as a coach, was that this work succeeded as well as it did because Mark was always in charge of how much he wished to reveal or engage with personal issues. The coaching was provocative but non-directive, leaving the client to determine which issues to explore and how far that exploration was still connected to goals, wants, and needs.

The ICF specifically emphasizes distinguishing coaching "from other personal or organizational support professions," including therapy, consulting, mentoring, and training.[21] Adhering to an articulated code of ethics is a vital correlative of this differentiating capability. Calling these capabilities "competencies" makes more visible what is virtually invisible without coach-specific training. The 11 core competencies discussed earlier are somewhat subtle, but are used as criteria for assessing both the rudimentary ICF's Associate Certified Coach level of coach certification up to the mastery of the ICF's Master Certified Coach level of coach certification. Yet we all need a beginner's mind to understand that ethical issues are often murky and hard to work through with absolute clarity. Coaches must continually assess their relationship with the client to assure ongoing ethical management of that relationship. Indeed, a well-honed awareness intelligence joined with personal accountability drives dedicated coaches to embody all core competencies at whatever level of skill mastery they are.

In addition, the ICF has recently updated the coding standards for the Professional Certified Coach (PCC) assessment markers in an effort to attain more consistent assessment in the ICF credentialing process.[22] Using these markers, assessors will be better able to provide concrete, specific, and useful feedback to candidates about their coaching (Figure 8.4). By incorporating markers as evidence-based assessment, the ICF intends to "develop and implement a performance evaluation that is fair, consistent, valid, reliable, repeatable and defensible." ICF's strategic goal is to construct a global-standards system in service of creating an attractive, credible presence and voice for professional coaching.[23]

Figure 8.4 PCC Marker Scoring Sheets for ICF Core Competencies*

ICF Core Competency 2: Establishing the Coaching Agreement

Assessor Name: _____ Applicant Name or ID: _____

PCC Markers	Observed?	Evidence
2.1 Coach helps the client identify, or reconfirm, what s/he wants to accomplish in the session.		
2.2 Coach helps the client to define or reconfirm measures of success for what s/he wants to accomplish in the session.		
2.3 Coach explores what is important or meaningful to the client about what s/he wants to accomplish in the session.		
2.4 Coach helps the client define what the client believes he/she needs to address or resolve in order to achieve what s/he wants to accomplish in the session.		
2.5 Coach continues conversation in direction of client's desired outcome unless client indicates otherwise.		

* Used with permission from the International Coach Federation. ICF's formula for using the assessment markers to determine a successful pass is not included.

ICF Core Competency 3: Establishing Trust and Intimacy with the Client

Assessor Name: _____ Applicant Name or ID: _____

PCC Markers	Observed?	Evidence
3.1 Coach acknowledges and respects the client's work in the coaching process.		
3.2 Coach expresses support for the client.		
3.3 Coach encourages and allows the client to fully express him/herself.		

ICF Core Competency 4: Coaching Presence

Assessor Name: _____ Applicant Name or ID: _____

PCC Markers	Observed?	Evidence
4.1 Coach acts in response to both the whole person of the client and what the client wants to accomplish in the session.		
4.2 Coach is observant, empathetic, and responsive.		
4.3 Coach notices and explores energy shifts in the client.		
4.4 Coach exhibits curiosity with the intent to learn more.		

4.5 Coach partners with the client by supporting the client to choose what happens in the session.		
4.6 Coach partners with the client by inviting the client to respond in any way to the coach's contributions and accepts the client's response.		
4.7 Coach partners with the client by playing back the client's expressed possibilities for the client to choose from.		
4.8 Coach partners with the client by encouraging the client to formulate his or her own learning.		

ICF Core Competency 5: Active Listening

Assessor Name: _____ Applicant Name or ID: _____

PCC Markers	Observed?	Evidence
5.1 Coach's questions and observations are customized by using what the coach has learned about who the client is and the client's situation.		
5.2 Coach inquires about or explores the client's use of language.		
5.3 Coach inquires about or explores the client's emotions.		
5.4 Coach inquires about or explores the client's tone of voice, pace of speech or inflection as appropriate.		

PCC Markers		
5.5 Coach inquires about or explores the client's behaviors.		
5.6 Coach inquires about or explores how the client perceives his/her world.		
5.7 Coach is quiet and gives client time to think.		

ICF Core Competency 6: Powerful Questioning

Assessor Name: _____ Applicant Name or ID: _____

PCC Markers	Observed?	Evidence
6.1 Coach asks questions about the client: his/her way of thinking, assumptions, beliefs, values, needs, wants, etc.		
6.2 Coach's questions help the client explore beyond his/her current thinking to new or expanded ways of thinking about himself/herself.		
6.3 Coach's questions help the client explore beyond his/her current thinking to new or expanded ways of thinking about his/her situation.		
6.4 Coach's questions help the client explore beyond current thinking towards the outcome s/he desires.		
6.5 Coach asks clear, direct, primarily open-ended questions, one at a time, at a pace that allows for thinking and reflection by the client.		

6.6 Coach's questions use the client's language and elements of the client's learning style and frame of reference.		
6.7 Coach's questions are not leading, i.e., do not contain a conclusion or direction.		

ICF Core Competency 7: Direct Communication

Assessor Name: _____ Applicant Name or ID: _____

PCC Markers	Observed?	Evidence
7.1 Coach shares observations, intuitions, comments, thoughts and feelings to serve the client's learning or forward movement.		
7.2 Coach shares observations, intuitions, comments, thoughts and feelings without any attachment to them being right.		
7.3 Coach uses the client's language or language that reflects the client's way of speaking.		
7.4 Coach's language is generally clear and concise.		
7.5 The coach allows the client to do most of the talking.		
7.6 Coach allows the client to complete speaking without interrupting unless there is a stated coaching purpose to do so.		

ICF Core Competency 8: Creating Awareness

Assessor Name: _____ Applicant Name or ID: _____

PCC Markers	Observed?	Evidence
8.1 Coach invites client to state and/or explore his/her learning in the session about her/his situation (the what).		
8.2 Coach invites client to state and/or explore his/her learning in the session about her/himself (the who).		
8.3 Coach shares what s/he is noticing about the client and /or the client's situation, and seeks the client's input or exploration.		
8.4 Coach invites client to consider how s/he will use new learning from the coaching.		
8.5 Coach's questions, intuitions and observations have the potential to create new learning for the client.		

ICF Core Competencies 9, 10, and 11: Designing Actions, Planning and Goal Setting, and Managing Progress and Accountability

Assessor Name: _____ Applicant Name or ID: _____

PCC Markers	Observed?	Evidence
9-10-11.1 Coach invites or allows client to explore progress towards what s/he wants to accomplish in the session.		
9-10-11.2 Coach assists the client to design what actions/thinking client will do after the session in order for the client to continue moving toward the client's desired outcomes.		
9-10-11.3 Coach invites or allows client to consider her/his path forward, including, as appropriate, support mechanisms, resources and potential barriers.		
9-10-11.4 Coach assists the client to design the best methods of accountability for her/himself.		
9-10-11.5 Coach partners with the client to close the session.		
9-10-11.6 Coach notices and reflects client's progress.		

Beyond coaching our students in Gestalt-based competencies, we further mentor our students in meeting ICF competencies by offering some guideline tips and sample phrasings for the coaches to demonstrate their use of the evidence-based markers and to avoid negative assessments (Figure 8.5).

Figure 8.5 Guideline Tips and Sample Phrasings That Align with ICF Competencies[24]

ICF COMPETENCY	SAMPLE PHRASING TO USE	WHAT TO AVOID (NEGATIVE ICF ASSESSMENT)
2. Coaching Agreement	* What would you like to achieve from this session? * What do you want from our work together? * By the end of this session, how will you know you have achieved your goal? * What do you wish to focus on today? *[for ongoing sessions]* * I hear you want to explore this, this, and this. How would you like to go on with these—one at a time? together? * How are we doing so far in regards to your goals? *[checking in between sessions]* * How does this session serve your long-term goals?	* Suggesting what the client needs to work on. * Telling the client what the issue is and what work needs to happen. * Setting the coaching agenda in a directive, non-collaborative way.
3. Trust and Intimacy	* Asking permission to inquire, give feedback, enter into sensitive areas. * Staying in the not-knowing and containing. * What supports you in learning? * What interferes with your learning? * What holds you back from trying new learning?	* Not asking permission. * Failing to inquire as to what the client wants/does not want.
4. Coaching Presence	* Completely connected as an observer. * Partnership—not leading. * Allowing space to say no. * Can I share my perspective? * Can I tell you what I notice? * Can I offer you a metaphor for this issue? * I feel a bit uncomfortable. What is happening for you?	* Dominating the session with one's own stories and perceptions without sensitivity to one's impact.

5. Active Listening	* Paraphrasing * I notice your voice becomes quiet as you talk about this challenge. * You are moving your hands as you speak. What might your hands be saying? * I notice you just sighed. What is happening right now? * I heard your cognitive description, but I wonder about your inner emotions. * What do you tell yourself about this issue? * What do you want others to hear from you?	* Appearing to be unaware of the client's voice, either emotionally, somatically, or cognitively. * Failing to register or appear to hear the differences in any of the above dimensions.
6. Powerful Questioning	* Questions that interrupt and/or reframe the moment and capture the client's interest and energy * Open-ended questions that take the client to a new place of thinking * One question at a time * As you talk about this issue, what's familiar about this story? * What do you always say "yes" to? * What do you always say "no" to? * In this story, what are you attached to? * Who do you have strong feelings for? * What is happening to you right now?	* Not being able to interrupt the client's narrative with a pithy question that creates interest or reframes the client's energy for new possibilities.
7. Direct Communications	* So you mentioned "confusion." Can you describe the picture of your confusion? * Can I ask you to repeat what you just said, but say it more slowly? * Can you repeat your statement but use the pronoun "I" instead of "you"? * Can you say those words in a louder tone? . . . Can you say that even louder?	* Being vague, circumlocutionary. * Restating and re-explaining observations or requests that need to be pithy and direct. * Too much talking from the coach.

Universal Coaching Competencies | 235

8. Creating Awareness	* Questions that promote awareness * Observations that promote awareness * Are you aware that you are talking [or breathing] very quickly? * I notice that you are laughing while talking about this sad story. * I notice the way you are moving back and forth as you talk. What are you aware of that is in front of you and behind you? * As you speak about this important achievement, your face seems very still. What are you holding in your stillness?	* Unable to offer observations or disclosures or questions that heighten client awareness. * Explaining to clients rather than having them engage in their own reflective awareness.
9. Designing Actions	* Imagine that you are talking to your boss right now about this issue. Could you speak to me as if you were talking to him? * You have just named a challenge. For the next two minutes, can you say all the ways that this challenge keeps you stuck? * Your fears about giving presentations can be eased by the power of practice. Can we try a test run of your presentation, and you can ask for support in the moment to strengthen your delivery? * If these thoughts that limit you were a character, what would he/she look like? What would he/she say? Can you act that out?	* Engaging the client in cognitive, "talk about" strategies rather than using experiential moments for experimental learning efforts.

10. Goal Setting	* Let's state your goal with a plan or a strategy that works for you. * Does this plan feel doable for you over the next two weeks? * When can you achieve this? * That sounds like a commitment. When can you do that? * Is this plan too ambitious? If you were guaranteed success, what can you do? * If you were guaranteed success, what would be a less ambitious and more realistic plan?	* Missing opportunities to have clients reframe their goal or plan or strategy. * Avoiding commitment language to a goal.
11. Managing Progress and Accountability	* What tells you that you have achieved this goal? * As we close, what are your learnings from this session? * How will you take this awareness into your everyday life? * What actions will you take to continue this work? * If you were to take a little first step, what would that first step be? * Who or what can support you to hold you to this learning? * How will you make sure to continue this work? * How will you keep yourself accountable?	* Avoiding or missing the trajectory of follow-up which the client needs to have developed before ending the session. * Lack of language around anticipation, whether visualization or cognitive strategy about steps needed to maintain the success of the coaching agreement. * Failing to marry future actions to the original coaching agreement, which is the ROI of the coaching effort. * * Consult the ICF chart that "provides guidelines about coach intervention(s) which are seen as competency failure(s)"—"ICF Core Competencies Ratings Levels," *Coachfederation.org*.

While Gestalt coaching and certainly most other 21st-century coaching approaches are holistic, the markers suggest a universal structure of basic competencies for professionally certified coaches according to the ICF. As we mentor our students, they often ask too many questions in a given coaching session; or in trying to establish a coaching agreement, they tend to move on before they have an agreement (what the client wants or needs); or, once they have an agreement, they don't use it to close out the session. The presumed obviousness of the core competencies requires close observation of coaching sessions and mentor coaching. We offer our guidelines of what to say with the caution that our ACTP students not take these as a kind of rote checklist of acceptable phrasing, but simply as guidelines toward competent coaching practice that incorporates wisdom from the Gestalt approach embedded in ICF accreditation evidence-based markers of the core competencies.

In supporting our students to complete the ICF competencies in our ACTP program, we offer them detailed feedback as well as suggest guideline tips that adhere to the ICF markers and uphold Gestalt coaching principles and expectations. Even so, we find that the "obviousness" of ICF certification remains a challenge because of the evaluation component involving credentialing. Students need mentor coaching around their competencies, but they also typically need supervision about their use of self and their use of self as coach. Because of this, we have until this writing been recommending Pamela McLean's excellent *The Completely Revised Handbook of Coaching: A Developmental Approach,* 2nd ed. Gestalt coaching places a high value on equipotentiality and the myriad ways of meeting the client, yet the performance accreditation demands of ICF suggest a mastery of these competencies that continues to challenge those who are facing accreditation evaluation. In part, the incentive to write this book (and specifically this chapter) emerges out of the goal to give more direct and understandable information to our students, which we are now providing. We ourselves offer a mastery program to assist our students in the development of the technical competencies as well as the more adaptive vertical development challenges around use of self as instrument. For an example of how to use Gestalt coaching competencies with the ICF competencies, see Appendix C on Supervision. It is also our goal to assist our students and practitioners to achieve their dream of being a "remarkable coach," in Philippe Rosinski's words.[25]

Gestalt coaching invites us to call upon the full breadth and depth of our awareness intelligence to become masterful awareness agents. We are expected to practice active listening and to adapt to the client's agenda: the client's needs, wants, and resistances drive the coaching engagement, not the coach's. Because coaching is often categorized as a helping profession, "the challenge is to unlearn [our] deeply embedded, directive model of helping in favor of one that is more mutual, more collaborative, and more centered on the needs and preferences of the [client]," and to forego our natural tendencies toward "advice giving, problem-solving, and theorizing."[26] The ICF's definition of coaching stresses this adaptive model:

> [Coaching is] partnering with clients in a thought-provoking and creative process that inspires them to maximize their personal and professional potential, which is particularly important in today's uncertain and complex environment. Coaches honor the client as the expert in his or her life and work and believe every client is creative, resourceful, and whole. Standing on this foundation, the coach's responsibility is to:

- Discover, clarify, and align with what the client wants to achieve
- Encourage client self-discovery
- Elicit client-generated solutions and strategies
- Hold the client responsible and accountable

This process helps clients dramatically improve their outlook on work and life, while improving their leadership skills and unlocking their potential.[27]

When Ed Nevis brought Gestalt theory, concepts, and methods into the field of organizational consulting, he introduced a new element of relational, collaborative ways to work with clients. Even so, often it has been the consultant's expertise that remained the determining voice for how to best and most effectively move the organizational system forward. The consultant was perceived to be the one accountable for setting the agenda and driving the work to meet larger system needs. In Gestalt coaching, however, the client is always in charge, and coaches defer to the client's wisdom regarding which issues to focus on. Coaching can be an OD tool, and OD consulting can be a logical career shift for coaches. But Gestalt coaching is not a "subset" of either consulting or psychotherapy, Gestalt or otherwise.

Now that coaching is recognized as a profession, the horizontal tasks that demonstrate qualification for a professional coaching credential represent a commitment to the structures of coaching excellence. The ICF's code of ethics and core competencies, which so closely parallel the principles and practices of Gestalt coaching, are at the core of all Gestalt Center for Coaching coach training programs as well. Gestalt coaches are also strongly committed to learning along a vertical developmental axis, however, which importantly enhances and expands the foundations of coaching excellence.

As we close this chapter on the relationship between ICF core competencies and Gestalt coaching concepts, the power of what these two "languages" offer is compelling. ICF core competencies can be considered to be the ground variables that constitute competent, effective, and trustworthy coaching. A reasonable self-assessment for any coaching encounter could be to engage in a self-assessment as to one's use of these ICF competencies. Learning to engage these competencies is an act of horizontal development, especially as we move toward evidence-based coaching assessments that identify use of the ICF core competencies. On the other hand, Gestalt coaching competencies augment coaching practice by activating process variables that enhance the vibrancy of the coaching encounter. Gestalt coaching concepts make visible the range of awareness variables that are honed through vertical development and the integration of one's awareness intelligence.

Gestalt coaching is strengthened by the ICF core competencies, particularly in creating the coaching agreement and in the call for continued accountability. In turn, the ICF core competencies are strengthened and enhanced when the existential, experiential, and experimental variables of Gestalt coaching are introduced. We are proud of the integration of these two forces in the service of professional coaching. We invite you to practice them both, and to reflect on your successes and failures and on your capacities to grow into a coaching professional who makes a difference with the work you are able to offer others.

CHAPTER 9

The Relevance of Gestalt Coaching Today

By Barbara Singer, President & CEO of Executive Core

Be patient towards all that is unresolved in your heart. Try to love the questions themselves.
—RAINER MARIA RILKE *(LETTERS TO A YOUNG POET)*

Our greatness lies not so much our being able to remake the world as in being able to remake ourselves.
—MAHATMA GANDHI

My esteemed colleague and dear friend, Dorothy Siminovitch, honored me by inviting me to contribute some thoughts to this important book on Gestalt coaching. I do not espouse to be an expert in Gestalt theory, but I can tell you that Gestalt thinking has guided my career in organizational development, C-suite/executive coaching, and talent management strategy for over 20 years. Over those last 20 years, I have also observed that executive coaches with training in a Gestalt way of thinking tend to be successful when working with C-suite executives in companies like McKinsey & Company, Cisco Systems, Egon Zehnder, Heidrick & Struggles, General Electric, the Ford Motor Company, and other organizations filled with intelligent people who demand smart thought partners. These coaches frequently get at hidden assumptions, faulty beliefs, hidden fears, or blind spots in awareness faster than those not trained in a Gestalt approach. Furthermore, these Gestalt practitioners are in the habit of doing self-work with regard to their personal presence and self-management. They can hold their own in board meetings and top management team meetings, and they leave a memorable impression of playfulness, credibility, and almost immediate trust. They also tend to show up as trusted advisors and not consultants.

As an executive coach, CEO of Executive Core, an international coaching and consulting firm, and occasionally considered one of the pioneers in the field, I am constantly reminded that each of us stands on the shoulders of other great minds.[1] In the early 2000s, I conducted my first certification around executive coaching. I remember summarizing the underpinning of the practice by discussing the forefathers of psychology who have influenced how we do leadership development today. For many of us who work primarily in business, we have closeted our ties to the psychological pioneers of the last 100 years, preferring instead to cite John Kotter, Peter Senge, Warren Bennis, Daniel Goleman, Jim Collins, Lisa Lahey, Sheryl Sandberg, Dale Carnegie, Norman Vincent Peale, Stephen Covey, and Richard Boyatzis. But before there were leadership gurus that we followed, there were great minds in psychology teaching us to think differently about helping others navigate their life in healthy and self-affirming ways. And prior to that were the great philosophers—Plato, Aristotle, Socrates, Descartes, Thomas Aquinas, John Locke, Immanuel Kant, Confucius, and the list goes on. It is important in our careers to remember the roots of our ways of thinking even as we look to evolve our wisdom and practice.

In considering how Gestalt thinking has changed the way we approach helping people, we can reflect upon four pioneers in psychology—Alfred Adler, Carl Jung, Carl Rogers, and Frederick "Fritz" Perls. Adler taught us that business leaders need to have unified goals that put an emphasis on our stakeholders. In coaching, we call this the ecosystem approach (Marshall Goldsmith calls it "stakeholder-centered" coaching).[2] Carl Jung taught us that personality types can help us adapt our communication and plan our interactions more strategically for people who process information and make decisions differently than we do. Jung also taught us that much of what we experience is subjective, and we must honor people's own sense of self before helping them expand their self-awareness. And Carl Rogers encouraged us to ensure that clients take an active stance and assume responsibility for their own success—essentially coining the philosophy that we must define success for ourselves. Fritz Perls, the father of Gestalt theory and practice, taught us to take action and to measure the results, which today is the hallmark of good executive coaching at the top of the house in corporations. Perls taught us that experiential learning and action, rather than cognitive "talking about" challenges, feelings, problems, or goals, is what unlocks a person's potential.

Today there are many ways we measure the impact of growing talent, but it all depends on the perceptions and measures of the system, not just individuals' perceptions alone. The chart below reminds us when we work with leaders that they have the ability to positively impact revenue (often measured in OIBTDA, Operating Income Before Taxes and Depreciation and Amortization). We can use pre- and post-testing of valid 360-degree survey reports to see if leaders improve their behavior. We can gather anecdotal examples from stakeholders (bosses, peers, direct reports, and those outside of the organization) to demonstrate that the person has made positive changes. We can also begin to measure increased self-awareness when we see a person's own evaluation of themselves matching how others evaluate them. A Gestalt way of thinking helps a person take action faster in a way that can be seen and reported on by others around them (Figure 9.1).

Figure 9.1 Tracking Leadership Impact

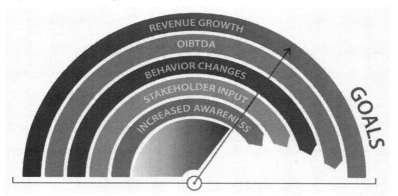

A Gestalt approach continues to resonate with leaders today because it reminds us to think about how we behave as a way of recognizing and enhancing our inner creative potential. Gestalt thinking reminds us to slow time down and to clarify our intention so that our behaviors can become congruent and authentic—so that our presence is warm and memorable. As practitioners, when we see that a client isn't congruent, we are signaled that the person may be slowed down unintentionally by a basic inner conflict.

After coaching thousands of leaders, we often find them in conflict or challenged to navigate relationships with supervisors, direct reports, and colleagues. Leaders need ways to motivate and engage teams to achieve tangible results. Leaders who become distracted, for example, forget to keep their eye on how to best serve customers. Additionally, leaders often report they worry about what others think about their rapid promotion over peers. Perhaps they don't agree with senior leadership's direction, so they send mixed messages to colleagues about what needs to be done in the business. Or leaders might want to successfully execute a team project but are afraid team members will let them down by performing at substandard levels. As leaders and as people, common basic conflicts can cause anyone to get "stuck" and disconnected from their creative juices—people may react without fully tapping into all information and forms of intelligence.

As a quick assessment, which of these have you seen in yourself, in your colleagues, or in your clients?

- Isolating/withdrawing
- Not asking for feedback from those who can tell you the difficult truth
- Making decisions based on fears
- Pleasing people (wanting to be liked/accepted at your own expense)
- Being impatient
- Demonstrating anger that is more than the situation calls for
- Not forgiving
- Not demonstrating gratitude for what you have
- Losing a sense of humor and playfulness
- Distorting reality/turning a blind eye to important facts
- Not synthesizing all the available data/facts into a good course of action
- Missing key themes/patterns when making a decision
- Forgetting to assess how people will be impacted and adjusting accordingly
- Failing to act because you fear failing
- Winning at all costs—others get hurt
- Not clearly understanding how others perceive you

- Not being clear in your intentions

Coming to terms with inner conflicts or hidden assumptions that repeat potentially destructive behaviors, or are simply focused on accelerating success, requires more than a single, simplistic technique to shed light on everything holding you back. It asks for a process of discovering new insights about yourself in a dynamic way. Gestalt coaching encourages leaders to start taking small, experimental risks with new ways of being. Gestalt coaching encourages people to practice new behaviors, seek feedback, and try again. A Gestalt way of thinking encourages all of us to try to take on the perspective of another person so that we can better communicate and understand his/her motivations. This is at the heart of mindset shifts and influence. Gestalt coaching requires that we approach leadership in an integral way, tapping into all aspects of humanity. A Gestalt approach considers values, physical well-being, cognitive intelligence, spirituality (a sense of something greater than ourselves or a higher purpose) and morality, emotional intelligence, influence through presence and interpersonal skills, and a social network or sense of belonging.

Too often, we neglect critical aspects of ourselves. Where do you see this in yourself, in your colleagues, or in your clients? To ascertain if you, a colleague, or a client is in the zone of self-awareness, consider if that person is evolving toward:

- Constantly making new discoveries about themselves
- Taking ownership of their experience—not blaming others for their misfortunes
- Developing new strategies, skills, and ways of thinking that allow them to satisfy their needs with little detriment to others
- Accepting the consequences of their actions

- Developing a way of thinking that helps them remain resilient during tough times without overly relying on others to help
- Asking for and offering help to others in a way that demonstrates balanced reciprocity

After Dorothy launched Awareness IQ in Istanbul, we partnered to create a new awareness index that measures all of the items above and allows people to get 360-degree feedback from others on their current state of Gestalt thinking. We've used simple business language to ensure that anyone can apply it. And as we've worked with Fortune 500 clients, we are getting feedback that a person's state of awareness is keenly predictive of his or her future success. One client recently wrote to us,

> The way their team managed the process and relationship with each leader was crucial for their development. Our top talent mentioned that one of the most relevant experiences throughout the program was the coaching sessions along with the 360° assessment to better understand where they needed to focus. The insights provided were of great value for them and for their development.

During an international rollout for a large financial services company, they ranked Executive Core's coaching as one of the very best aspects of the program in every country. One participant wrote last week,

> Coaching was very supportive and I felt this was one of the critical elements for the program. It gave me a chance to think what I should do to accelerate my growth. I clearly understood my current situation and logically

developed the plan for growth by going through the coaching process. Analyzing myself logically and clearly and understanding my strengths and weaknesses was very hard, and Anna's coaching helped a lot.

Data collected from more than 100 leaders who participated in this development show that their stakeholders (their supervising leaders, direct reports, colleagues, etc.) reported improvement in the following areas:

- Increased self-awareness
- Listening, and influencing goals based on perceived gaps and alignment around priorities
- Enterprise thinking/collaboration/working across the functions/product offerings
- Mindshift change as one moves from manager to more senior leader
- More fluid navigation within market complexity/volatility—being more mindful and more thoughtful, e.g., managing market growth along with regulatory/compliance
- Collaboration—especially outside of one's function across the enterprise
- Constructive debate to forward new ideas without damaging relationships
- Team alignment, motivation, and development
- Executive Presence
- Adaptive communication upward and influencing the strategy
- Receiving sponsorship/champions from more senior leaders to grow/evolve and be more aligned with strategy from headquarters

Early on, Fritz Perls wrote that "a client's posture, movements, gestures, voice, hesitations, and other cues tell the real story."[3] I could not agree more. One of our jobs as consultants and executive coaches is to determine when there are hidden or underlying needs. Perls was known for his colorful warning that most verbal communication is a lie, and if you are too logical and fact-based, focused only on the content, you may just miss the essence of the person. In today's world, Perls's way of delivering his insights and knowledge would be judged arrogant, chauvinistic, and even demeaning. But 50 years ago, he was a fresh voice speaking against a dogmatic post-WWII mentality that adhered to Freudian psychoanalytic constructs of conformity over innovation, commonality over originality, and accommodation over self-liberation. Perls's voice has since evolved in the excellent writing of Barry Johnson on polarity management, on organizational consulting by the late Edwin Nevis, and on resistance by Hank Karp.[4] There are also the "muses" of Gestalt practice—and Dorothy's coach training program in Istanbul is regarded as the latest evolution of the fire of innovation which can be traced back to Fritz Perls. Whether it is self-awareness or recognizing awareness in other people, a true understanding of self and others is often beyond words because it draws from a holistic, multi-dimensional approach. This book helps make that clear.

Which leads to my next point: Gestalt theory adds to the important work of emotional and social intelligence. One reason I was drawn to Gestalt theory was that it grew out of a negative reaction to analytical theory. In professional coaching, we tend to work with heads of business units, technology gurus, graduates of top business schools, and other strategists who have received accolades their entire life for analytical prowess. To become a more inspiring and adaptable leader, they need something more than analytical skills. They need a little help from their friends. Gestalt thinking helps intelligent people get in touch with their other senses and sources of intelligence beyond the cognitive realm. The coaches that serve smart leaders need to be able to keep up cognitively, but they need to bring something else to the table besides logical reasoning.

Those who are familiar with Gestalt thinking aren't afraid to be direct. I find this to be a necessary skill if you are working with a busy CEO or the head of R&D. They don't have much time and they need you to quickly get to the point. They do appreciate hearing new and different things they haven't figured out on their own, but they do not suffer fools gladly. So they need their coaches and consultants to be precise and insightful. They aren't afraid if you are affirming and let them know your only agenda is to be a champion for their ethical and moral success and the happiness of their employees and customers. They don't mind a little confrontation, especially when it is accurate and playfully delivered. Let them set the pace and discuss a topic when they are ready. And a great executive coach is going to give these leaders challenges that aren't easy. They will appreciate being stretched and having a trusted advisor by their side to help them face things that can be a little frightening.

One caring executive coach I know encouraged a CEO of a Fortune 500 company to share his feelings over the last economic crisis with his top management team. This CEO had been known for showing "heart" in the past, but this particular economic crisis was challenging his entire industry. In a state of fear, he defaulted to holding highly analytical meetings and bringing in experts who could describe various business strategies. There wasn't much heart left in the top management meetings, and his coach pointed this out in her gentle, quiet, and wise way. So this CEO tried an experiment suggested by his coach, which challenged him to share his hopes and fears in the next top-management team meeting. He also shared what he thought the company could evolve to generations in the future. The result was that the top-management team equally shared their feelings, and instead of analytical reports and banter, they opened up about their hopes and fears. The company executives even tightened their belts and took less compensation in order to reduce layoffs and downsizing. The rest is a history of a successful outcome, but employees and that industry still talk about the innovation that took place afterwards across the entire enterprise.

This is the power of experiment applied in the moment that makes the difference. It takes courage to take a risk. It takes presence, use of self, and the willingness to fail. These qualities are also why successful innovation is so inspiring to others: it marries truth to possibility. Dorothy's "Gestalt coaching primer" will act to help coaches and consultants be more mindful about their presence, their use of self, and how they can create experiments that serve their clients.

Those who embrace Gestalt thinking have worked on themselves in order to become the agents of awareness that Dorothy describes. This means they often achieve the ability to demonstrate a deep respect for individual experience. They often live their lives in a spirit of gratitude. Practitioners who are seeking higher levels of self-awareness reveal that work in their client interactions. Here are some Gestalt techniques that anyone can use to help develop awareness and talent in client organizations.

- I've often requested that a client who is in conflict with another person's perspective assume *that* person's perspective, while someone else plays the client himself. By talking as if they are the other person, clients often achieve the capacity to understand the other person's perspective and gain deeper awareness about what issue, assumption, or value might be contributing to the conflict. This allows both parties to be more creative and thoughtful.

- Another technique you can try is playful exaggeration. Have people exaggerate the various ways they may be playing a rigid role in their career/life. For instance, if a client shows she has a proclivity for playing the victim in certain relationships, try having her exaggerate this behavior. This also works when a person may be playing a dominating or perhaps even an aggressive role (using threatening negative outcomes or insinuation to get her way). Taking things to the ridiculous, in a safe context, makes people laugh while they are also gaining insight. It often helps them return to a more balanced state of thinking and allows them to be adaptive when life requires it—instead of immediately reverting to a more rigid role, being flexible when an alternative approach emerges could be far more effective.

Balancing assertiveness and empathic listening is a theme that we see woven through most leadership challenges. Leaders who can both listen deeply and assert succinctly are often more successful than those who can't. People often struggle with the sense of when to be passive and when to be aggressive, yet this polarization is what gets them in trouble with relationships. This is the issue of communication and voice that Dorothy has addressed in the qualities of presence, which apply both to leaders and the coaches who work with them. Here are other examples of where relationships in business/organizations become polarized in destructive ways when the challenge of managing resistances is not met:

- Directive boss vs. passive direct report
- Keeping a plan vs. being spontaneous

- Compliance vs. innovation
- Traditionalist vs. novelty
- Autonomy/freedom vs. regulation
- Dedication to work vs. quality of life outside of work
- Delegation vs. command and control

Gestalt thinking helps us see that these are not opposing problems to be solved but rather equally viable forces to be managed. If you haven't had the chance to read Barry Johnson's work on polarity management, it's worth the time. Through a creative reframe, the Gestalt coach can help a client see that both are valid perspectives and, through understanding the other person's motivation, can be managed. If you address the resistance that is connected to the fear, oftentimes the person who was most polarized will become a champion of the opposing side.

Fritz Perls also talked about a technique called "making the rounds." Today, we use this technique when we encourage leaders to reach out to their stakeholders to ask for feedback, take risks, put issues on the table, disclose, and especially to seek out affirmations when they were at their best. In one women's program held at the SVP and C-suite level, women were asked to "make the rounds" among their colleagues and have them write a few paragraphs about when they have seen this female leader at her very best. Many of the female leaders were shocked and pleasantly surprised at the major positive impact the little things they've done have made among their colleagues. They often don't realize that they have a personal brand of leadership that matters and can impact and improve people's working lives every day.

Gestalt practitioners also ask clients to take responsibility for consequences. One very successful successor to a CEO called his team together and shared his performance review and 360-degree leadership report with them. Before leaving the room, the CEO asked each person to think of something he could do to radically improve (this CEO was already much respected, and his revenue numbers in his division were impressive). The CEO returned to take responsibility for anything they had to share. It turned out that his team, while they had learned a great deal from watching him set strategy for his division, were now ready to ask that he let them make more of the decisions. The leader was delighted and surprised. At the end of the meeting, the team followed the CEO's example, and all agreed to take responsibility for improving one aspect of their communication with him to ensure that future execution of the strategy went smoothly.

Another important aspect of Gestalt practice is to challenge leaders who complain about others. Many times leaders project their own weaknesses onto others. If a leader says she does not trust someone, you can ask that leader to take on the perspective (play the role) of the other person. As a coach, you can help the leader discover to what degree the distrust is an inner conflict or tied to a faulty assumption. Just hearing aloud the statements the leader may be making about other people can help her realize these are blocks to working with others effectively. In one instance, an SVP of a UK firm was constantly complaining about the emotional outbursts of her CEO; he, in turn, was complaining about her emotional outbursts. While the SVP felt she was extremely professional and polished, the truth was that she was overly criticizing her colleagues in front of her boss. She was being perceived as whining and non-collaborative. When her coach exaggerated both her statements and her boss's statements, this executive realized the negativity she was emitting. She found it to be far more effective to start meetings with shared goals and progress made to date. So when discussing challenges/problems, she began with a list of what her team was doing to improve the situation and asked her boss what she might be missing. They both discovered the approach to be far more productive and satisfying.

Having fun in our work also helps because laughter is actually known to support trust. I love to have leaders exaggerate the behavior they fear expressing. On many occasions, I have had introverted leaders get ready for an important meeting by exaggerating their nonverbal behaviors. Their fear is that they will look fake, not logical, or not composed. Typically, they fear they will become "too animated"—too physically expressive, will smile too much, and will use their hands too much for emphasis. Yet when we have them exaggerate what they think "over-the-top" gestures and facial expressions might look like, and then capture them on video with a smart device, they invariably see how naturally animated and lively they look. And they appreciate the positive reinforcement others give them when they "exaggerate" something they have routinely avoided.

Perls was also known for having people rehearse their interactions. In organizational development and executive coaching, we'd be lost without this technique, which actually moves people toward their own success. Gestalt coaching is committed to these useful techniques, along with other best cognitive methods to honor the person in an integral way.

The new Leadership Awareness Index that Dorothy and I are launching is a 360-degree instrument that draws on Gestalt theory, conceptual models, methodologies, and insights. We hope this instrument will be a groundbreaking way to measure a person's mindfulness, using both coaching insights and observations and stakeholder input. Consider the questions for the index for yourself and use the following scale to recognize and assess your own awareness capacity, an essential aspect of Gestalt coaching mastery (Figure 9.2).

Figure 9.2 Leadership Awareness Index Scoring Scale

0	1	2	3	4	5
No Evidence	**Does Not Meet Standard**	**Developing**	**Basic**	**Proficient**	**Mastery**
Shows no evidence of learning or reflection regarding this skill	Little demonstration of this skill in a way that positively impacts the business	Nearly meets standard but does not consistently demonstrate or show depth/insight/generalizations in a way that positively impacts the business	Consistently demonstrates a basic level of this skill but lacks breadth of demonstration at all levels or agility across levels, platforms, functions, regions	Demonstrates skill consistently in a way that has positive impact on the business	Demonstrates this skill at all levels, across functions/platforms, inside and outside the organization. Can teach/coach/model this skill for others in a way that helps everyone positively impact the business

- Takes action with appropriate urgency yet refrains from acting impulsively
- Sees complete environment and long-term implications of a situation in order to react to the higher good
- Creates a sense of alignment (between oneself and stakeholders) by sharing meaningful stories and examples
- Helps others make sense of a situation
- Has a can-do attitude to try something new
- Enjoys tackling novel and/or difficult issues and consistently maintains self-confidence/personal efficacy
- Conveys positive contagious energy about ideas or new projects/people
- Invites balanced participation to explore multiple ways of achieving an end goal and fosters commitment to the decision-making process
- Follows ideas through to completion, even in the face of adversity
- Distills complex ideas into a clear plan of action
- Extends others' ideas and is able to synthesize/combine normally unrelated thoughts, ideas, and actions

- Shares information and resources openly and graciously in order to prepare others to face the unknown
- Sees possibilities to improve or try something completely new
- Does not become overly invested in a single idea or plan of action
- Seeks out new information and others' perspectives to get the full picture
- Invites and brainstorms opposing perspectives and playfully asks everyone to take on the perspective of others
- Invites and allows for experimentation in a way that reassures others that it's okay to fail as part of successful learning
- Constantly seeks a higher-level understanding of things that benefits the team, the organization, society, and the greater good
- Strives for clarity around each unit's (team, organization, society) higher purpose
- Tends to avoid relying on heuristics and prior attitudes; open to new/conflicting information
- Sees the unknown as an adventure and can remain comfortable with ambiguity
- Connects with others on a personal level and shows compassion and understanding of others' problems
- Is able to gather information concerning others' thoughts and feelings, even if they are reticent to speak up
- Includes others in important decisions and activities, even when they hold conflicting views, possess less-formal authority, or are not primary contributors
- Mobilizes groups of people to actively work toward same mission and goals without constant direction

- Can clearly describe where (s)he fits into the workgroup and organization
- Demonstrates humility and a lack of concern for status
- Where appropriate, puts others' needs first in order to facilitate employee development and performance
- Improvises ways to connect with others in unexpected and useful ways
- Identifies/articulates common themes
- Communicates the value of belonging to groups in a way that energizes others (optimistic, hopeful, resilient)
- Has a healthy concern for others as well as self
- Believes all people (self and others) have value
- Works to surface his/her own hidden biases as well as illuminate the hidden biases of others when it comes to stereotyping certain groups of people
- Creates followership/inspires affiliation—people want to connect with this individual
- Makes a clear decision and shows how the group contributed to it in a way that people feel heard and honored

As a next step, you can ask people you trust to share their observations about when you are at your best and also under extreme stress. How does your mindfulness factor hold up? Where might you do some additional work? Our colleagues in San Francisco, the Search Inside Yourself Leadership Institute (SIYLI), are making a big impact in bringing these developmental best practices to the workplace and into contemporary coaching practice.[5] In our turbulent times, these practices provide added value for improving work, personal relationships, leadership development, and personal well-being. It is heartening to add that the focus of this practice has always been the domain of Gestalt work. In a very real sense, Dorothy's "modest" book on Gestalt coaching is a gift—it demystifies what has always sounded like a mysterious practice. That demystification is the challenge of any approach based on awareness, itself a deep and elusive concept. This elusive quality of awareness is what 21st-century leaders most need to understand and to manage, and a Gestalt approach is precisely the way to achieve such understanding, for coaches and those whom they coach.

One of the more powerful aspects of Gestalt thinking is that it transcends cultures, regions, and different perspectives extremely well. Culturally diverse organizations can tailor these techniques in a way that accommodates regional or cultural differences. Such flexibility breaks down resistance caused from lack of understanding, and helps put people of diverse perspectives "in the driver's seat" as they navigate their own development. Much has also been written about the polarities that exist in society, organizations, and individuals. Gestalt thinking helps us realize that there is wide range in thinking and behaviors—that there always exist multiple perspectives. When a person has been deeply influenced by two different cultures, he may often feel he has "unfinished business" when contradictions occur between the cultures. One German executive that we worked with had married a woman born and educated in Mexico. This executive led LATAM Airlines operations in Germany, and later took on a bigger role in the company to manage the Americas. By becoming aware of his various aspects, he began to appreciate his ability to focus on results, to lead a team in an expansive and collaborative way, and to successfully consult with his North American colleagues to make them part of the solution. He acculturated the best of his experiences, both European and Mexican, into an amazing leadership style that got noticed at headquarters.

I ask the reader to look back to the roots of some of your thinking and the techniques you have learned to apply in your life and in your work. There is always additional work we can personally do, and you must do it for yourself and on your own. Your clients will benefit deeply. Then have the courage to challenge your clients to try new things to enrich their understanding of the world and how they make their way through their careers. I have noticed for many years that each time a leader is promoted, she has to make a mental shift in how she sees her role, the organization, the customers, and her team. The concepts, theory, and techniques offered in Dorothy's book provide an excellent toolkit to assist coaches in supporting leaders during their transition(s).

Early in our careers, as emerging high talents, we might be focused on a small set of deliverables. As we progress, we are challenged to see things from the perspective of the entire enterprise or organization, and to take on the perspective of our various clients, who may be operating in dispersed functions and regions. My own work in Gestalt thinking led me to acknowledge a new capacity in myself that I had previously overlooked. It allowed me to show up with both my cognitive and emotional senses, to be connected and part of the data I take in as I get to know each new client. This Gestalt perspective helped me remain humble and to laugh at my own foibles (and there are many), and to show up more confidently with very senior leaders and yet help them laugh through their own foibles. The holistic, systems-based approach that defines Gestalt coaching allows the executive coach many ways of meeting and coaching leaders to assist them in their integrity and challenges of growth. The stance of the Gestalt coach is always appreciative and understands that each client, no matter their challenges, is always trying his or her best, whether it appears so or not. It is worthy to honor the words of Marianne Williamson: "Our deepest fear is not that we are inadequate. Our deepest fear is that we are powerful beyond measure. It is our light, not our darkness, that frightens us. We ask ourselves, who am I to be brilliant, gorgeous, talented and fabulous? Actually, who are you *not* to be?"[6]

The Gestalt approach was first offered in the grand spirit of self-liberation. This primer on Gestalt coaching is a wonderful resource for coaches and consultants who wish to make a liberating difference with their presence and their practice.

APPENDIX A
The ICF Certification Process[1]

Being a credentialed coach is how I say to the world, "I am a professional coach."
—Julia Mattern, PCC

While there are now a number of certified Gestalt-based coach training programs, I take particular pride in having developed the first such program to have earned International Coach Federation (ICF) certification as an Accredited Coach Training Program (ACTP)—the International Gestalt Coaching Program, inaugurated in 2006. This was followed by my second, co-developed ACTP, the Gestalt Coaching Program in Istanbul (formerly the Eurasian Gestalt Coaching Program), in 2009.

To have earned ACTP standing, the top tier of ICF certification for coach training programs, means that the program administrators have submitted complete training curricula for review to ICF; have agreed to deliver training in alignment with ICF core competencies and with ICF ethical guidelines; and have agreed to provide supervision that confirms demonstrated coaching competencies that vary across three different individual credentials: the Associate Certified Coach (ACC), the Professional Certified Coach (PCC), and the Master Certified Coach (MCC).

To qualify for ACTP accreditation, a program's curriculum must include the following:

Program Requirements Overview

- Minimum of 125 student contact hours
- 80 percent of all training must be delivered in synchronous activities and focused on the ICF Core Competencies
- Compliance with operational standards
- Course list
- ICF-credentialed instructors, observers, mentors, and performance evaluation reviewers
- MCC-credentialed Director of Training
- Six observed coaching sessions for each student
- Ten hours of Mentor Coaching
- Performance evaluation
- Audit materials
- Statements of agreement, compliance and limitations, duty to notify, and payment agreements

Because there are multiple paths to becoming an ICF-certified coach, applicants are frequently challenged by the intricacy of the process. Three paths to individual certification at all levels include ACTP, ACSTH, and Portfolio. Graduates of an ACTP program may apply for an individual ICF Credential via the ACTP credential application path. To fully appreciate the distinctions between these certifications, and for further details, go to the Coachfederation.org "Individual Credentialing" website pages for Associate Certified Coach (ACC), Professional Certified Coach (PCC), and Master Certified Coach (MCC).

APPENDIX B
Sample Coaching Agreement

[Your company logo here]

Coaching Agreement

I give _____ permission to coach me. I understand that coaching is neither therapy nor consulting. She agrees to hold all content of our sessions completely confidential. I understand that we are both responsible for creating a successful coaching relationship, which will support me in reaching my goals and living my life to the best I am able. ***Indicate your agreement by checking the boxes below.***

I agree to work with _____ to shape our coaching relationship to best meet my needs by:	
Sharing relevant information with _____	
Making requests of _____ when my needs are not being met	
Disagreeing openly with _____ as appropriate	
Agreeing on what important words mean	
Testing our assumptions	
Dealing with other obstacles as they arise	

I give _____ permission to:	
Challenge me with powerful questions	
Make requests of me for homework	
Provide inquiries for me to consider	
Intrude, challenge, and hold me accountable	

I agree to the following business items:	
Fee of $ _____ per hour	
Fee will be paid at the beginning of each month	
Two 1-hour sessions per month, or a total of 2 hours per month	
Coaching for a maximum of 6 months	

I agree to the following scheduling items:	
If I am late for an appointment, my session is shortened accordingly	
If I miss an appointment without calling 24 hours in advance, I will be charged for the missed appointment	
Rescheduling more than 24 hours in advance results in no charge, provided the change is mutually convenient	

_____   _____

Signature   *Date*

Some Things to Consider

- What accomplishments or measurable events must occur during your lifetime so that you will consider your life to have been satisfying and well lived?
- If there were a secret passion in your life, something that is almost too exciting to actually do or do more of, what would it be?
- What do you consider your roles to be (e.g., in your family, local community, workplace, country, world)?
- How would you devote your time if money weren't an issue?
- If you had a five-year goal and you had the support to make it happen, what would your goal be and what kind of support would you have?
- What's missing in your life that would make it more fulfilling?
- Where is your life out of balance? What are you not getting enough of in your life? What do you want to get more of in the next few years?
- What's your life purpose? How does this impact your day-to-day living?
- What else would you like your coach to know about you?

Designing the Coaching Agreement

As we begin our work together, we will discuss the questions that follow. You are welcome to either send me your responses or simply consider them for our conversations.

- How do you want me to be as your coach?
- As a coach, how can I best support you?

- What would give you your money's worth?
- What would turn you off?
- What are some of your goals for coaching?
- When you attain these goals, how will you feel?
- What do I really need to know about you that will help me coach you?

APPENDIX C
Coaching Supervision

How do you get to Carnegie Hall? Practice!
— Lily Tomlin

After a great deal of review and conversation with other coaching schools, it seems that all too many people either confuse Gestalt coaching with Gestalt therapy or suggest that Gestalt coaching is too directive. The converse is the case that I have strived to articulate in this primer. The Gestalt approach to coaching is likely the most collaborative, inviting, and client-centered approach currently available within the field of professional coaching. If the coaching appears to be directive, it may be that the person delivering the coaching is still in development of her mastery, or the person observing the coaching has restrictive perceptual filters. To counter such misunderstandings, we include this Appendix concerning the need for supervision and mentorship to offer further development for the journey toward coaching mastery and also for the assessors who would evaluate and assess Gestalt coaching excellence.

Accredited coach training programs have been available since the ICF started in 1995, but an important phenomenon has since emerged: the need for ongoing coach supervision. Just taking an entry program on coaching, even one certified by the ICF, is not sufficient to assure coaching excellence. One measure of accountability and coaching excellence lies in having access to multiple perspectives that allow for greater understanding and choicefulness for client work. Continued improvement of skills, knowledge, and self-awareness serves to maintain enhanced quality in professional coaching endeavors.[1] The importance of multiple perspectives might playfully be further understood from the word itself—"super–vision," which, as an activity, transcends subjective perspectives and opens new insights into the possibilities that coaches could offer their clients.[2] The ICF has been prescient in understanding this new development, stating:

> *It has become recognized practice that coaches at every stage in their coaching journey continually seek development, both personally in terms of deepening their coaching presence and awareness, and professionally in terms of competencies, ethics and standards. One of the growing trends internationally for undertaking such development is engaging in the practice of "coaching supervision" similar in concept to the supervision which supports many behavioral science professions.*[3]

Toward the goal of embedding supervision into professional coaching practice, the ICF is working to more clearly distinguish between supervision and mentor coaching, acknowledging that the terms are often commonly confused. The ICF defines Mentor Coaching as *coaching for the development of one's coaching, rather than reflective practice, coaching for personal development or coaching for business development.* ICF defines Coaching Supervision differently, as *the interaction that occurs when a coach periodically brings his or her coaching work experiences to a coaching supervisor in order to engage in reflective dialogue and collaborative learning for the development and benefit of the coach and his or her clients.* The difference has become important particularly in terms of ICF credentialing:

> *Mentor Coaching focuses on the development of coaching skills mainly in the context of initial development. Coaching Supervision offers the coach a richer and broader opportunity for support and development. In Coaching Supervision, the coach is invited to focus much more on what is going on in their process and where the personal may be intruding on the professional.*

ICF's focus on supervision as offering "a richer and broader opportunity for support and development" in fact speaks to what Gestalt coaches, in particular, already teach: space and time need to be set aside for self-reflection in order for one's own awareness to best be able to serve and be useful for another. It takes reflection and analysis of one's limitations to become aware of one's umwelt, that which we failed to be aware of. We look to evolve our strengths and to benefit from informed feedback. A strong and purposeful use of self happens when coaches enrich their range of possible interventions by being involved in ongoing learning and development in collaboration with another coach.[4] As an approach that has truly made use of one's presence as the cornerstone of coaching mastery, the Gestalt approach is particularly sensitive to the committed self-work needed in the development of mastery. It is an act of commitment to personal mastery to invite observations, aware projections, feedback, and inquiry in relation to one's work. It is an act of commitment and mastery in coaching to be in a position to supervise others.

Peter Hawkins and Nick Smith offer another widely accepted definition of supervision: supervision is a "process by which a coach/mentor/consultant with the help of a supervisor, who is not working directly with the client, can attend to understanding better both the client system and themselves as part of the client-coach/mentor system, and transform their work." They define three main functions of supervision: Coaching the coach on their coaching; mentoring the coach on their development in the profession; providing an external perspective to ensure quality of practice.[5] Even here, there appears to be an area of conceptual confusion between supervision and mentor coaching, using the terms almost interchangeably. Yet the primary thrust is on stepping back from the coaching encounter and reflecting on practice, purpose, and process.

For our purposes, we wish to honor the ICF's efforts to differentiate the terms. As a coach training center, the Gestalt Center for Coaching accepts and agrees with the ICF's determination of the value of supervision for the coach. Supervision provides for:

- An environment for customized personal and professional growth
- An environment to bring ethical issues
- An environment to bring personal uncertainties and vulnerabilities
- An environment to bring boundary issues
- Diminished risk around ethical issues means diminished risk for the coach and for the coach's clients
- The opportunity to engage in a meta-view of client, competency, and/or practice
- The opportunity to engage in a matrix view of client, competency, and/or practice

Working in Istanbul, our esteemed Gestalt Coaching Program faculty member Belkıs Kazmirci offers that the value of supervision and mentor coaching, particularly for our fellow Gestalt coaches, is as follows[6]:

- To have a space for reflection on both the content and process of the work
- To look at and see from another perspective
- To be aware of what the coach does not see, hear, and feel—what is happening and not mentioned
- To get feedback
- To increase the quality of work through continuous professional development
- To express personal stress and reactivity that may be brought up by the work
- Not to carry one's difficulties, problems, and projections alone
- To develop the internal supervisor

Let's return to the opening idea, that access to multiple perspectives is a measure of coach accountability and a factor in coaching excellence through enhanced understanding and choicefulness for client work. Gestalt coaching is a process approach which is focused on attending to phenomena that the coach senses and discerns in herself, the client, and/or the shared field. The following Gestalt coaching case study offers teaching points, followed by thoughts for meta-level reflections after the case presentation. This case is offered, with permission, from my dear colleague Dost Deniz, MCC, who has presented it as a way of illustrating how to work with the Gestalt process concepts of: Resistance, Cycle of Experience (COE), and experiments and Unit of Work (UOW). Dost remarks: "This is a small case example that illustrates how I use not only the COE, the resistances, and the UOW and their interrelations, but also other Gestalt concepts like level of system, use of self, the relational field, and body process. None of these concepts are stand-alone tools."

While there are many examples of coaching issues and choice points throughout this primer, in order to demystify Gestalt coaching, a case study with a master Gestalt coach is best to illustrate these points. This excellent case illustrates how to use Gestalt concepts to assist new possibilities for high-level executives. What is not obvious to the reader may be those choice points and embedded experiences that defy linear presentation. As Dost's long-time colleague and partner, I offer his case with meta-commentary and questions for further illumination. And I offer these observations with a great deal of respect, as any observation or question asked immediately insinuates a corrective perspective. I adhere instead to the ideas of equipotentiality and appreciation. Equipotentiality suggests that there are always other ways of coaching, but appreciation offers the stance of looking with eyes of gratitude.

A Case Study in Working with Resistance Using Gestalt Coaching Concepts and Methodology, with Meta-Commentary

The Work—A	Teaching Points	Work–A: Meta-level Commentary
Hannah is a 37-year-old executive who works in marketing at a large global pharmaceutical company. Although she is high up in the organization, this is the first time she is managing a 25-person team that requires her to present herself as more of a leader than an individual contributor, and she wishes to be "impactful" in that position. We worked together for 4 sessions, mostly around some "technical challenges" about management (e.g., hiring and firing people, giving performance reviews, etc.).		The issue of "leader impact" seems to hold the essence of the work. What framing of coaching agreement served this client?
		What in particular supports you to be sensitive to her pace? How do you recognize the larger somatic issue when she is more drawn to the technical issue?
		Response-A
From the very first session, what caught my attention was her speed and energy of talking and how she pulled herself up physically (a lot of visible tension and rigidness on her shoulders, back, neck, and abdomen), which ended up making her short of breath when talking.	These somatic cues can be signs of a client desensitized to bodily experience and emotions. Most probably, other ways of breaking contact (i.e., other resistances) will be accompanying this. I am already using the Cycle of Experience lens to assess where the client is and what might be stopping her from making better contact with herself, her wants, and her environment.	Contracting for this engagement took place in the most concrete way, as this was a corporate-sponsored project and involved the boss, HR, peers, and direct reports. Yet when we moved into contracting with Hannah, even though she was interested in the "leadership impact," she seemed more interested in the technical issues, and she indeed needed the technical information support, being a first-time executive. As our theory says, the coach's role is to provide the presence that is missing.

The answer to the second question: My awareness of what is going on somatically lies in tracking the client's physical process, verbal choices, and how she is using her voice, her body, her speech and mind (as Buddhists would say), and my awareness of my own internal reactions to what I see, hear, and feel. |

Appendix C: Coaching Supervision | 275

The Work—B	Teaching Points	Work-B: Meta-level Commentary
In the first few sessions, my shared observations about her way of talking ended with her either making "introjective" statements ("I should talk slower, shouldn't I?") or with dismissing the observations as nothing important to pay attention to ("I always talk like this", "My whole family talks fast"—which is actually interesting and important information). She would deflect: "Yes, but what do you think I should do with this employee?" I continued to make the same observations, and she ditched them all, stating that she had very urgent "technical information needs." In response, I stated my position: I am OK to support you where you want me to, yet I am not letting go of this and will bring it back when the opportunity presents itself.	Again, these are signs of a client not making somatic contact with self and choosing to stay with the "cognitive narrative." It is sometimes a good idea not to try to go through closed doors and not to push, yet to also maintain your position as a coach by making your assessment of the situation transparent to the client.	You offered the client somatic observations that she turned away or deflected. How do you support yourself to hold on to this important observation when the client is not willing or ready to accept what appears so relevant? You made visible the doorway to somatic work with support for her technical requests. Can you speak to how that served to create more trust and intimacy?

Response-B

This early in the engagement, it is more important to build trust and intimacy than to push figures that the client isn't ready for. My stance is one of adaptive learning support: Real adaptive learning happens through disturbing people at a rate they can tolerate. I use my internal sense of where the client is and what work the ground is ready for. The energy of the client and the relationship need to be ready for deeper work to move forward, and this readiness is created only when we allow for the trust and intimacy to be built—in this case, supporting the client where she is while also not letting go of my observations and interest for the client, which I need to state openly. This is how we provide the emotional support—i.e., the heart—while also inviting clients to step toward their learning edge.

Appendix C: Coaching Supervision

The Work—C	Teaching Points
The truly pivotal opportunity presented itself in the 4th session. Hannah said that she received feedback from several people, including her boss, about her impact. The feedback was mostly about her abruptness and pushiness, her not taking into account other people's viewpoints and feelings, and dominating meetings and conversations. She also had been videotaped in a workshop, which was a simulated project meeting, and it was a total shock to her to watch herself doing all the things people told her she was doing that she denied doing. She said, "I have known people like this and always detested them."	The client's self-description is again an indication that she has very little awareness of her own process. She does not collect data about herself (i.e., what she is desensitized to) around what she is doing and how she is impacting others. Also in her narrative there is the very basic issue of projection, where what we react to most in others is what we alienate in ourselves. The COE and the more revealing resistances of introjection and projection began to form the pivotal UOW.

Work-C: Meta-level Commentary
You describe that she was in shock about how she saw herself on the videotape. Was there a place for awareness experiments?

Response–C
There are always choice points, and there was certainly room for awareness experiments here. But our experiments are always a function of the figure we are most paying attention to, the boundary we assess as the most potent for having more contact, and definitely, our own richness of ground. So I understand your question to suggest you may have followed a different path. Given who I am as a coach and as a meditation and Qi Gong practitioner, and given my assessment of where the client's energy was that particular day, I probably chose different in-the-moment awareness experiments, which would involve her slowing down and making contact with herself in support of greater awareness.

The Work	Teaching Points	Work: Meta-level Commentary
After talking a little bit about the feedback she had gotten and creating some agreement/contract about the work, I made a statement about her speed of talking. I asked her to pay attention to her speed and to report out what she was aware of.	In our role as awareness agents, we work with the COE and with resistances not to make "diagnoses" that we present to client, but to construct experiments. The experiments are not shaped from an assessment ("she is desensitized") but from the observed phenomenological data ("she is talking too fast, she is not breathing, she is pushing/holding herself up physically"). Working collaboratively, we invite her interest about what she is unaware of (what she is desensitized to). Using the COE assessment as background and using the phenomenological data gives more room for creativity as we invite the client to choose what to attend to. This is beginning of the second stage in the UOW.	[We see Dost taking an appreciative stance to attend to the client's process and to invite her interest into what she may not have been aware of. Agreement here is implicit, and appears to suggest an open-ended coaching agreement directed at Hannah gaining greater awareness of her leadership.]
		Response

Appendix C: Coaching Supervision | 279

The Work	Teaching Points	Work: Meta-level Commentary
She again wanted to dismiss my observation, but this time I asked her, "I can let go and follow you, or I can challenge you a little bit. Which do you want?"	It is always a good idea to give the choice (and the control) to the client, as it creates safety and trust, and allows the client to potentially move further forward than she would otherwise.	[This shows Dost using the paradoxical theory of change: supporting Hannah to pay attention to her process invites movement. Dost reports always establishing the coaching agreement as a holder of the work.]
She thought a few seconds, then said, "As much as I want to run away, I probably need to go with the challenge!"	(To date, in my experience, there has not been one client who didn't choose the challenge.)	
	Recognize that she is already making a shift—she is moving outside her habitual pattern by choosing the challenge and moving toward making contact with her issue. We could create other work out of this—"How is it for you to choose the challenge?," which would become a new UOW. Or we could choose to continue with the present figure. In either case, it is a good idea to acknowledge and bring into the client's awareness the shift she is now making.	
I thanked her for her honesty and acknowledged her courage.		Response

The Work—D	Teaching Points	Work-D: Meta-level Commentary
		We hold the concept of equifinality in constructing experiments. What thematic experiments are possible here?
I asked her to pay attention to her speaking speed and what was uppermost for her. She said the speed felt normal to her—it didn't feel fast. She said, "When I speak this fast I can feel my energy!" I asked her to slow down and see how that was for her. She briefly did so, then said, with a lot of facial expression and gestures, "Boring!" and returned to talking fast again.	We are creating small experiments with the client as we are searching for meaningful ways to move into action in the UOW. It starts with a small "awareness" experiment and moves into a directed behavior ("slow down") experiment.	
I made another observation about how she was holding herself up physically. Using her language, I asked her, "Where do you feel your *energy* in your body?"	When constructing experiments, it is always good to pay attention to and work with the client's own language—vocabulary, metaphors, and so on (in this case "energy").	

Response–D
"Boredom" is a word often used when people wish to avoid feeling. One thematic experiment could be to invite Hannah to pay attention to what she is calling boring and to speak about what she notices.

Appendix C: Coaching Supervision | 281

The Work	Teaching Points	Work: Meta-level Commentary
She responded by saying, "In my upper chest." I asked her to pay attention to this experience of feeling the energy in her upper chest, and she reported feeling breathless and anxious when she feels her energy there. I suggested to her to try something different, to try to bring the energy down lower in her body and to see how that felt. She could bring it down to her middle abdomen, and I asked her to continue speaking while feeling the energy in her abdomen and tell me what that was like. Her speech slowed down remarkably, her voice got deeper, and some of the tightness in her upper body relaxed. At first, she again reported it was "boring!", accompanied with all the previous gestures and minimizing facial expressions. I asked her to stay with her experience a little bit longer, and to see if there was anything more besides boring. After a few seconds, she said, "And I also feel calmer." After a few iterations, she reported she could feel her body, and also the chair supporting her. She said, "I feel much more grounded and stronger when I am in my stomach."	With the client, we are co-creating an experiment which will allows her to make contact with her bodily experience while also making contact with the exterior, which is based on my own COE, i.e., my assessment that she is not making contact with both her inside and the exterior. Do not let go of your experiment when the client seems to be opposing or resisting. It is the resistance playing out, and as coaches our job is to support our clients to pay attention to what is going on exactly at that moment. This is why we are called awareness agents, and we are hired to help clients look into things they wouldn't otherwise.	[This is an example of how staying present to the client's resistance invites her to experience her polarity—"I am feeling more grounded." Dost's staying with the experiment demonstrates the power of working energetically with resistance, which requires patience and awareness.]

Response

The Work	Teaching Points	Work: Meta-level Commentary
At this moment, I realized I was experiencing her as being much more present than she ever had been in this room. I actually felt as if this were the first time I felt her with me. I shared this with her, and she said, "I feel the same. This is the first time I feel not rushed to tell a story or feeling anxious to make myself clear, but just to be here with you and experience myself."	Use of self is our most important contribution to change. By selectively sharing our own experiences, observations, and ideas, we allow clients to make better contact with themselves and their environment. Our UOW figure was "making contact with myself and others." As coach, we need to work "relationally" with clients and offer ourselves as the immediate environment, i.e., "the other" in the room. Note that here there is also a shift in the level of system. Before this intervention, the work was mostly at the intrapersonal level (in the client). By this intervention, now we are at the interpersonal level. When used intentionally, LOS is a very powerful lens and tool, too.	[This is an articulation of the concepts of presence and use of self described in Chapter 5 that the executive client can develop across the levels of systems she is responsible for. One of the great strengths of the Gestalt approach is the capacity to use LOS interventions, which Dost illustrates so well.]
		Response

Appendix C: Coaching Supervision | 283

The Work—E	Teaching Points	Work-E: Meta-level Commentary
I asked, "And how is it for you to be in this state?" She responded, "A completely new way of being." "How so?" I asked. She replied, "I feel much more grounded, stronger, clearer. I feel as if I was lost in a fog before and now the fog just got cleared. And I can feel my body . . . on the chair . . . and I can see you!" We stayed with her experience a little longer to support her to fully experience herself and the environment.	We move forward in the experiment. It is important to move step by step, and also to stay with the little shifts the client has. These shifts are what we are after, and we need to help clients stay with them long enough so they can both experience and assimilate them. Also note how the client is now attending to both the intrapersonal and interpersonal level ("I can feel my body and I can see you"). This is what she had asked for as a leader.	How does this illustrate the paradoxical theory of change?
		Response-E
I asked her to go back to her usual style—to pull herself up, to speed up her speech—and see what that was like. She did not like it at all, and she actually had difficulty doing it. Afterwards, she said, "I realize that I am as if in a state of terror in here. I am scared that you won't get me, or I will not be able to persuade you or others, or you won't take me into account. I want to tell you what to do and I will not let you go until you say yes, because I am scared otherwise." Then she said, "Can I go back down now?"	When we started, the client was totally unaware of the effects of her natural state, which she reported to be normal. It may be a good idea to take her to that state again after having experienced the other "polarity." In this case, having some other experience she can compare to, she became aware of the impact of her habitual style on her way of making meaning about the world and herself (or vice versa).	The formulation and orchestration of the work was based on the PTC, as is all my work. The simplest thing I did was help Hannah be in her natural state and experience it directly. Our awareness and attention are often held hostage to our ideas, thoughts, emotions, and stories about what we are experiencing, without having direct contact with that experience. Not having made contact with our experience, having never "touched" it, how can we understand it, let alone change it? Before we make direct contact with an experience, we don't really "have" it. There may have been more radical experiment opportunities for this case. However, what is needed is not a "dramatic" experience, but a fully integrated contact experience with who we are at any given moment, during which we stay aware of and interested in our cognitive and emotive faculties in order for any shift or change to create itself.

The Work	Teaching Points	Work: Meta-level Commentary
After going down, she said, "This is much, much more grounded. I am amazed how much stronger and calmer I feel when I allow myself to feel my body." We stayed a little while longer here to help her become more grounded in her new what is.	Now, having had the other experience, she is able to make better contact with her new behavior/state.	[This illustrates how the coach must be holding the original figure framed as the coaching agreement in his awareness to bring the client to a closure that assesses the ROI for the client. It is a gift of accountability toward client learning for the coach to return to the coaching agreement and, collaboratively with the client, work to encourage the client to assess what is different and what can be continued. Dost illustrates how accountability for the work is enhanced by reclaiming the original figure of the coaching agreement as a closure assessment.]
"Wonderful," I said, then asked, "So how impactful do you feel now?" She lit up, and looked as if surprised. "I feel very strong here," she said. "It is as if I still care about you, but I don't care if you accept my ideas or not."	Now we move to closure. We bring back the original figure of wanting to be more impactful, which is why we went through this process in the first place. We say that 80% of the work gets done in the last 20% of the session, as most of the meaning-making and assimilation of the experience take place here.	

Response

Appendix C: Coaching Supervision | 285

The Work—F	Teaching Points	Work-F: Meta-level Commentary
She thought a few minutes more, and said, "I still know who I am even if you don't accept my point." I asked her to repeat the sentence. She did, slower. I asked her to change her language to "I still know who I am even if you don't accept me," which created a shift in her tone of voice, face, and breathing. I made an observation about that, and we talked a little while about what that might mean and its implications. We made a contract to explore this further in future sessions.	Because of this, even though we are closing, as coaches we need to strengthen accountability by paying close attention to new shifts clients may have and how to use those opportunities. As clients process their experience (the UOW), they make new formulations to guide their future and create new meaning. We witness many sentences like the one in this session ("I still know . . ."). Our job is to catch them and use them to help our clients experience them and create new shifts. In this case, my own Cycle came into play when I asked her to change her language. This came from my own ground, my own experience, my own formulations of how we make meaning of the world and ourselves. We also know that everything we do is a little projection—we project our identity into our ideas, our observations, words, and the offered work. Using this awareness, I created a little experiment, which ended up being meaningful. It could just as well have been totally off the mark, in which case we would simply have moved on.	You mention accountability, which is how ICF core competencies strengthen Gestalt coaching. What are the possible examples of how she can extend the work outside the session?
		Response-F
		That was actually discussed for the last 30 minutes of our session. We created some mindfulness practices (i.e., homework experiments) that she was to do every day to build her habit of grounding and returning to her center. She co-designed and agreed to do these short practices at least twice a day to start, adding more as she needed. We also explored ways she could become aware of when she had fallen back into her usual style, using her awareness of somatic reactions and cues. Hannah also enlisted some of her trusted colleagues to be her support team. She shared with them what she was working on and asked for their feedback after specific events, such as meetings, and their periodic feedback on her progress. Both of these strategies—mindfulness practices and support team feedback—were effective.

The Work—G	Teaching Points	Work–G: Meta-level Commentary
I asked, "What are you aware of, as a result of all that we talked about?" She said, "If I can be in this state in the meetings, I will not need to dominate." I asked her to repeat that statement. She did so, while letting out a big breath, and her face lit up. For the rest of the session, we focused on strategies she could use to stay centered and keep herself grounded in her work and other parts of her life.	As coaches, we need to work with our clients and assist them in their being accountable to themselves as they bring this related learning into their life. Such self-accountability is also the outcome of one of the ICF core coaching competencies (*ability to hold attention on what is important for the client, and to leave responsibility with the client to take action*).	What strategies of accountability can be reinforced that haven't been mentioned?

Response–G
This was just the beginning of the work. We worked on her presence and use of self in the following sessions. There were many successes but also many setbacks, as we were working with habitual patterns that had been developed over a lifetime, and for good reasons: they had worked in the settings where they were developed, and even still worked to a degree, yet at great cost to Hannah. We created experiments that helped her become more aware and in contact with the existential reality of how she organized her world and how she was in relationship with it. We explored why and how these habitual patterns were formed and how they sustained themselves. Hannah's growth and change was not immediate but gradual—most of the time, two steps forward, one step back. Yet her development as a leader was demonstrated in the post-engagement 360-degree interviews we made, as people identified the change she herself observed as "impressive." Since our final session, Hannah has received two promotions: one a position promotion, the other involving moving into larger responsibilities in terms of budget and headcount.

It is a wonderful opportunity to present this case. Dost is a master certified practitioner and is well known in Turkey for his supervision to other coaches. This case illustrates the idea of "solo supervision" that is described as the coach "reflecting on each coaching session in a methodical manner that aligns with the [ongoing] goals of the coach."[7] As a practitioner, Dost has been on a path of mindfulness, which infuses all of his work, and the "self-work" on his presence consistently leads to self-inquiry about his use of self. This case is used to offer an example of a high level of solo supervision and reflection on Gestalt coaching, which focuses on supporting the client to become aware and mobilized to realize goals that are concrete, achievable, and deliverable.

Dost's **teaching points** are as follows:

RESISTANCE PHENOMENA

- Resistances are interruptions to "contact," a concept of the Cycle of Experience which we use to assess a client system and create a Unit of Work by choosing what to attend to.
- Resistances are formed as a creative adaptation in response to perceived threats in the environment to one's integrity or livelihood. Resistances decrease, avert, or redirect energy, action, and contact to ensure we get what we want or don't get what we don't want. On a basic physical level, for example, body resistance is what keeps us healthy and alive by regulating what is taken into the body itself (e.g., food intake). But further, resistance serves the system's boundary management when what is present in the environment is perceived as too much, too quick, or too soon.
- Resistances are creative when they are an aware, spontaneous, and choiceful response to a perceived threat in the environment. When a resistance is unaware and habitual, it is not adaptive and not a reasonable response

to the here-and-now phenomenology of the system and/or environment. The resistance becomes a "fixed gestalt" that now prevents the organism from responding appropriately and creatively to what is being offered by the environment, thus resulting in not getting what we want or getting what we don't want.
- Resistances need to be approached with respect. They are not inherently something "bad" that "must be changed." They definitely serve a purpose currently or once served a purpose in the past. The coaching work is to bring habitual, unaware resistances that are part of the self (and so difficult to see) into the client's awareness, so that the client can determine the "cost" of holding on to that resistance.

RESISTANCE AND CYCLE OF EXPERIENCE
- The COE is not just a model of how people move through and toward their needs and wants, but also a tool to identify how they are stopping themselves, and thus where "the work" needs to happen—i.e., the resistances. We are always in contact with something; we break contact with one thing in favor of or to benefit another. Resistances in this respect are not stand-alone concepts but are, instead, integral to the COE.
- When we are paying attention to clients' process (COE), we are mostly assessing what they are doing to move toward (or to not move toward) meeting their needs and wants, both in their presenting story and in the phenomenologically observable data. What we are paying attention to are how resistances manifest in the client's language and voice (e.g., choice of words, sentence structure, details, flow, pitch, speed), in the client's body process (e.g., posture,

gestures, breathing), and in the congruence or incongruence between all of these. We are paying attention to what gets our attention (using our own COE) in terms of what the client makes or breaks contact with.
- The COE, and the resistances integral to it, is our lens and assessment tool for identifying potential Units of Work.

UNIT OF WORK
- Unit of Work is our "intentional change" tool. Through UOWs, we co-create meaningful behavioral experiments for the client from the in-the-moment phenomenology of the here-and-now, thus facilitating learning for the client and for ourselves.
- The UOW guides us in how to join with the client to identify a single figure—theme—to pay attention to during our time together. Robert Kegan has said there are two important change questions: What do you really want? and What will you do to keep from getting it?[8] This perfectly captures the definition of a "theme"—the client's want and the client's resistance. When constructing Units of Work, we identify such themes that include wants and resistances, and sometimes polarities, and the direction the client wants to move toward.
- The UOW guides us in managing the flow of the work. It makes the beginning, middle, and end of the work visible and amendable. It assists us in determining, along with the client, what the next step of the work might be.

PARADOXICAL THEORY OF CHANGE AS OVERARCHING LENS
- As awareness agents, our work is not to help clients "correct," directively change, or eradicate any particular behavior.

Instead, our work is to support clients to discover, become aware, get curious, accept, embody, understand, and integrate. We support clients to become more choiceful, adaptive, and fresh in their responses.
- We use the COE, UOW, and experiments not to create change, but to create awareness, choice, and new possibilities for clients.

One needs to continue self-development, reflect on oneself, and gain ever greater clarity and awareness to be able to serve and be useful for another. As mentioned in previous chapters, a strong and purposeful use of self happens when coaches enhance their competencies by being involved in an ongoing process of integrating horizontal and vertical development enrichment. This process develops coaches' competencies by providing them with knowledge of and practice with different approaches around the work they are doing with their clients, as well as supporting them to see additional opportunities through their internal supervisor. This case is a successful coaching case, with the client voicing appreciation for the shifts that have taken place and where her own return on the coaching investment was "two promotions: one a position promotion, the other involving moving into larger responsibilities in terms of budget and headcount."

The case is offered with the understanding that meta-level thinking, or the opportunity for another perspective, supports the coach in creating awareness of different possibilities and possible alternative interventions with their clients to move them toward their goals. I typically have engaged with colleagues such as Joan Kofodimos, a well-known and respected executive coach who follows a different coaching model, the Constructive-Developmental (C-D) model, that expands my own perspective in approaching clients' dilemmas. Joan's use of C-D theorists assists me to understand clients by moving beyond Gestalt's process approach toward an alternative model that has history and predictive power.[9] This approach offers a capacity to help coaches better understand developmental forces and challenges that impact clients. Working with Dost's case has made me aware of what a great opportunity supervision offers, and how important an appreciative and validating stance is. It takes a highly trusting stance to invite supervision without feeling criticized. While Dost's case illustrates how Dost has been his own thought partner, for so many other coaches, a more formalized supervision may be of benefit. Various types of supervision are available, including not only "solo supervision," but also peer supervision, conducted with a coaching buddy or small group; formal individualized supervision, which involves meeting with a senior master coach; formal group supervision, which has a consistent group of participant colleagues meeting for one to two years; spot supervision, which allows for short-term consultations between coach and supervisor regarding a specific dilemma; and internal coach supervision, where organizations invite external supervisors in for the development of the organization's internal coaches.[10] What is interesting about coach supervision is that consistent supervision is also linked to coaches feeling more confident and developing a more successful coaching practice.[11]

Philippe Rosinski has recently argued for an "integrative coaching supervision" that takes into account global coaching practices, identifying it as "a holistic approach that calls upon multiple and interconnected perspectives" that lead to more effective and more creative supervisory work.[12] Rosinski suggests an integrative model that adopts six interconnected perspectives to provide the holistic value that we as Gestalt coaches adhere to. The six-fold perspectives Rosinski recommends as required lenses for all coaches are: physical, cultural, political, spiritual, managerial, and psychological.

The physical perspective, as we have discussed earlier in Chapter 5, includes our bodies and our bodily sensations, which comprise what we call somatic intelligence. The cultural perspective entails supervisory coaching as an effective approach to overcoming what Robert Kegan describes as immunity to change, because the supervisor assists supervisees to make contact with different worldviews that may challenge their "limiting norms, values, and assumptions" and move toward "increasing complexity for greater creativity."[13] The third perspective is the political, which is often difficult for executive supervisees who see politics "as an evil activity that should be eliminated." But Rosinski argues that the political perspective is important to enable an appreciation of why politics in organizations is a basic fact of life and to develop adaptive ways to deal with it. The fourth perspective, the spiritual perspective, is seen as aligned with the growing focus on mindfulness, which is defined as "maintaining a moment-to-moment awareness of our thoughts, feelings, bodily sensations, and surrounding environment."[14] Mindfulness, which we have already defined as paying attention in the moment on purpose and without judgment, serves to support a stance of gratitude and emotional equanimity, and because of greater calmness, we reap the benefits of better thinking. While perhaps more ephemeral as an evidence-based example, mindfulness researchers, particularly those at the Search Inside Yourself Leadership Institute, are gathering growing evidence that mindfulness both in coaching and in coaching supervision enlarges the adaptive capacity of all involved. The managerial perspective is identified with important areas such as "time management, personal organization, project management, and more generally, practices aimed at increasing results and productivity." This perspective involves metrics and surveys to demonstrate results and describe productivity. Rosinski observes that while most coaching supervisors may be more familiar with managerial models, this would not necessarily be true for supervisors with a psychotherapy background. Finally, for the psychological perspective, Rosinski argues that having a healthy and mature ego that allows the coaching supervisor to engage her supervisees in a constructive and fluid manner is a required condition for an effective supervisory coaching relationship. Rosinski adds that supervisory coaches would do well to learn from various schools of psychology to expand their coaching effectiveness.[15]

Supervising coaches who aim to support the development of supervisees need to have reached a level of development at least equal to the supervisee's level, and preferably superior to it. This concept is consistent with the work of Petrie and other developmental theorists. Rosinski's work on the phenomenon he identifies as global coaching includes everything of concern to a coach's development, linking multiple perspectives as possible leverages to address alternative viewpoints in order to manage complex challenges. He notes that "[a]s avid and polyvalent learners, integrative coaching supervisors are aware of their limitations and are therefore keen to collaborate with other professionals with complementary know-how to serve their supervisees, or to refer the latter to the former. This way, supervisees' growth is not restricted by the supervisor's inevitable limitations but can be further enabled by combining diverse standpoints."[16]

Recently, for example, I was the mentor coach and supervisor for two colleagues attempting to gain their ICF MCC certification. The process of attaining this credential has become arduous. My responsibility was to question my own capacity to serve them well, as these colleagues had suffered previous application rejections.

Actually, this issue of MCC certification has become a larger credentialing issue, as globally there has been a serious pattern of credentialing failure. Worried about my colleagues' failures, I intentionally recused myself and, to avoid any suggestion of bias, recommended a formal ICF assessor who was not Gestalt-oriented for this important activity. I honored myself and my colleagues by being more expansive and calling in another colleague to work with them. My concern was, and is, that many people equate Gestalt coaching with Gestalt therapy, and therefore have preconceptions about our style of coaching. This concern in part motivated this book, but in this instance, my calling in another mentor coach sent a message to my colleagues that said, "I am willing to do whatever is needed to support your success." It was unclear to me whether one reason my colleagues were being failed was because there might have been a bias against Gestalt coaching. In supervision, as in all coaching, we are ethically required to speak to our strengths and limitations, and we must take responsibility for the shugyo of serving our supervisees with the accountability for effectiveness that they deserve.

At the same time, Rosinski also lists the arguments against *mandatory* coaching supervision. These arguments include: 1) Blurring the distinction between coaching and psychotherapy, where coaching supervision has a flavor of the supervision experience from the psychotherapy model; 2) A one-size-fits-all approach, which discourages diverse learning across multiple domains; 3) Technical or "mechanistic" interpretations of coaching competencies that erode the necessary humanistic values; and 4) Rigid or narrow frameworks that undermine and diminish alternative possibilities.[17]

"Coaching supervision," Rosinski notes from the start, "is a relatively new but already somewhat controversial discipline."[18] Our challenge in a supervisory position is to move from being the superficial coach or the expert coach or the nice coach—coaches

Appendix C: Coaching Supervision | 295

who lack knowledge or caring or complexity, or all of these—to become the "remarkable coach," who is committed to ongoing learning and growth in all areas of knowledge and skills while engaging in coaching as a transcendent encounter that seeks connection with clients as well as supervisees in deeply contactful ways (Figure 1).

Figure 1 Rosinski Superficial, Nice, Expert, and Remarkable Coaches[19]

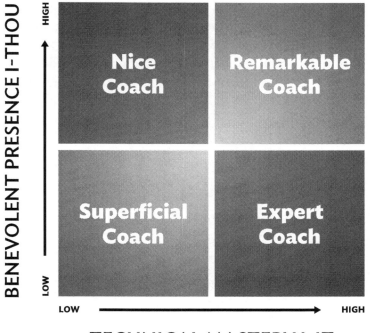

Maybe remarkable coaches are most self-evident because they seem to "reveal" themselves as deeply human and deeply credible. They do the self-work necessary to address the challenges of head and heart and technical know-how in order to best serve their clients and supervisees.

Let me close this discussion with an invitation to coach and to learn at any level of your competence. With practice, commitment, feedback, and good intention, you will be on the road to becoming the coach you desire to be. Self-compassion is a strong ally for this journey. As my dear colleague Marcia Reynolds says, "Clients don't expect you to be perfect. They need you to be present."[20] In "Gestalt-speak" we would say: Be present in your presence and in your use of self. Do the horizontal development work of learning both the Gestalt coaching and ICF competencies, and then, in vertical development mode, learn to leverage the gifts of your presence so that you have used all of your awareness with greater choice and satisfying interventions. You and your clients deserve this satisfaction.

Bibliography

Bacon, Terry R., and Karen I. Spear. *Adaptive Coaching: The Art and Practice of a Client-Centered Approach to Performance Improvement.* Mountain View, CA: Davies-Black, 2003.

Beisser, Arnold. "The Paradoxical Theory of Change." 1970. In *Gestalt Therapy Now: Theory, Techniques, Applications,* edited by Joen Fagan and Irma Lee Shepherd, 77–80. Gouldsboro, ME: Gestalt Journal Press, 2006. Also at *Gestalt.org,* accessed June 5, 2015. http://www.gestalt.org/arnie.htm.

Bergquist, William H., and Dorothy E. Siminovitch. "Coaching High Potential and High Performance Clients." *International Journal of Coaching in Organizations* 8, no. 1 (2010): 78–93.

Bluckert, Peter. "The Gestalt Approach to Coaching." In *The Complete Handbook of Coaching,* edited by Elaine Cox, Tatiana Bachkirova, and David Clutterbuck, 80–93. London & Thousand Oaks, CA: Sage, 2010.

———. *Gestalt Coaching: Right Here, Right Now.* Maidenhead, UK: Open University Press, 2015.

Bowman, Charles E. "The History and Development of Gestalt Therapy." In *Gestalt Therapy: History, Theory, and Practice,* edited by Ansel L. Woldt and Sarah M. Toman, 3–20. Thousand Oaks, CA: Sage, 2005.

Britton, Jennifer J. *Effective Group Coaching: Tried and Tested Tools and Resources for Optimal Group Coaching Results.* Mississauga, Ontario: Wiley, 2010.

Brock, Vikki G. *Sourcebook of Coaching History.* 2nd ed. N.p.: Vikki G. Brock, 2014.

Carroll, Michael. "From Mindless to Mindful Practice: On Learning Reflection in Supervision." *Psychotherapy in Australia* 15, no. 4 (2009): 43–51. Accessed August 29, 2016. http://emergesupervision.nz/wp-content/uploads/2014/11/learning_reflection.pdf.

Cashman, Kevin. *Leadership from the Inside Out: Becoming a Leader for Life.* 2nd ed. San Francisco: Berrett-Koehler, 2008.

Chidiac, Marie-Anne, and Sally Denham-Vaughan. "The Process of Presence: Energetic Availability and Fluid Responsiveness." *British Gestalt Journal* 16, no. 1 (2007): 9–19. Accessed February 9, 2016. http://www.relationalchange.org/pdf/03-chidiac.pdf.

Clarkson, Petrūska. *Gestalt Counselling in Action.* 1989. 4th ed. Updated by Simon Cavicchia. Los Angeles: Sage, 2014.

Cooper, Robert K., and Ayman Sawaf. *Executive E.Q.: Emotional Intelligence in Leadership and Organizations.* New York: Perigee, 1998.

Cuddy, Amy. *Presence: Bringing Your Boldest Self to Your Biggest Challenges.* New York: Little, Brown, 2015.

Duhigg, Charles. *The Power of Habit: Why We Do What We Do in Life and Business.* New York: Random House, 2014.

Eoyang, Glenda H. *Coping with Chaos: Seven Simple Tools.* Circle Pines, MN: Lagumo, 2009.

Feder, Bud, and Jon Frew, eds. *Beyond the Hot Seat Revisited: Gestalt Approaches to Group.* New Orleans: Gestalt Institute Press, 2008.

Gillie, Marion. "Commentary III: Applying Gestalt Theory to Coaching." *Gestalt Review* 13, no. 3 (2009): 254–260. Accessed

June 5, 2015. http://www.gisc.org/gestaltreview/documents/
SSimon_GRArticle_with_Responses_GR13.3.pdf.

Gillie, Marion, and Marjorie Shackleton. "Gestalt Coaching or Gestalt Therapy? Ethical and Professional Considerations on Entering the Emotional World of the Coaching Client." *International Gestalt Journal* 32, no. 1 (2009): 173–196.

Glaser, Judith E. *Conversational Intelligence: How Great Leaders Build Trust and Get Extraordinary Results.* Brookline, MA: Bibliomotion, 2014.

Goleman, Daniel. *Emotional Intelligence: Why It Can Matter More than IQ.* 1995. New York: Bantam, 2005.

———. *Social Intelligence: The New Science of Human Relationships.* New York: Bantam, 2007.

Hanafin, Jonno. "Rules of Thumb for Awareness Agents: With a Tip o' the Hat to Herb Shepard." *OD Practitioner* 36, no. 4 (2004): 24–28.

Heifetz, Ronald, Alexander Grashow, and Marty Linsky. *The Practice of Adaptive Leadership: Tools and Tactics for Changing Your Organization and the World.* Boston: Harvard Business Press, 2009.

Huckabay, Mary Ann. "An Overview of the Theory and Practice of Gestalt Group Process." 1992. In *Gestalt Therapy: Perspectives and Applications*, edited by Edwin C. Nevis, 303–330. Cambridge, MA: GestaltPress, 2000.

Huffington, Arianna. *Thrive: The Third Metric to Redefining Success and Creating a Life of Well-Being, Wisdom, and Wonder.* New York: Harmony Books, 2014.

Johansen, Bob. Interview. "Speed in a VUCA World: How Leaders of the Future Will Execute Strategy." *Forum* 2010. Accessed May 25, 2015. http://www.forum.com/downloads/transcripts/VUCA-Interview-2010-Final.pdf.

———. *Leaders Make the Future: Ten New Leadership Skills for an Uncertain World.* 2nd ed. San Francisco: Berrett-Koehler, 2012.

Joyce, Phil, and Charlotte Sills. *Skills in Gestalt: Counselling and Psychotherapy*. 3rd ed. Los Angeles: Sage, 2014.

Karp, H. B. *The Change Leader: Using a Gestalt Approach with Work Groups*. San Francisco: Jossey-Bass/Pfeiffer, 1996.

Katzenbach, Jon R., and Douglas K. Smith. *The Wisdom of Teams: Creating the High-Performance Organization*. 1993. New York: HarperCollins, 2003.

Kegan, Robert, and Lisa Lahey. "The Real Reason People Won't Change." *Harvard Business Review* November 2001. Accessed May 26, 2015. https://hbr.org/2001/11/the-real-reason-people-wont-change.

Kegan, Robert, and Lisa Laskow Lahey. *Immunity to Change: How to Overcome It and Unlock the Potential in Yourself and Your Organization*. Boston: Harvard Business Press, 2009.

Kepner, Elaine. "Gestalt Group Process." 1980. In *Beyond the Hot Seat Revisited: Gestalt Approaches to Group*, edited by Bud Feder and Jon Frew, 17–37. New Orleans: Gestalt Institute Press, 2008.

Kitzler, Richard. "A Trialogue between Laura Perls, Richard Kitzler, and E. Mark Stern." In *Gestalt Voices*, edited by Edward W. L. Smith, 18–32. Gouldsboro, ME: Gestalt Journal Press, 1989.

Kolb, David A. *Experiential Learning: Experience as the Source of Learning and Development*. 2nd ed. Upper Saddle River, NJ: Pearson, 2014.

Latner, Joel. "Systems and Field Theories in Gestalt Therapy." *Gestalt Journal* 6, no. 2 (1983): 71–90.

———. "The Theory of Gestalt Therapy." In *Gestalt Therapy: Perspectives and Applications*, edited by Edwin C. Nevis, 13–56. Cambridge, MA: GestaltPress, 2000.

Mackewn, Jennifer. *Developing Gestalt Counselling: A Field Theoretical and Relational Model of Contemporary Gestalt Counselling and Psychotherapy*. 1997. London: Sage, 2009.

McKee, Annie, Richard Boyatzis, and Frances Johnston. *Becoming a Resonant Leader: Develop Your Emotional Intelligence, Renew*

Your Relationships, Sustain Your Effectiveness. Boston: Harvard Business Press, 2008.

McLean, Pamela. *The Completely Revised Handbook of Coaching: A Developmental Approach.* 2nd ed. San Francisco: Jossey-Bass, 2012.

Melnick, Joseph, and Sonia March Nevis. "Gestalt Therapy Methodology." In *Gestalt Therapy: History, Theory, and Practice*, edited by Ansel L. Woldt and Sarah M. Toman, 101–115. Thousand Oaks, CA: Sage, 2005.

Minahan, Matt. "The Foundations of Coaching Roots in OD." *OD Practitioner* 38, no. 3 (2006): 4–7.

Nevis, Edwin C. "Gestalt Therapy and Organization Development: A Historical Perspective, 1930–1996." *Gestalt Review* 1, no. 2 (1997): 110–130.

———. *Organizational Consulting: A Gestalt Approach.* 1987. Cambridge, MA: GestaltPress, 2001.

O'Neill, Mary Beth. *Executive Coaching with Backbone and Heart: A Systems Approach to Engaging Leaders with Their Challenges.* 2nd ed. San Francisco: Jossey-Bass, 2007.

Partlett, Malcolm. "Contemporary Gestalt Therapy: Field Theory." In *Gestalt Therapy: History, Theory, and Practice*, edited by Ansel L. Woldt and Sarah M. Toman, 41–63. Thousand Oaks, CA: Sage, 2005.

———. "The Unified Field in Practice." *Gestalt Review* 1, no. 1 (1997): 16–33. Accessed May 25, 2015. http://www.gisc.org/gestaltreview/documents/theunifiedfieldinpractice.pdf.

Perls, Frederick S., Ralph Hefferline, and Paul Goodman. *Gestalt Therapy: Excitement and Growth in the Human Personality.* Rev. ed. 1951. New York: Julian, 1994.

Petrie, Nick. "The How-To of Vertical Development Leadership—Part 2: 30 Experts, 3 Conditions, and 15 Approaches." *Center for Creative Leadership* 2015. Accessed July 28, 2015. http://insights.ccl.org/wp-content/uploads/2015/04/vertical-LeadersPart2.pdf.

———. "Vertical Leadership Development–Part I: Developing Leaders for a Complex World." *Center for Creative Leadership* 2014. Accessed May 26, 2015. http://insights.ccl.org/wp-content/uploads/2015/04/VerticalLeadersPart1.pdf.

Polster, Erving, and Miriam Polster. *Gestalt Therapy Integrated: Contours of Theory and Practice.* New York: Vintage Books, 1973.

Reynolds, Marcia. *The Discomfort Zone: How Leaders Turn Difficult Conversations into Breakthroughs.* San Francisco: Berrett-Koehler, 2014.

Rock, David. "SCARF: A Brain-Based Model for Collaborating with and Influencing Others." *NeuroLeadership Journal* 1 (2008): 1–9. Accessed May 25, 2015. http://www.scarf360.com/files/SCARF-NeuroleadershipArticle.pdf.

Rock, David, and Linda J. Page. *Coaching with the Brain in Mind: Foundations for Practice.* Hoboken: Wiley & Sons, 2009.

Rosenfeld, Edward. "An Oral History of Gestalt Therapy: Part One: A Conversation with Laura Perls." *Gestalt Journal* 1, no. 1 (1978): 8–31.

Rosinski, Philippe. "Integrative Coaching Supervision." *Global Coaching Perspectives* July 2016 Issue 10: 34–39. Accessed August 25, 2016. http://www.associationforcoaching.com/media/uploads/gcp_july_mag(9).pdf.

Seashore, Charles N., Edith Whitfield Seashore, and Gerald M. Weinberg. *What Did You Say? The Art of Giving and Receiving Feedback.* North Attleborough, MA: Douglas Charles Press, 1992.

Scharmer, C. Otto. *Theory U: Leading from the Future as It Emerges: The Social Technology of Presencing.* San Francisco: Berrett-Koehler, 2009.

———. "Uncovering the Blind Spot of Leadership." *Leader to Leader* 47 (2008): 52–59. Accessed May 25, 2015. http://www.allegrosite.be/artikels/Uncovering_the_blind_spot_of_leadership.pdf.

Scharmer, Otto, and Katrin Kaufer. *Leading from the Emerging Future: From Ego-System to Eco-System Economics*. San Francisco: Berrett-Koehler, 2013.

Senge, Peter. *The Fifth Discipline: The Art and Practice of the Learning Organization*. 1990. New York: Doubleday, 2006.

Silsbee, Doug. *Presence-Based Coaching: Cultivating Self-Generative Leaders through Mind, Body, and Heart*. San Francisco: Jossey-Bass, 2008.

Siminovitch, Dorothy. "Define Your Unique Identity." In *Ready, Aim, Soar! The Expert Insights System for Business Growth and Success in the 21st Century*, edited by Brynn Burger, 210–215. Charlotte, NC: Expert Insights Publishing, 2012.

———. "Gestalt Coaching with Dorothy Siminovitch." Interview by Katrina Burrus. Podcast audio, October 8, 2015. Accessed February 24, 2016. http://www.mkbconseil.ch/eeceec41-gestalt-coaching-with-dorothy-siminovich/.

———. "Interview with Edie Seashore: On Coaching." *International Journal of Coaching in Organizations* 8, no. 1 (2010): 19–39.

———. "The Pragmatic Magic of Gestalt Coaching." Interview by Robert Holmes. Podcast audio, January 16, 2014. Accessed February 24, 2016. http://www.frazerholmes.com/gestalt-coaching/.

———. "A Tale of Many Cities: Gestalt-Based Executive and Team Coaching and Awareness IQ." Interview by Krister Lowe. Podcast audio, November 11, 2015. Accessed February 24, 2016. http://www.teamcoachingzone.com/dorothysiminovitch/.

Siminovitch, Dorothy E. "Gestalt-Based Coaching Competencies: The Importance of Presence and Use of Self." *Choice* 13, no. 3 (2015): 41–43.

———. "Practicing Gestalt." *Coaching World* August 2013, no. 7: 36–39. Accessed January 11, 2016. http://www.joomag.com/magazine/mag/0163339001381775357?feature=archive.

Siminovitch, Dorothy E., and Ann M. Van Eron. "The Power of Presence and Intentional Use of Self: Coaching for Awareness, Choice and Change." *International Journal of Coaching in Organizations* 6, no. 3 (2008): 90–111.

———. "The Pragmatics of Magic: The Work of Gestalt Coaching." *OD Practitioner* 38, no. 1 (2006): 50–55.

Soosalu, Grant. *Coaching Wisdom: Coaching the Head, Heart and Gut with mBraining: Essays, Ideas and Explorations on Multiple Brain Integration Techniques (mBIT) Coaching.* N.p.: Worldwide Coaching Magazine, 2015. Kindle edition.

Storjohann, Ginny. "This Thing Called Coaching: A Consultant's Story." *OD Practitioner* 38, no. 3 (2006): 12–16.

Strozzi-Heckler, Richard. *The Leadership Dojo: Build Your Foundation as an Exemplary Leader.* Berkeley, CA: Frog, 2007.

Tan, Chade-Meng. *Search Inside Yourself: The Unexpected Path to Achieving Success, Happiness (and World Peace).* New York: HarperCollins, 2012.

Tolbert, Mary Ann Rainey, and Jonno Hanafin. "Use of Self in OD Consulting: What Matters Is Presence." In *The NTL Handbook of Organization Change and Development: Principles, Practices, and Perspectives*, edited by Brenda B. Jones and Michael Brazzel, 69–82. San Francisco: Pfeiffer, 2006.

Uhl-Bien, Mary, Russ Marion, and Bill McKelvey. "Complexity Leadership Theory: Shifting Leadership from the Industrial Age to the Knowledge Era." *Leadership Quarterly* 18, no. 4 (2007): 298–319. Accessed May 25, 2015. http://digitalcommons.unl.edu/leadershipfacpub/18.

Vaill, Peter B. *Managing as a Performing Art: New Ideas for a World of Chaotic Change.* San Francisco: Jossey-Bass, 1989.

Wheatley, Margaret J. *Leadership and the New Science: Discovering Order in a Chaotic World.* 3rd ed. San Francisco: Berrett-Koehler, 2006.

Williamson, Sally. *The Hidden Factor: Executive Presence: How to Find It, Keep It, and Leverage It.* Atlanta: Sally Williamson & Assoc., 2011.

Woldt, Ansel L., and Sarah M. Toman, eds. *Gestalt Therapy: History, Theory, and Practice.* Thousand Oaks, CA: Sage, 2005.

Yontef, Gary M. "Gestalt Therapy Theory of Change." In *Gestalt Therapy: History, Theory, and Practice*, edited by Ansel L. Woldt and Sarah M. Toman, 81–100. Thousand Oaks, CA: Sage, 2005.

Zinker, Joseph. *Creative Process in Gestalt Therapy.* New York: Vintage Books, 1977.

Endnotes

Introduction

[1] From the start, I embraced the International Coach Federation's leadership in the field, and encouraged our training programs to do so as well.

[2] See Dorothy E. Siminovitch and Ann M. Van Eron, "The Pragmatics of Magic: The Work of Gestalt Coaching," *OD Practitioner* 38, no. 1 (2006): 50–55.

[3] Laura Perls, in Edward Rosenfeld, "An Oral History of Gestalt Therapy, Part One: A Conversation with Laura Perls," *Gestalt Journal 1*, no. 1 (1978): 24.

[4] See, for example, the essays collected in Ansel L. Woldt and Sarah M. Toman, eds., *Gestalt Therapy: History, Theory, and Practice* (Thousand Oaks, CA: Sage, 2005).

[5] Richard Kitzler, "A Trialogue between Laura Perls, Richard Kitzler, and E. Mark Stern," in *Gestalt Voices,* ed. Edward W. L. Smith (Gouldsboro, ME: Gestalt Journal Press, 1989), 24.

[6] Charles E. Bowman, "The History and Development of Gestalt Therapy," in *Gestalt Therapy: History, Theory, and Practice,* ed. Ansel L. Woldt and Sarah M. Toman (Thousand Oaks, CA: Sage, 2005), 17.

[7] As Elaine Kepner, a noted Gestalt practitioner and preeminent faculty member at GIC, stated: "We have had a community process at the Gestalt Institute of Cleveland which makes it difficult to ascribe a formulation to any one individual. Since we began offering workshops and training

programs to the public in 1958, the majority of programs have been planned, designed and led by staff teams in varying combinations. Because of this there has been a continuous and reciprocal faculty learning process, so that the formulations and practices of any one person tend to be that person's unique synthesis rather than that person's unique contribution. However, there are several persons whose inputs and perspectives on group dynamics and system processes have been highly important and influential. They are Edwin Nevis, . . . Leonard Hirsch, and Richard Wallen . . . ." In *Beyond the Hot Seat: Gestalt Approaches to Groups,* ed. Bud Feder and Ruth Ronall (New York: Brunner/Mazel, 1980), 10.

[8] See, for example, Peter Bluckert, *Gestalt Coaching: Right Here, Right Now* (Maidenhead, UK: Open University Press, 2015).

Chapter 1

[1] Bob Johansen, "Speed in a VUCA World: How Leaders of the Future Will Execute Strategy," interview with *Forum* 2010, accessed May 25, 2015, http://www.forum.com/downloads/transcripts/VUCA-Interview-2010-Final.pdf. See also Bob Johansen, *Leaders Make the Future: Ten New Leadership Skills for an Uncertain World,* 2nd ed. (San Francisco: Berrett-Koehler, 2012).

[2] For an historical overview of this evolving theory, see Edwin C. Nevis, "Gestalt Therapy and Organization Development: A Historical Perspective, 1930–1996," *Gestalt Review* 1, no. 2 (1997): 110–130.

[3] Joel Latner, "The Theory of Gestalt Therapy," in *Gestalt Therapy: Perspectives and Applications,* ed. Edwin C. Nevis (Cambridge, MA: GestaltPress, 2000), 15.

[4] Jon Kabat-Zinn, *Wherever You Go, There You Are: Mindfulness Meditation in Everyday Life* (New York: Hyperion, 1994), 4.

[5] "Bracketing . . . is not about attempting to be free from preconceptions, attitudes or reactions. It is an attempt to keep us close to the newness of the here-and-now moment." Phil Joyce and Charlotte Sills, *Gestalt Skills: Counselling and Psychotherapy,* 3rd ed. (Los Angeles: Sage, 2014), 18.

[6] Michael Carroll, "From Mindless to Mindful Practice: On Learning Reflection in Supervision," *Psychotherapy in Australia* 15, no. 4 (2009): 43, accessed August 29, 2016, http://emergesupervision.nz/wp-content/uploads/2014/11/learning_reflection.pdf.

7   See, for example, his *Theory U: Leading from the Future as It Emerges: The Social Technology of Presencing* (San Francisco: Berrett-Koehler, 2009).

8   Scharmer, *Theory U,* 134.

9   Juriah Mosin, "Optical Illusion Created by Clay Columns," accessed May 22, 2015, http://www.dreamstime.com/royalty-free-stock-photography-optical-illusion-created-clay-columns-image5967577.

10 Arnold Beisser, "The Paradoxical Theory of Change," in *Gestalt Therapy Now: Theory, Techniques, Applications,* ed. Joen Fagan and Irma L. Shepherd (Palo Alto: Science and Behavior Books, 1970/2006), 77–80.

11 Gary M. Yontef, "Gestalt Therapy Theory of Change," in *Gestalt Therapy: History, Theory, and Practice,* ed. Ansel L. Woldt and Sarah M. Toman (Thousand Oaks, CA: Sage Publications, 2005), 83.

12 Mel Zuckerman, "How I Did It: Mel Zuckerman, Chairman, Canyon Ranch," *Inc.com,* December 1, 2007, accessed December 31, 2015, http://www.inc.com/magazine/20071201/how-i-did-it-mel-zuckerman-chairman-canyon-ranch.html.

13 For a similarly rich understanding of multiple intelligences, see Judith E. Glaser, *Conversational Intelligence: How Great Leaders Build Trust and Get Extraordinary Results* (Brookline, MA: Bibliomotion, 2014).

14 We explore Awareness IQ in different ways throughout the following chapters.

15 Joel Latner, "Systems and Field Theories in Gestalt Therapy," *Gestalt Journal* 6, no. 2 (1983): 72.

16 "Kurt Lewin." *New World Encyclopedia,* accessed February 24, 2016, http://www.newworldencyclopedia.org/entry/Kurt_Lewin.

17 C. Otto Scharmer, "Uncovering the Blind Spot of Leadership," *Leader to Leader* 47 (2008), 52–59, accessed May 25, 2015, http://www.allegrosite.be/artikels/Uncovering_the_blind_spot_of_leadership.pdf.

18 Nick Petrie, "Vertical Development Leadership–Part I: Developing Leaders for a Complex World," *Center for Creative Leadership* 2014, accessed May 26, 2015, http://insights.ccl.org/wp-content/uploads/2015/04/VerticalLeadersPart1.pdf, and "The How-To of Vertical Development Leadership–Part 2: Experts, 3 Conditions, and 15 Approaches," *Center for Creative Leadership* 2015, accessed May 26, 2015, http://insights.ccl.org/wp-content/uploads/2015/04/verticalLeadersPart2.pdf.

[19] Petrie, "Vertical Development Leadership," 7.

[20] Malcolm Partlett, "Contemporary Gestalt Therapy: Field Theory," in *Gestalt Therapy: History, Theory, and Practice*, ed. Ansel L. Woldt and Sarah M. Toman (Thousand Oaks, CA: Sage, 2005), 47.

[21] Gary M. Yontef, qtd. in Malcolm Partlett, "Contemporary Gestalt Therapy," 47.

[22] See Giacomo Rizzolatti and Corrado Sinigaglia, *Mirrors in the Brain: How Our Minds Share Actions and Emotions* (New York: Oxford UP, 2006).

[23] In part, a distinction is enforced because of inherent differences between personal therapy and organizational consulting and expected outcomes. See Marion Gillie's concise overview of the issue in "Commentary III: Applying Gestalt Theory to Coaching," *Gestalt Review* 13, no. 3 (2009): 254–260. Also see Marion Gillie and Marjorie Shackleton, "Gestalt Coaching or Gestalt Therapy? Ethical and Professional Considerations on Entering the Emotional World of the Coaching Client," *International Gestalt Journal* 32, no. 1 (2009): 173–196.

[24] As an example, the International Coach Federation's definition of coaching is "partnering with clients in a thought-provoking and creative process," and asserting the client to be "the expert in his or her life and work" and mutually "responsible and accountable" for the coaching work. "Coaching FAQs," *Coachfederation.org*, accessed April 18, 2016, http://coachfederation.org/need/landing.cfm?ItemNumber=978&_ga=1.77825684.1821737589.1449688935.

[25] "Safe emergency" is from Frederick S. Perls, Ralph Hefferline, and Paul Goodman, *Gestalt Therapy: Excitement and Growth in the Human Personality*, rev. ed. (New York: Julian, 1994/1951). We explore safe emergency and safety in the coaching encounter in more depth in Chapter 6.

[26] See the International Coach Federation's list, "Core Competencies," *Coachfederation.org*, accessed May 25, 2015, http://www.coachfederation.org/credential/landing.cfm?ItemNumber=2206&navItemNumber=576.

[27] See, for example: David Rock and Linda Page, *Coaching with the Brain in Mind: Foundations for Practice* (Hoboken, NJ: Wiley, 2009); Margaret J. Wheatley, *Leadership and the New Science: Discovering Order in a Chaotic World*, 3rd ed. (San Francisco: Berrett-Koehler, 2006); Peter M. Senge, *The Fifth Discipline: The Art & Practice of the Learning Organization* (New York:

Doubleday, 2006); Annie McKee, Richard Boyatzis, and Frances Johnston, *Becoming a Resonant Leader: Develop Your Emotional Intelligence, Renew Your Relationships, Sustain Your Effectiveness* (Boston: Harvard Business Press, 2008); Daniel Goleman, *Social Intelligence: The New Science of Human Relationships* (New York: Bantam Books, 2007); Robert K. Cooper and Ayman Sawaf, *Executive EQ: Emotional Intelligence in Leadership and Organizations* (New York: Perigee, 1998).

Chapter 2

[1] Robert Kegan and Lisa Lahey, "The Real Reason People Won't Change," *Harvard Business Review* November 2001, accessed May 25, 2015, https://hbr.org/2001/11/the-real-reason-people-wont-change/ar/1. See also Robert Kegan and Lisa Laskow Lahey, *Immunity to Change: How to Overcome It and Unlock Potential in Yourself and Your Organization* (Boston: Harvard Business Press, 2009).

[2] David Livingstone Smith, *Why We Lie: The Evolutionary Roots of Deception and the Unconscious Mind* (New York: St. Martin's Press, 2004), 3, 21.

[3] Ellen J. Langer, *Mindfulness* (Boston: DaCapo, 2014), 21.

[4] "Learning from within" is from Kevin Cashman, *Leadership from the Inside Out*, 2nd ed. (Berrett-Koehler, 2008).

[5] Michael Carroll, "From Mindless to Mindful Practice: On Learning Reflection in Supervision," *Psychotherapy in Australia* 15, no. 4 (2009): 45, accessed August 29, 2016, http://emergesupervision.nz/wp-content/uploads/2014/11/learning_reflection.pdf.

[6] Jan Koenderink, *World, Environment, Umwelt and Innerworld* (De Clootcrans Press, 2012), accessed May 25, 2015, http://www.gestaltrevision.be/pdfs/koenderink/Umwelts.pdf.

[7] David M. Eagleman, "The Umwelt," *Edge.org*, accessed May 25, 2015, http://www.edge.org/response-detail/11498.

[8] Edwin C. Nevis, *Organizational Consulting: A Gestalt Approach* (Cambridge, MA: GestaltPress, 2001), 102.

[9] A "safe emergency" allows for client anxiety when engaging the risk of change—it is "a felt emergency, but the emergency is safe and controllable and known to be so by both [client and coach]." Perls, Hefferline, and Goodman, *Gestalt Therapy*, 64.

10   The term "amygdala hijack" is Daniel Goleman's. It refers to emotional responses that are immediate, overwhelming, and out of proportion with the original stimulus. Daniel Goleman, *Emotional Intelligence: Why It Can Matter More than IQ* (New York: Bantam, 2005).

11   Arnold Beisser, "The Paradoxical Theory of Change," in *Gestalt Therapy Now: Theories, Techniques, Applications,* ed. Joen Fagan and Irma Lee Shepherd (Gouldsboro, ME: Gestalt Journal Press, 2006), 77–80.

12   Kevin Cashman, *Leadership from the Inside Out*, 2nd ed. (Berrett-Koehler, 2008). Neuroscience research further confirms that deep change (that is, new and assimilated learning) occurs most strongly from *self-generated* insights and meaning-making.

13   Graham Lee, qtd. in Marion Gillie, "Commentary III: Applying Gestalt Theory to Coaching," *Gestalt Review* 13, no. 3 (2009): 255, accessed June 5, 2015, http://www.gisc.org/gestaltreview/documents/SSimon_GRArticle_with_Responses_GR13.3.pdf.

14   Amy Cuddy, *Presence: Bringing Your Boldest Self to Your Biggest Challenges* (New York: Little, Brown, 2015), 25.

15   Bob Johansen, "Speed in a VUCA World: How Leaders of the Future Will Execute Strategy," interview with *Forum* 2010, accessed May 25, 2015, http://www.forum.com/downloads/transcripts/VUCA-Interview-2010-Final.pdf.

16   Jennifer Mackewn, *Developing Gestalt Counselling: A Field Theoretical and Relational Model of Contemporary Gestalt Counselling and Psychotherapy* (London: Sage, 2009), 67.

17   Chade-Meng Tan, *Search Inside Yourself: The Unexpected Path to Achieving Success, Happiness (and World Peace)* (New York: HarperCollins, 2012).

18   Holly Finn, "How to End the Age of Inattention," *WSJ.com,* June 1, 2012, accessed May 25, 2015. http://www.wsj.com/articles/SB10001424052702303640104577436323276530002.

19   Kirk Lawrence, "Developing Leaders in a VUCA Environment," UNC Kenan-Flagler Business School, UNC Executive Development, 2013, 7, accessed June 5, 2015, http://www.growbold.com/2013/developing-leaders-in-a-vuca-environment_UNC.2013.pdf.

20   Nick Petrie, "Vertical Leadership Development–Part I: Developing Leaders for a Complex World," *Center for Creative Leadership,* 2014,

accessed May 26, 2015, http://insights.ccl.org/wp-content/uploads/2015/04/VerticalLeadersPart1.pdf.

[21] Otto Scharmer and Katrin Kaufer, *Leading from the Emerging Future: From Ego-System to Eco-System Economics* (San Francisco: Berrett-Koehler, 2013).

[22] Scharmer and Kaufer, *Leading from the Emerging Future,* 68.

[23] George Kohlrieser, "10 'People' Mistakes Leaders Make," *IMD.org*, June 2012, accessed June 5, 2015, http://www.imd.org/research/challenges/damaging-leadership-mistakes-management-george-kohlrieser.cfm.

Chapter 3

[1] Originally developed at the Gestalt Institute of Cleveland (GIC) over 40 years ago.

[2] Joseph Melnick and Sonia March Nevis, for example, call it the "continuum of experience" ("Gestalt Therapy Methodology," in *Gestalt Therapy: History, Theory, and Practice,* ed. Ansel L. Woldt and Sarah M. Toman (Thousand Oaks, CA: Sage, 2005), 103). Jennifer Mackewn points out that the "Gestalt theory of self-regulation . . . has always encompassed the whole irreducible complexity of the individual within the field and could perhaps more consistently be called self-other regulation . . . ." For that reason, she prefers to call it "the cycle of the interdependence of the organism and environment," or more briefly (using Joseph Zinker's caption), "the interactive contact cycle." Mackewn, *Developing Gestalt Counselling: A Field Theoretical and Relational Model of Contemporary Gestalt Counselling and Psychotherapy* (London: Sage, 2009), 18–19.

[3] Viktor E. Frankl, *Man's Search for Meaning* (New York: Beacon Press, 1959/2006).

[4] Unfinished business can absorb a person's attentional energy until closure is reached. The concept is taken from the work of psychologist Bluma Zeigarnik, who discovered that we tend to most remember or hang on to tasks or objectives that are uncompleted, and is known as the Zeigarnik effect.

[5] Daniel Kahneman, "The Riddle of Experience vs. Memory," *TED Talks*, February 2010, accessed May 25, 2015, http://www.ted.com/talks/daniel_kahneman_the_riddle_of_experience_vs_memory?language=en.

⁶ Sonia Nevis is a co-founder of the Gestalt Institute of Cleveland.

⁷ Adam Bryant, "Google's Quest to Build a Better Boss," *New York Times,* March 12, 2011, accessed May 25, 2015, http://www.nytimes.com/2011/03/13/business/13hire.html?_r=0.

⁸ Charles N. Seashore, Edith Whitfield Seashore, and Gerald M. Weinberg. *What Did You Say? The Art of Giving and Receiving Feedback* (North Attleborough, MA: Douglas Charles Press, 1992).

⁹ "360 Degree Evaluation: Delivering Feedback," *CustomInsight.com*, n.d., accessed May 25, 2015, http://www.custominsight.com/360-degree-feedback/360-delivering-feedback.asp.

¹⁰ David Rock, "SCARF: A Brain-Based Model for Collaborating with and Influencing Others," *NeuroLeadership Journal* 1 (2008): 1–9, accessed May 25, 2015, http://www.scarf360.com/files/SCARF-NeuroleadershipArticle.pdf.

¹¹ Edwin C. Nevis, *Organizational Consulting: A Gestalt Approach* (Cambridge, MA: GestaltPress, 2001), 79 (original italics).

Chapter 4

¹ Arianna Huffington, *Thrive: The Third Metric to Redefining Success and Creating a Life of Well-Being, Wisdom, and Wonder* (New York: Harmony Books, 2014), 159.

² Charles Duhigg, *The Power of Habit: Why We Do What We Do in Life and Business* (New York: Random House, 2014), 19.

³ Marcia Reynolds, *The Discomfort Zone: How Leaders Turn Difficult Conversations into Breakthroughs* (San Francisco: Berrett–Koehler, 2014), 5.

⁴ H. B. Karp, *The Change Leader: Using a Gestalt Approach with Work Groups* (San Francisco: Jossey-Bass/Pfeiffer: 1996), 108.

⁵ Alan Sieler, "The Transformative Power of Ontological Coaching," in *Further Techniques for Coaching and Mentoring,* ed. David Megginson and David Clutterbuck (Oxford: Butterworth-Heinemann, 2009), 53.

⁶ Miriam Orriss, "The Karpman Drama Triangle," *Coaching Supervision Academy,* 2004, accessed May 26, 2015, http://coachingsupervisionacademy.com/thought-leadership/the-karpman-drama-triangle.

⁷ Ibid.

8   Reynolds, *The Discomfort Zone*, 5.

9   Robert Kegan and Lisa Lahey, "The Real Reason People Won't Change," *Harvard Business Review* November 2001 (original italics), accessed May 26, 2015, https://hbr.org/2001/11/the-real-reason-people-wont-change.

10 Edwin C. Nevis, *Organizational Consulting: A Gestalt Approach* (Cambridge, MA: GestaltPress, 2001), 61.

11 A Gestalt colleague has suggested that our habitual resistance patterns could perhaps more valuably be redefined as different and nuanced styles of contact. We each meet the world we live and work in with certain skills and resources. Contact is a Gestalt term used to assess how successful—or unsuccessful—we are in affecting others and being ourselves affected by others. Gordon Wheeler, *Gestalt Reconsidered: A New Approach to Contact and Resistance,* 2nd ed. (Cambridge, MA: GICPress, 1998).

12 Erving Polster and Miriam Polster, *Gestalt Therapy Integrated: Contours of Theory and Practice* (New York: Vintage Books, 1973), 79.

13 Ibid., 84.

14 Joseph Luft and Harry Ingham, "The Johari Window: A Graphic Model of Interpersonal Awareness," in *Proceedings of the Western Training Laboratory in Group Development* (Los Angeles: UCLA, 1955). Our version of the Johari Window is an adaptation.

15 Ellen Schall, "Learning to Love the Swamp: Reshaping Education for Public Service," *Journal of Policy Analysis and Management* 14, no. 2 (1995): 203. "The 'swamp,'" Schall tells us, is Donald A. Schön's metaphor for "the important, complex, and messy problems that resist technical analysis." See Ronald Heifetz, Alexander Grashow, and Marty Linsky, *The Practice of Adaptive Leadership: Tools and Tactics for Changing Your Organization and the World* (Boston: Harvard Business Press, 2009).

16 Qtd. in Jack Kornfield, *A Path with Heart: A Guide through the Perils and Promises of Spiritual Life* (New York: Bantam, 1993), 25.

Chapter 5

1   Marie-Anne Chidiac and Sally Denham-Vaughan, "The Process of Presence: Energetic Availability and Fluid Responsiveness," *British Gestalt Journal* 16, no. 1 (2007): 10.

2   Ibid.

3   "Core Competencies," *Coachfederation.org*, accessed February 9, 2016, http://www.coachfederation.org/credential/landing.cfm?ItemNumber=2206&navItemNumber=576.

4   Chidiac and Denham-Vaughan, "The Process of Presence," 12.

5   Terrence E. Maltbia, Rajashi Ghosh, and Victoria J. Marsick, "Trust and Presence as Executive Coaching Competencies: Reviewing Literature to Inform Practice and Future Research," Teacher's College Columbia University, 2011, accessed January 2, 2016, http://devweb.tc.columbia.edu/i/a/document/15966_Final_Trust.pdf, 19–20.

6   Richard Strozzi-Heckler, *The Leadership Dojo: Build Your Foundation as an Exemplary Leader* (Berkeley, CA: Frog, 2007).

7   Amy Cuddy's TED Talk on "power posing" and related body language is an example of the popularization of a concept that has implicitly been a part of the Gestalt understanding of presence for a long time. Amy Cuddy, "Your Body Language Shapes Who You Are," *TED*, June 2012, accessed February 10, 2016, https://www.ted.com/talks/amy_cuddy_your_body_language_shapes_who_you_are?language=en.

8   Research on emotional communication, by Albert Mehrabian, suggests the impact of other people's presence as 55% visual, 38% as from the speaker's voice tone, and 7% as derived from the words themselves. Cited in John Neffinger and Matthew Kohut, *Compelling People: The Hidden Qualities That Make Us Influential* (New York: Hudson Street Press, 2013), 76.

9   Amy Cuddy, *Presence: Bringing Your Boldest Self to Your Biggest Challenges* (New York: Little, Brown, 2015), 25.

10 Mary Ann Rainey Tolbert and Jonno Hanafin, "Use of Self in OD Consulting: What Matters Is Presence," in *The NTL Handbook of Organization Change and Development: Principles, Practices, and Perspectives,* ed. Brenda B. Jones and Michael Brazzel (San Francisco: Pfeiffer, 2006), 72.

11 Dorothy E. Siminovitch, "Gestalt-Based Coaching Competencies: The Importance of Presence and Use of Self," *Choice* 13, no. 3 (2015): 41–43.

12 Grant Soosalu, *Coaching Wisdom: Coaching the Head, Heart and Gut with mBraining: Essays, Ideas and Explorations on Multiple Brain Integration Techniques (mBIT) Coaching* (N.p.: Worldwide Coaching Magazine, 2015), Kindle edition; Jayne Warrilow, *Resonantcoaching.com,* accessed August 5, 2016—see also her video presentation, "The Resonance Project:

A Collaborative Journey into Life, Love, and Leadership," *YouTube* video, 20:32, December 10, 2014, accessed August 5, 2016, https://www.youtube.com/watch?v=C2dUoutUEHY.

[13] Milton Rokeach, *The Nature of Human Values* (New York: Free Press, 1973), 5.

[14] Crisis Communication Strategies, "Analysis: The Johnson and Johnson Tylenol Crisis," Univ. of Oklahoma Dept. of Communications, accessed August 5, 2016, http://www.ou.edu/deptcomm/dodjcc/groups/02C2/Johnson%20&%20Johnson.htm.

[15] Ibid.

[16] James Burke's handling of the Tylenol crisis continues to be taught at Johnson & Johnson as a means of guiding both seasoned executives and new hires in the organizational values that J&J holds around their for-profit endeavors. Burke's case is classic because his responses illustrate the kind of behavior that organizes and embodies right action.

[17] Robert E. Franken, *Human Motivation,* 3rd ed. (New York: Brooks/Cole, 1993), 396.

[18] Scott Barry Kaufman and Caroline Gregoire, "Ten Habits of Highly Creative People," *Greater Good* (Univ. of California, Berkeley), January 20, 2016, accessed August 5, 2016, http://greatergood.berkeley.edu/article/item/ten_habits_of_highly_creative_people.

[19] David Slocum, "The Rise of Creativity as a Key Quality in Modern Leadership," *Forbes,* January 27, 2015, accessed August 5, 2016, http://www.forbes.com/sites/berlinschoolofcreativeleadership/2015/01/27/the-rise-of-creativity-is-a-key-quality-in-modern-leadership/#649f0c973173.

[20] You can see the ads here: "1984," *YouTube* video, 1:03, accessed August 5, 2016, https://www.youtube.com/watch?v=2zfqw8nhUwA; "Think Different," *YouTube* video, 1:00, accessed August 5, 2016, https://www.youtube.com/watch?v=nmwXdGm89Tk.

[21] Aaron Taube, "How the Greatest Super Bowl Ad Ever—Apple's '1984'—Almost Didn't Make It to Air," *Business Insider,* January 22, 2014, accessed August 5, 2016, http://www.businessinsider.com/apple-super-bowl-retrospective-2014-1.

[22] "Apple: Think Different," *Creative Criminals,* n.d., accessed August 5, 2016, http://creativecriminals.com/celebrities/apple/think-different.

23 Walter Isaacson, *Steve Jobs* (New York: Simon & Schuster, 2015), 328.

24 Even as I searched for a more contemporary example, I kept returning to the primal boldness of Steve Jobs's demonstrated creativity. He sought to "make a dent in the universe," in his words (Isaacson, *Steve Jobs*, 94), which he seems to have done. And Jobs continues to inspire—it was his immense capacity for creativity that allowed him to remake himself after a disruptive dismissal from Apple in 1985 and to return in 1997 to remake the company's image.

25 Robert W. Levenson, "Human Emotions: A Functional View," in *The Nature of Emotion: Fundamental Questions*, ed. Paul Ekman and Richard J. Davidson (New York: Oxford UP, 1994), 123.

26 Ibid.; "Micro-Expressions," Paul Ekman Group, accessed August 7, 2016, http://www.paulekman.com/micro-expressions.

27 Institute for Health and Human Potential, "What Is Emotional Intelligence?" n.d., accessed August 7, 2016, http://www.ihhp.com/meaning-of-emotional-intelligence. The term was popularized by Daniel Goleman in his book *Emotional Intelligence: Why It Can Matter More than IQ* (New York: Bantam, 1995/2005).

28 The amygdala "is the specialist [part of the brain] for emotional matters." The neocortex is "the thinking [part of the] brain." Goleman, *Emotional Intelligence*, 14–15, 10.

29 Recently, a Stanford psychologist has articulated a useful distinction regarding self-management: having access both to will power—e.g., facing or doing something one has been avoiding or wanting—and "won't power"—breaking an unhealthy habit or saying "no" to what one doesn't want. Kelly McGonigal, *The Willpower Instinct: How Self-Control Works, Why It Matters, and What You Can Do to Get More of It* (New York: Avery, 2012), 7.

30 Daniel Goleman and Cary Cherniss, "Guidelines for Promoting Emotional Intelligence in the Workplace," Consortium for Research on Emotional Intelligence in Organizations, n.d., accessed August 7, 2016, http://www.eiconsortium.org/pdf/guidelines_for_best_practice.pdf.

31 *BrainyQuote*, accessed August 7, 2016, http://www.brainyquote.com/quotes/quotes/v/viktorefr160380.html.

32 HeartMath Institute, "Science of the Heart: Heart-Brain Communication," n.d., accessed August 7, 2016, https://www.heartmath.org/research/science-of-the-heart/heart-brain-communication.

33 Noetics Systems International, "Heart Science: Neurocardiology," n.d., accessed August 7, 2016, http://noeticsi.com/heart-science-neurocardiology.

34 Ibid.

35 "Heart Intelligence," HeartMath Institute, accessed August 7, 2016, https://www.heartmath.org/articles-of-the-heart/the-math-of-heartmath/heart-intelligence.

36 Qtd. in "Former Malden Mills CEO Aaron Feuerstein Speaking at Heroes of Professional Ethics Event March 30," Xavier University, March 24, 2009, accessed August 9, 2016, http://www.xavier.edu/campusuite25/modules/news.cfm?seo_file=Former-Malden-Mills-CEO-Aaron-Feuerstein-speaking-at-Heroes-of-Professional-Ethics-event-March-30&grp_id=1#.V6nIBfkrK70.

37 "The Mensch of Malden Mills," *60 Minutes,* CBS News, accessed August 3, 2016, http://www.cbsnews.com/news/the-mensch-of-malden-mills.

38 See this chapter's endnote 8.

39 Thomas Putnam, "The Real Meaning of *Ich Bin ein Berliner,*" *The Atlantic Monthly,* Fall 2013, accessed August 7, 2016, http://www.theatlantic.com/magazine/archive/2013/08/the-real-meaning-of-ich-bin-ein-berliner/309500. The summary of the speech and its impact is from this article.

40 *Merriam-Webster, s.v.* "intuition," accessed August 8, 2016, http://www.merriam-webster.com/dictionary/intuition.

41 *Online Etymology Dictionary, s.v.* "intuition," Douglas Harper, accessed August 8, 2016, http://www.etymonline.com/index.php?term=intuition.

42 Roger Frantz, "Herbert Simon: Artificial Intelligence as a Framework for Understanding Intuition," *Journal of Economic Psychology* 24 (2003): 266.

43 Nalini Ambady, "The Perils of Pondering: Intuition and Thin Slice Judgments," *Psychological Inquiry* 21, no. 4 (2010): 271, accessed August 9, 2016, http://ambadylab.stanford.edu/pubs/2010Ambady_PsychInquiry.pdf.

44 Malcolm Gladwell, *Blink: The Power of Thinking without Thinking* (New York: Back Bay-Little, Brown, 2007), 21–22 (original italics).

45 Melissa Carver and Leo Carver, "5 Ways to Develop Your Intuition," The Chopra Center, accessed August 9, 2016, http://www.chopra.com/ccl/5-ways-to-develop-your-intuition.

46 See Belleruth Naparstek, *Your Sixth Sense: Unlocking the Power of Your Intuition* (New York: Harper Collins, 1997).

47 "Core Competencies Comparison Table," *Coachfederation.org*, accessed August 8, 2016, http://coachfederation.org/credential/landing.cfm?ItemNumber=3175&RDtoken=37378&userID=&navItemNumber=3176.

48 See Anders Ericsson and Robert Pool, *Peak: Secrets from the New Science of Expertise* (New York: Houghton Mifflin Harcourt, 2016).

49 Malcolm Partlett, "Contemporary Gestalt Therapy: Field Theory," in *Gestalt Therapy: History, Theory, and Practice*, ed. Ansel L. Woldt and Sarah M. Toman (Thousand Oaks, CA: Sage, 2005), 47.

50 C. Otto Scharmer, *Theory U: Leading from the Future as It Emerges: The Social Technology of Presencing* (San Francisco: Berrett-Koehler, 2009).

51 Doreen Hemlock, "Riding Out the Slump," *Sun Sentinel*, March 1, 2009, accessed August 9, 2016, http://articles.sun-sentinel.com/2009-03-01/business/0902270158_1_largest-auto-retailer-auto-dealers-autonation.

52 "Mission Statement," *Berggruen.org*, accessed August 14, 2016, http://berggruen.org/about#mission-statement.

53 "Berggruen Philosophy Prize," *Berggruen.org*, accessed August 14, 2016, http://philosophyandculture.berggruen.org/councils/5; "History," Berggruen.org, accessed August 14, 2016, http://berggruen.org/about#history.

54 Peter Bluckert, *Gestalt Coaching: Right Here, Right Now.* (Maidenhead, UK: Open University Press, 2015), 52.

55 See, for example: Doug Silsbee, *Presence-Based Coaching: Cultivating Self-Generative Leaders through Mind, Body, and Heart* (San Francisco: Jossey-Bass, 2008); Mary Beth O'Neil, *Executive Coaching with Backbone and Heart*, 2nd ed. (San Francisco: Jossey-Bass, 2007); Sally Williamson, *The Hidden Factor: Executive Presence: How to Find It, Keep It, and Leverage It* (Atlanta: Sally Williamson & Assoc., 2011).

56 Gestalt's paradoxical theory of change (see Chapter 2) emphasizes bringing into awareness those habitual behavioral or ideational patterns that interfere with clients' capacity to meet their needs and achieve their desired

goals. Awareness of these patterns is often obstructed by powerful, unaware resistances.

57   Cuddy, *Presence*, 24.

58   Strozzi-Heckler, *The Leadership Dojo*, 27.

59   Ed Nevis cautions that "forces in the client may have much to do with what is evoked and a particular response may say as much about the client as it does about the consultant" (*Organizational Consulting*, 135).

60   Tolbert and Hanafin, "Use of Self in OD Consulting," 78–79.

61   Coaches are asked to skillfully and artfully "respond to the total circumstances pertaining to a situation [e.g., the coaching encounter] in ways that are creative and effective." The total circumstances comprise the field, including "the different conventions and tacit assumptions that operate in that field . . . and . . . what is 'appropriate' or 'called for' in a situation." Malcolm Partlett, "Contemporary Gestalt Therapy: Field Theory," in *Gestalt Therapy: History, Theory, and Practice*, ed. Ansel L. Woldt and Sarah M. Toman (Thousand Oaks, CA: Sage, 2005), 48.

62   Nick Petrie, "Vertical Leadership Development–Part I: Developing Leaders for a Complex World," *Center for Creative Leadership*, 2014, accessed May 26, 2015, http://insights.ccl.org/wp-content/uploads/2015/04/VerticalLeadersPart1.pdf.

63   Ibid., 9 (original italics).

64   Bluckert, *Gestalt Coaching*, 52.

65   Daniel Goleman and Richard E. Boyatzis, "Social Intelligence and the Biology of Leadership," *Harvard Business Review* September 2008, accessed November 6, 2014, http://hbr.org/2008/09/social-intelligence-and-the-biology-of-leadership/ar/pr.

66   Experiments are discussed in Chapter 6.

67   System boundaries are discussed in Chapter 7.

68   See Pamela McLean, *The Completely Revised Handbook of Coaching: A Developmental Approach*, 2nd ed. (San Francisco: Jossey-Bass, 2012).

69   Tolbert and Hanafin, "Use of Self in OD Consulting," 79.

70   Peter Bluckert, "The Gestalt Approach to Coaching," in *The Complete Handbook of Coaching*, 2nd ed., ed. Elaine Cox, Tatiana Bachkirova, and David Clutterbuck (Los Angeles: Sage, 2014), 87.

Chapter 6

1   Phil Joyce and Charlotte Sills, *Skills in Gestalt: Counselling and Psychotherapy,* 3rd ed. (Los Angeles: Sage, 2014), 40.

2   Petrie's "heat experience"—"a challenge that is so difficult to solve from your current stage of development that you almost *have* to grow to survive it"—is a necessary component of vertical development. Nick Petrie, "The How-To of Vertical Leadership Development–Part 2," *Center for Creative Leadership* 2015, 8, accessed July 28, 2015, http://insights.ccl.org/wp-content/uploads/2015/04/verticalLeadersPart2.pdf.

3   Joseph C. Zinker, *Creative Process in Gestalt Therapy* (New York: Vintage Books, 1978), 123.

4   Erving Polster and Miriam Polster, *Gestalt Therapy Integrated: Contours of Theory and Practice* (New York: Vintage Books, 1973), 233–284.

5   Ibid., 252.

6   Ibid., 255.

7   Ibid., 268.

8   Ibid., 282.

9   Joyce and Sills, *Skills in Gestalt,* 95.

10 Ibid., 40.

Chapter 7

1   In terms of offering a Gestalt response to the call for "learning organizations" that nurture and sustain ongoing adaptability and performance excellence, Jon Frew makes a point of differentiating between workplace groups and teams and other institutional settings. Jon Frew, "Keeping the Spirit in the Organization: A Classroom as a Learning Experience," in *Beyond the Hot Seat Revisited: Gestalt Approaches to Group,* ed. Bud Feder and Jon Frew (New Orleans: Gestalt Institute Press, 2008), 301–320. Frew of course also references the seminal work on organizational teams: Jon R. Katzenbach and Douglas K. Smith, *The Wisdom of Teams: Creating the High-Performance Organization* (New York: HarperCollins, 2003).

2   John M. Levine and Richard L. Moreland, "Small Groups: An Overview," in *Small Groups: Key Readings,* ed. John M. Levine and Richard L. Moreland (New York: Psychology Press, 2006), 1–3.

3   Since every whole is a part of yet a larger whole, and since every part of a whole is itself a self-contained and functional whole, the term "part" here obviously refers to *subsystem*.

4   For a clear introduction to complexity science applied to organizational change management, see Esther Cameron and Mike Green, "Complex Change," in *Making Sense of Change Management: A Complete Guide to the Models, Tools, and Techniques of Organizational Change*, 4th ed. (Philadelphia: Kogan Page, 2015), 367–386.

5   Malcolm Partlett, "Contemporary Gestalt Therapy: Field Theory," in *Gestalt Therapy: History, Theory, and Practice*, ed. Ansel L. Woldt and Sarah M. Toman (Thousand Oaks, CA: Sage, 2005), 47.

6   See, for example: Mary Uhl-Bien, Russ Marion, and Bill McKelvey, "Complexity Leadership Theory: Shifting Leadership from the Industrial Age to the Knowledge Era," *Leadership Quarterly* 18, no. 4 (2007): 298–319, accessed May 25, 2015, http://digitalcommons.unl.edu/leadershipfacpub/18.

7   This is the "flip" of the VUCA deficits (Volatility, Uncertainty, Complexity, and Ambiguity), known as the VUCA Prime. Kirk Lawrence, "Developing Leaders in a VUCA Environment," UNC Executive Development 2013, 6, accessed July 27, 2016, http://www.growbold.com/2013/developing-leaders-in-a-vuca-environment_UNC.2013.pdf.

8   Elaine Kepner, "Gestalt Group Practice," in *Beyond the Hot Seat Revisited: Gestalt Approaches to Groups*, ed. Bud Feder and Jon Frew (New Orleans: Gestalt Institute Press, 2008), 17–37.

9   Mary Ann Huckabay, "An Overview of the Theory and Practice of Gestalt Group Process," in *Gestalt Therapy: Perspectives and Applications*, ed. Edwin C. Nevis (Cambridge, MA: GestaltPress, 2000), 303–330.

10 Paul Schoenberg and Bud Feder, for example, premise that "all organisms can be understood only in context of the system(s) or field(s) . . . within which they operate," and add the parenthetical acknowledgement that "field theorists may take issue with the lumping of systems theory and field theory together." Paul Schoenberg and Bud Feder, "Gestalt Therapy in Groups," in *Gestalt Therapy: History, Theory, and Practice*, ed. Ansel L. Woldt and Sarah M. Toman (Thousand Oaks, CA: Sage, 2005), 223.

11 Uhl-Bien, Marion, and McKelvey, "Complexity Leadership Theory," 302.

[12] Glenda H. Eoyang, *Coping with Chaos: Seven Simple Tools* (Circle Pines, MN: Lagumo, 2009), x–xi.

[13] Ibid.

[14] Katherine J. Klein, Jonathan C. Ziegart, Andrew P. Knight, and Yan Xiao, "Dynamic Delegation: Shared, Hierarchical, and Deindividualized Leadership in Extreme Action Teams," *Administrative Science Quarterly* 51 (2006): 617, accessed May 25, 2015, http://www-management.wharton.upenn.edu/klein/documents/New_Folder/Klein-Ziegert-Knight-Xiao_ASQ-Dynamic-Delegation.pdf.

[15] Ibid.

[16] Donelson R. Forsyth, *Group Dynamics,* 4th ed. (Boston: Thomson Wadsworth, 2006), 6, 10.

[17] See Jennifer J. Britton, *Effective Group Coaching: Tried and Tested Tools and Resources for Optimal Group Coaching Results* (Mississauga, Ontario: Wiley, 2010).

[18] The group coach's personal presence and her use of self as an instrument will have a distinctive impact on the group as a whole. Coaching presence and use of self are discussed in Chapter 5.

[19] Huckabay, "An Overview," 319.

Chapter 8

[1] See, for example, Pamela McLean, *The Completely Revised Handbook of Coaching: A Developmental Approach,* 2nd ed. (San Francisco: Jossey-Bass, 2012), and Dianne R. Stober and Anthony M. Grant, eds., *Evidence Based Coaching Handbook: Putting Best Practices to Work for Your Clients* (Hoboken: Wiley & Sons, 2006).

[2] "Coaching FAQs," *Coachfederation.org*, accessed May 26, 2015, http://coachfederation.org/need/landing.cfm?ItemNumber=978&_ga=1.8214705.223658093.1428429807&RDtoken=24574&userID.

[3] "Create Positive Change and Achieve Extraordinary Results," *Coachfederation.org,* accessed April 3, 2016, http://becomea.coach/?navItemNumber=4090.

[4] "About," *Coachfederation.org,* accessed May 25, 2015, http://www.coachfederation.org/about/?navItemNumber=557.

⁵ I often think that were he alive now, Fritz Perls, the so-called father of Gestalt psychotherapy, would have become a coach. He would find that coaching, in its accessibility to all walks of life and in its democratic appeal, captured his desire to "gift" the deep insights and effectiveness of Gestalt processes to every human being. He would find the ICF's vision of "the flourishing of humanity [through] coaching's creative and thought-provoking process to maximize professional and personal growth" to be a familiar ambition.

⁶ Robert Dilts, qtd. in Vikki G. Brock, *Sourcebook of Coaching History*, 2nd ed. (Vikki G. Brock, 2014), 64.

⁷ For full descriptive detail regarding ICF core competencies, see "Core Competencies," *Coachfederation.org*, accessed April 24, 2016, https://www.coachfederation.org/credential/landing.cfm?ItemNumber=2206&navItemNumber=576.

⁸ Brock, *Sourcebook of Coaching History*, 249. See "Code of Ethics," *Coachfederation.org*, accessed May 26, 2015, http://www.coachfederation.org/about/ethics.aspx?ItemNumber=854&navItemNumber=634.

⁹ T. J. Sork and B. Welock, qtd. in Brock, *Sourcebook of Coaching History*, 248.

¹⁰ Qtd. in Brock, *Sourcebook of Coaching History*, 248.

¹¹ See, for example, Matt Minahan, "The Foundations of Coaching: Roots in OD," *OD Practitioner* 38, no. 3 (2006): 4–7; Marion Gillie, "Commentary III: Applying Gestalt Theory to Coaching," *Gestalt Review* 13, no. 3 (2009): 254–260; and Ginny Storjohann, "This Thing Called Coaching: A Consultant's Story," *OD Practitioner* 38, no. 3 (2006): 12–16. Figure 8.1 is adapted from these and other sources.

¹² See Chapter 2, "Negotiating Expectations," in Terry R. Bacon and Karen I. Spear, *Adaptive Coaching: The Art and Practice of a Client-Centered Approach to Performance Improvement* (Mountain View, CA: Davies-Black, 2003), 21–36.

¹³ Kevin Cashman, *Leadership from the Inside Out,* 2nd ed. (San Francisco: Berrett-Koehler, 2008), 20.

¹⁴ For an example of a Coaching Agreement, see Appendix B.

[15] "Part One: Definition of Coaching," *Coachfederation.org*, accessed May 25, 2015, http://coachfederation.org/about/ethics.aspx?ItemNumber=854&_ga=1.25297019.770761598.1410366801&RDtoken=15010&userID.

[16] Solomon Asch (1907–1996), Gestalt psychologist and pioneer in social psychology, is known for his work establishing that behavior is not in response to the world as it is but to the world as it is perceived.

[17] "Core Competencies Comparison Table," *Coachfederation.org*, accessed August 8, 2016, http://coachfederation.org/credential/landing.cfm?ItemNumber=3175&RDtoken=37378&userID=&navItemNumber=3176.

[18] Students frequently assume that successfully completing an ICF-accredited coach training program automatically grants them ICF-certified coach status. This is not true: Documented proof of successful completion of an ICF-accredited coach training program only allows the student to apply for ICF coach certification and to begin the ICF certification process itself. There are multiple paths to becoming an ICF-certified coach and three levels of certification. See Appendix A for more on the process and requirements.

[19] Bacon and Spear, "The Ten Red Flags," *Adaptive Coaching*, 76–78.

[20] Kenneth P. De Meuse and Guangrong Dai, "The Effectiveness of Executive Coaching: What We Can Learn from the Research Literature," Korn/Ferry Institute, 2009, accessed May 26, 2015, http://www.kornferryinstitute.com/sites/all/files/documents/briefings-magazine-download/The%20Effectiveness%20of%20Executive%20Coaching-%20What%20We%20Can%20Learn%20from%20the%20Research%20Literature%20.pdf.

[21] "Coaching FAQs: How Is Coaching Distinct from Other Support Professions," *Coachfederation.org*, accessed April 3, 2016, https://www.coachfederation.org/need/landing.cfm?ItemNumber=978&navItemNumber=567.

[22] ICF Core Competency 1 is "Meeting ethical guidelines and professional standards." All ICF-credentialed coaches agree to pledge themselves and their work to ICF's ethical code of conduct ("Code of Ethics," *Coachfederation.org*). There are no designated PCC Markers for ICF Core Competency 1. "The Professional Certified Coach (PCC) Markers," *Coachfederation.org*, accessed August 25, 2016, http://coachfederation.org/files/FileDownloads/0614PCCMarkers.pdf.

²³ "New Assessment Markers for PCC Candidates," *Coachfederation.org*, accessed August 25, 2016, http://coachfederation.org/credential/landing.cfm?ItemNumber=3740&navItemNumber=765.

²⁴ Developed by Dorothy Siminovitch for the Gestalt Center for Coaching, with special assistance from Belkıs Kazmirci, Zeynep Evgin Eryımaz, and Gila Şeritçioğlu.

²⁵ See Appendix C: Supervision, p. 295.

²⁶ Bacon and Spear, *Adaptive Coaching*, xx, ix.

²⁷ "Coaching FAQs," *Coachfederation.org*, accessed May 26, 2015, http://www.coachfederation.org/need/landing.cfm?ItemNumber=978&navItemNumber=567.

Chapter 9

¹ Along with Marshall Goldsmith, I was awarded the Thought Leader of Distinction award in 2013 by the Association of Corporate Executive Coaches for pioneering work in standards and practices for executive coaching with corporations around the world. I was also given the status of Master Certified Executive Coach for my 20 years of contributions to the field.

² Marshall Goldsmith, *Leadership Is a Contact Sport* (2014). Two comprehensive studies were carried out by Marshall Goldsmith and Howard Morgan. The first one was in 2004 with 86,000 executives globally. The second was completed in 2014 with 248,000 people. In those studies, 95% of people showed improvement as measured by their stakeholders. The premise is that people who are engaged in a system that is engaged in their development are more likely to make real changes and mindshifts.

³ From Frederick S. Perls, *Gestalt Therapy Verbatim* (Moab, UT: Real People Press, 1969).

⁴ Barry Johnson, *Polarity Management: Identifying and Managing Unsolvable Problems* (Amherst, MA: HRD Press, 2014); Edwin C. Nevis, *Organizational Consulting: A Gestalt Approach*. 1987. (Cambridge, MA: GestaltPress, 2001); H. B. Karp, *The Change Leader: Using a Gestalt Approach with Work Groups* (San Francisco: Jossey-Bass/Pfeiffer, 1996).

⁵ Search Inside Yourself Leadership Institute, accessed August 23, 2016, https://siyli.org.

⁶ Marianne Williamson, *A Return to Love: Reflections on the Principles of A Course in Miracles* (New York: HarperOne, 1996), 90.

Appendix A

¹ All information regarding program accreditation and individual credentialing can be found on the Coachfederation.org website.

Appendix C

¹ Belkıs Kazmirci (PCC, Faculty, Gestalt Center for Coaching), personal communication to author, July 2016.

² Gila Şeritçioğlu (MCC, Faculty and Supervisor, Gestalt Coaching Program), personal communication to author, July 2016.

³ For full details on ICF's stance, see "Coaching Supervision," *Coach federation.org,* accessed July 28, 2016, http://coachfederation.org/credential/landing.cfm?ItemNumber=2212. The following ICF definitions are also taken from this online document.

⁴ Gila Şeritcioğlu (MCC, Gestalt Coaching Program Faculty and Supervisor), personal communication to author, July 2016.

⁵ Peter Hawkins and Nick Smith, *Coaching, Mentoring and Organizational Consultancy: Supervision and Development* (Maidenhead, UK: Open University Press, 2007), 35.

⁶ In Turkey, mentor coaching and supervision are seen as one.

⁷ Pamela McLean, *The Completely Revised Handbook of Coaching: A Developmental Approach,* 2nd ed. (San Francisco: Jossey-Bass, 2012), 239.

⁸ Robert Kegan and Lisa Laskow Lahey, *How the Way We Talk Can Change the Way We Work: Seven Languages for Transformation* (San Francisco: Jossey-Bass, 2001), 1.

⁹ Joan describes C-D theory as one that focuses on how one's thinking shapes, and limits, one's actions according to developmental transitions in the life span of a person, defined by patterns in how one constructs self and world (personal communication to author, August 2016). For some examples of the use of C-D theory, see: Jennifer Garvey Berger, *Changing on the Job: Developing Leaders for a Complex World* (Stanford, CA: Stanford UP, 2012); Suzanne R. Cook-Greuter, "Making the Case for a Developmental

Perspective," *Industrial and Commercial Training* 36, no. 7 (2004), accessed August 25, 2016, http://www.cook-greuter.com/Making%20the%20case%20for%20a%20devel.%20persp.pdf; Lisa Lahey, Emily Souvaine, Robert Kegan, Robert Goodman, and Sally Felix, *A Guide to the Subject-Object Interview: Its Administration and Interpretation* (Cambridge, MA: Minds at Work, 2011); Bill Torbert and Associates, *Action Inquiry: The Secret of Timely and Transforming Leadership* (San Francisco: Berrett-Koehler, 2004).

[10] Pamela McLean, *The Completely Revised Handbook of Coaching*, 239–241.

[11] Pamela McLean, "Coaching Supervision: Building Capacity, Deepening Impact" (presentation at the Hudson Institute of Coaching Annual Learning Conference, 2014).

[12] Philippe Rosinski, "Integrative Coaching Supervision," *Global Coaching Perspectives* July 2016 Issue 10, 34, accessed August 25, 2016, http://www.associationforcoaching.com/media/uploads/gcp_july_mag(9).pdf.

[13] Ibid., 36.

[14] Ibid., 37.

[15] Ibid. Rosinski also discusses the reasonable caution around the distorting effects of "transference" and "countertransference" in the supervisory coaching relationship. As Rosinski explains, coaching supervisors need to be "mature, psychologically savvy" coaches who are highly self-aware and "able to manage [their] own emotional and affective reactions." This takes the kind of self-work that we describe in Chapter 5.

[16] Ibid., 38.

[17] Ibid., 35.

[18] Ibid., 34.

[19] Ibid., 36.

[20] Marcia Reynolds, Coaching Teleclass, presented for the Gestalt Center for Coaching, July 22, 2016.

Index

Numbers
360-feedback method, 69, 243, 247, 253

A
accountability. *See also* responsibility, taking
    access to multiple perspectives and, 270, 273
    client self-accountability and, 286
    codes of ethics and, 209
    for coaching work, 44–46, 127
    for use of presence, 127, 133
    group and team coaching and, 203
    in homework experiments, 163
    in therapy, consulting, coaching, 212
    in Unit of Work, 24, 150
    intuition and, 122
    managing progress and, 217–219, 231, 236
    systems thinking principles and, 168
accreditation, coaching, 205–206, 237
Accredited Coach Training Program (ACTP), GCC's, 237
"acting on the choice," step in UOW creation, 152–153

action, in Cycle of Experience, 23, 59, 62–63, 78, 93
active listening, ICF core competency of, 122, 215, 234
adaptability, figure recognition and, 19
Adler, Alfred, 243
Akın, Ahmet, 8
alienated aspects of self, 47–48, 51, 69, 72, 74, 97, 102, 146, 155
"amygdala hijacking," 45, 114–115
anxiety, in Cycle of Experience, 59, 62, 92–93
appearance, aspect of presence, 108
Arrien, Angeles, 118
Asch, Solomon, 215
Associate Certified Coach (ACC), ICF's, 264
awareness
    awareness experiments. *See under* experiments, Gestalt
    awareness intelligence and, 54
    coach as agent of, 46–49, 137
    coach's self-observation and, 75–77
    creating awareness core competency, 216–217, 235
    Cycle of Experience (COE) and, 22–26, 56–58, 61–62, 78–80, 92

331

eco-system, 52–53
eco-system awareness, 243
figure/ground and, 16–22
leadership effectiveness and, 247–249
relationship to change, 39–54
resistance and, 83, 94–103
role in Gestalt theory, 14–16
self-assessment of, 246–247
threats assessed through, 70–75
use of self and, 137–139
awareness agents, Gestalt coaches as, 40, 46–49, 137
awareness experiments. *See under* experiments, Gestalt
awareness intelligence, 54
Awareness IQ, 21–22, 30, 247

B
Barbaro, Ron, 53
Beisser, Arnold, 20, 46, 49
Ben Ziv, Eti, 8
Boyatzis, Richard, 242
Burke, James, 111

C
Canyon Ranch Spas, 21
Case, Rick, 123
case study, coaching supervision, 273–290
Cashman, Kevin, 47
certifications, ICF's, 224, 263–264
change
    Gestalt theory of, 46–49
    Gestalt values and, 36
    resistance and, 82–91
    role of awareness in, 39–54
change agent, vs. awareness agent, 46–49
closure, in Cycle of Experience, 23, 60, 64–65, 93
coaching, defined, 34
coaching agreements
    ICF core competency involving, 213–214, 233
    sample coaching agreement, 265–268
coaching contracts, 45
coaching presence, core competency of, 214. *See also under* presence
Code of Ethics, ICF's, 213
collaboration, coach-client, 34–35, 41–42
Collins, Jim, 242
"Columns of People" illusion, 19–20
communication and voice, quality of presence, 110, 119–120
compassionate inquiry, coach's stance of, 42–44
competing commitments, 90–91, 206
concept, element of integrated Gestalt coaching, 11–12
conflict, group, 193–195
confluence, resistance pattern of, 99–100, 201
contact, in Cycle of Experience, 23, 59, 63–64, 93
core competencies, ICF
    active listening, 122, 215, 234
    coaching agreements, 233
    coaching presence, 214, 218, 233
    creating awareness, 216–217, 235
    designing actions, 217
    direct communication, 216, 234
    establishing the coaching agreement, 213–214
    establishing trust and intimacy with the client, 214, 233
    Gestalt principles and, 38, 205–208
    importance of, 239–240
    managing progress and accountability, 217–218
    meeting ethical guidelines and professional standards, 207, 209–213

planning and goal setting, 217, 236
powerful questioning, 215–216, 234
Covey, Stephen, 242
creating awareness, ICF core competency of, 216–217, 235
"creative indifference," 155–156
creativity, quality of presence, 110, 112–113
criticizing others, 254–255
Csíkszentmihályi, Mihály, 141
Cycle of Experience (COE)
  assessment questions for, 61–65
  awareness and, 22–26, 137–139
  awareness experiments and, 145–148
  coaching presence and, 132–133
  coach's self-knowledge and, 75–77
  complexity of experience and, 78–80
  defined, 55
  experiential, data-based feedback and, 65–70
  group and team coaching and, 180, 202
  importance of, 57–58
  in group development work, 194–198
  integrated with Unit of Work, 138–139
  learning, 37
  representations of, 55–56
  resistance case study and, 273, 277, 281, 288–290
  resistance and, 91–100
  six points of, 58–65
  use of self in, 132–133

D

deep learning, 74
deflection, resistance pattern of, 99, 200
Deniz, Dost, 8, 273–274, 287, 291
desensitization, resistance pattern of, 94–95, 198
designing actions, core competency of, 217
direct communication, core competency of, 216
direct communication, ICF core competency of, 234
directed behavior experiments, 160–161
diversity, Gestalt approach and, 259
dreams/dreamwork experiments, 162–163

E

Eastern philosophy, influence on Gestalt theory, 32
eco-system awareness, 52–53, 243
Einstein, Albert, 159
Elhadef, Meyzi, 8
embodiment, self and, 107, 137
emotional intelligence, 114–116, 249
emotions, emotional range; and quality of presence, 110, 113–116
enactment experiments, 159–160
energy, in Cycle of Experience, 23, 62–63
Enker, Paul, 8
entropy/negentropy system principle, 169
equifinality system principle, 170
Eryılmaz, Zeynep Evgin, 8
establishing the coaching agreement core competency, 213–214
establishing trust and intimacy with the client core competency, 214, 233
ethics, coaching, 206, 213
"Ethics Pledge," ICF's, 209
evoking-provoking distinction, 33
exaggeration, 146–149, 160, 252, 254–255
excitement, in Cycle of Experience, 59, 62, 92–93
Executive Core, 4, 242, 247

existential approach, Gestalt's, 4, 35, 50, 144–145, 240
experiential approach, Gestalt's, 4, 25, 35–36, 48, 65, 73, 144–145, 240
experiential learning, 50–51
experimental approach, Gestalt's, 4, 35, 38, 48, 54, 144–145, 240. *See also* experiments, Gestalt
experiments, Gestalt
    awareness experiments and, 145, 149–150, 154–156, 159
    data-based feedback and, 66
    directed behavior experiments and, 160–161
    dreams/dreamwork experiments and, 162–163
    enactment experiments and, 159–160
    fantasy experiments and, 161–162
    homework experiments and, 163–164
    overview of, 143–145
    resistance case study and, 273, 277–278, 280–281, 283, 285–286, 289–290
    thematic experiments and, 145, 149–152, 154–156
    Unit of Work (UOW) in, 150–158, 164–166
    use of self in, 76

F

fantasy experiments, 161–162
Fantz, Rainette, 3
feedback, data-based, experiential, 65–70
feedback system principle, 170
Feuerstein, Aaron, 118
field, defined, 123
field sensitivity, quality of presence, 110, 123–125. *See also* scanning
field theory (field dynamics), 28–31, 38, 171–175

figure satisfaction, 59–61, 63–64
figure/ground
    element of Gestalt awareness work, 16–22
    in Cycle of Experience, 57
    system, field theory and, 38
figures of interest
    overwhelmed by, 67–68
    place in Gestalt coaching, 16–22
Fourfold Way, Arrien's, 118
Frankl, Viktor, 57, 116
Freudian psychotherapy, 4, 81, 83
"frozen gestalt," 68

G

Gandhi, Mahatma, 103
gestalt, meaning of term, 13
Gestalt Center for Coaching, 7–8, 204, 208–209, 218, 239, 272
Gestalt Coaching Program, 263
Gestalt Institute of Cleveland, 3, 4, 7
Gestalt psychotherapy, Gestalt coaching vs., 34, 210–212, 239
Gestalt theory, basics of, 13–16
Goleman, Daniel, 242
Google, 68–69
Gottman, John, 121
group and team coaching
    entropy/negentropy principle and, 169
    equifinality principle and, 170
    feedback principle and, 170
    field theory and, 171–172
    group developement and, 175–180, 187–196
    holism and, 168
    interruptions to contact and, 196–198
    intervention tools and, 186–191
    leadership effectiveness and, 201–204

levels of system and, 26–27, 180–187, 202–203
models of coaching, consulting presence and, 204
need for, 167
open/closed system principle and, 168–169
resistance and, 198–201, 203
self-regulation principle and, 169–170
suboptimization principle and, 170–171
systems theory and, 168–171
group development, stages of, 175–180
group system level, 185–186

H
"habit loop," 82
habituation, 71–73, 82–84. *See also* unaware patterns
Hadari, Avi, 8
Halinski, Deb, 8
Hanafin, Jonno, 109
Hawkins, Ann, 8
Hawkins, Peter, 272
"heart brain," 117
"heart intelligence," 117–118
heart-based relations, quality of presence, 110, 116–118
HeartMath Institute, 116–117
Heifetz, Ron, 101–102
Hippocratic oath, 206
holism, system principle of, 168
homework experiments, 163–164
horizontal and vertical development, 29–30, 52–53, 133–136, 159, 208, 239–240, 290
Huckabay, Mary Ann, 173
Huxley, Aldous, 15
Hyundai USA, response to 2008 financial crisis, 123

I
Integrated Gestalt Coaching graphic, 11–12
integrative coaching supervision, 291. *See also* supervision, coaching
International Coaching Federation (ICF)
  certification and, 224, 263–264
  certifications and, 293–294
  coaching supervision and, 270–272
  Code of Ethics of, 213, 239
  core competencies. *See* core competencies, ICF
  Ethics Pledge of, 213
  mentoring coaching and, 270–271
  Professional Certified Coach assessment of, 224–231
International Gestalt Coaching Program, 6–7, 206
interpersonal system level, 183
introjection, resistance pattern of, 92, 94–96, 103, 148–149, 160, 199, 203
intuition, quality of presence, 110, 120–123

J
Jobs, Steve, 112–113
Johari Window, 101
Johnson, Barry, 249
Johnson & Johnson, response to Tylenol Murders, 111
Jung, Carl, 243

K
Kahneman, Daniel, 65
Karp, Hank, 86–88, 249
Karpman Drama Triangle, 88–89
Kaufer, Katrin, 52
Kazmirci, Belkıs, 8, 273
Kegan, Robert, 90–91, 292
Kennedy, John F., 120
Kepner, Elaine, 172–173

Kitzler, Richard, 5
Kofodimos, Joan, 8, 290
Kotter, John, 242

L

Lahey, Lisa, 90–91, 242
Land, Pamela, 8
language/speech, aspect of presence, 108
Lannoch, Martha, 8
Leadership Awareness Index, 4, 255–258
leadership effectiveness
  awareness and, 247–249
  group and team coaching and, 201–204
  measuring, 243–244
  presence and, 201
  self, use of as instrument and, 201
levels of system
  boundaries of, 180–186
  Cycle of Experience (COE) and, 79
  group level and, 185–186
  interpersonal level and, 183–184
  intervention at, 180–186
  resistances at various, 93–94
  self/individual level and, 182–183
  subgroup level and, 184–185
Lewin, Kurt, 22, 172

M

"making the rounds" technique, 253
Maltbia, Terrence, 107
managing progress and accountability, core competency of, 217–218
manner, aspect of presence, 108
Master Certified Coach (MCC) credential, ICF's, 122, 215, 264, 293–294
McLean, Pamela, 237
meeting ethical guidelines and professional standards core competency, 209–213. *See also* ethics, coaching
Mehrabian, Albert, 119
mentoring coaching, 269–273, 293–294
method, element of integrated Gestalt coaching, 11–12
mindfulness, 17, 20, 51, 75, 122, 146, 258, 292. *See also* present, Gestalt theory centered on
mirror neurons, 32
mood state, aspect of presence, 108

N

Naparstek, Belleruth, 8
need fulfillment, 14–15, 58, 63–64, 78
Nevis, Ed, 80, 92, 107, 239, 249
Nevis, Sonia, 66
"new what is," step in UOW creation, 153–155
norms, group, 176

O

obsolescence, 12, 18
Önen, Yeşim Özlale, 8
open/closed system principle, 168–169
organizational consulting, Gestalt; vs. Gestalt coaching, 34, 210–212, 239
organizational development, change agents and, 40
orientation questions, 37

P

paradoxical theory of change (PTC), 20, 46–50, 74, 148, 150, 289–290
perception. *See also* awareness
  figure/ground and, 16–22
  motivation and, 17
  subjectivity of, 15–16, 42–43, 140
Perls, Fritz, 17, 20, 46, 243, 249, 253, 255
Personal Weirdness Index (PWI), 129, 140
perspective, of the other, 251–252, 254

Petrie, Nick, 29–31, 133, 143, 208, 293
phenomenological inquiries, 73
planning and goal setting, core competency of, 217, 236
playful exaggeration technique, 252. *See also* exaggeration
Polster, Erving, 159, 161, 163–164
Polster, Miriam, 159, 161, 163–164
power of resistance model, Karp's, 86–88
powerful questioning, core competency of, 215–216, 234
presence. *See also* self, use of as instrument
    as vertical development, 133–136
    aspects of, 108–109
    coaching presence and, 31–35, 44, 106–107, 109, 125–133, 204, 214, 218, 233
    defined, 105–106
    leadership effectiveness and, 201
    qualities of, 110–125
    Theory U and, 29
"presencing," 123
present, Gestalt theory centered on, 11–12, 14, 17, 21, 28, 35, 48–50
Professional Certified Coach (PCC) credential, ICF's, 224–231, 264
projection, resistance pattern of, 96–98, 199, 254

R

"ready, fire, aim," 78
rehearsing interactions, 255
resistance
    case study of, 273–275, 277–278, 281, 287–289
    confronting in coaching, 100–103
    Cycle of Experience (COE) and, 60, 91–100
    failure to complete COE and, 60
    Gestalt view of, 81–91
    in groups, 198–201
    in Unit of Work creation process, 151–152
    resistance patterns and, 94–100
responsibility, taking, 22, 24, 88, 150, 190, 199, 217, 243. *See also* accountability
retroflection, resistance pattern of, 98–99, 200
Reynolds, Marcia, 89–90, 296
Rock, David, 71, 114
Rogers, Carl, 243
roles, group, 176–177
role/title, aspect of presence, 108
Rosinski, Philippe, 238, 291–295

S

"safe emergencies," 45–46, 74, 126, 145
Sandberg, Sheryl, 242
scanning, 61, 78, 110, 123–125
SCARF model, 71, 114
Scharmer, Otto, 18, 29, 52, 123
Schuster, John, 8
Search Inside Yourself Leadership Institute (SIYLI), 258, 292
Seashore, Edie, 69
self, use of as instrument. *See also* presence
    both coach and client, 75–77
    coaching presence core competency and, 218–219
    developing skill with, 136–141, 290
    evoking-provoking distinction and, 33–34, 125–133
    leadership effectiveness and, 201
    presence and, 33–34, 125–136
self-concept, 49–50
self-deception, awareness of, 41–42. *See also* awareness
self-identity, in groups, 177
self-image, 50–51
self/individual system level, 182–183

self-knowledge, 49–51, 75–77. *See also* awareness
self-mastery, 22, 115, 127–128
self-regulation system principle, 169–170
self-work, coach's, 127–130, 203, 251–252
Senge, Peter, 29, 242
sensation, in Cycle of Experience, 23, 58, 61, 92
Şeritçioğlu, Gila Ancel, 8
Sertoglu, Esra, 8
sexuality, aspect of presence, 108
shugyo, 115, 127–128
Siminovitch, Dorothy, 241, 247
Siminovitch, Jeffrey, 8
Simon, Herbert, 121
Singer, Barbara, 4
Slocum, David, 112
Smith, Nick, 272
social intelligence, 68, 249
somatic intelligence, 292
somatic portrayal, 67, 109
Soosalu, Grant, 110
Strozzi-Heckler, Richard, 107, 127–128
subgroup system level, 184–185
suboptimization system principle, 170–171
Suner, Elif Biçer, 8
supervision, coaching, 269–296
systems theory, 26–28, 30, 38, 168–171, 173–175

T
Thatcher, Margaret, 119–120
thematic experiments. *See under* experiments, Gestalt
theory, element of integrated Gestalt coaching, 11–12
Theory U, 29, 123
Thich Nhat Hanh, 48
"thin slicing," 121–123
threats, reassessed through awareness, 70–75
time management, UOW and, 158
Toffler, Alvin, 12
Tolbert, Mary Ann Rainey, 109
Tylenol murders, 111

U
umwelt, 42–43, 47–48, 74, 102
unaware patterns, 39–41, 48, 49–50, 70–73, 82–83, 85–88. *See also* awareness
uniqueness, aspect of presence, 108
Unit of Work (UOW)
    Gestalt conception of, 23–26
    Gestalt experiments and, 150–158, 164–166
    integrated with Cycle of Experience, 138–139
    learning, 37
    resistance case study and, 273–274, 277–280, 282, 289–290
    steps in creation of, 150–158
Utku, Alper, 8

V
Vaill, Peter, 12
values
    aspect of presence, 108
    central to Gestalt coaching, 36–37
    embodied, 110–111
Van Eron, Ann, 8
vertical development. *See also* horizontal and vertical development
    awareness and, 30
    Gestalt experiments and, 143–144
    use of self as, 133–136
Virag, Leslie, 8
voice, aspect of presence, 108
Volatility, Uncertainty, Complexity, and Ambiguity (VUCA), 12–13, 172
von Uexküll, Jakob, 42

W
War College, US Army, 12–13
Warner, William, 107
Warrilow, Jayne, 110
"what is" process analysis, 151
Whyte, David, 91
Williamson, Marianne, 260–261
withdrawal, in Cyle of Experience, 60, 64–65, 93. *See also* closure, in Cycle of Experience

Z
Zinker, Joseph, 159
Zuckerman, Mel, 21

Made in the USA
San Bernardino, CA
28 March 2017